Muslim European Youth

Reproducing ethnicity, religion, culture

Edited by
STEVEN VERTOVEC
ALISDAIR ROGERS

Routledge
Taylor & Francis Group
LONDON AND NEW YORK

First published 1998 by Ashgate Publishing

Reissued 2018 by Routledge
2 Park Square, Milton Park, Abingdon, Oxon, OX14 4RN
711 Third Avenue, New York, NY 10017, USA

Routledge is an imprint of the Taylor & Francis Group, an informa business

Copyright © Steven Vertovec and Alisdair Rogers 1998

All rights reserved. No part of this book may be reprinted or reproduced or utilised in any form or by any electronic, mechanical, or other means, now known or hereafter invented, including photocopying and recording, or in any information storage or retrieval system, without permission in writing from the publishers.

Notice:
Product or corporate names may be trademarks or registered trademarks, and are used only for identification and explanation without intent to infringe.

Publisher's Note
The publisher has gone to great lengths to ensure the quality of this reprint but points out that some imperfections in the original copies may be apparent.

Disclaimer
The publisher has made every effort to trace copyright holders and welcomes correspondence from those they have been unable to contact.

A Library of Congress record exists under LC control number: 98070995

ISBN 13: 978-1-138-32290-5 (hbk)
ISBN 13: 978-1-138-32291-2 (pbk)
ISBN 13: 978-0-429-45173-7 (ebk)

Contents

	List of Contributors	vii
1	Introduction *Steven Vertovec and Alisdair Rogers*	1
2	Islam in France: Social Challenge or Challenge of Secularism? *Jocelyne Cesari*	25
3	Islam and Interest Struggle: Religious Collective Action Among Turkish Muslims in the Netherlands *Thijl Sunier*	39
4	Imagining a British Muslim Identification *Yunas Samad*	59
5	Islam and Socialization Among Turkish Minorities in Denmark: Between Culturalism and Cultural Complexity *Lars Pedersen*	77
6	Young Muslims in Keighley, West Yorkshire: Cultural Identity, Context and 'Community' *Steven Vertovec*	87
7	Continuity and Change: Young Turks in London *Talip Kucukcan*	103

8	Gender and Generation: Young Muslims in Copenhagen *Yvonne Mørck*	133
9	Good Girls, Bad Girls: Moroccan and Turkish Runaway Girls in the Netherlands *Lenie Brouwer*	145
10	Growing Up as a Muslim in Germany: Religious Socialization Among Turkish Migrant Families *Lale Yalçin-Heckmann*	167
11	Educational Needs of Muslim Children in Britain: Accommodation or Neglect? *Marie Parker-Jenkins and Kaye Frances Haw*	193

List of Contributors

Lenie Brouwer is Lecturer in Ethnic Studies, Free University of Amsterdam

Jocelyne Cesari is Chargée de Recherches, Institute for the Research and Study of the Arab and Muslim World, Aix-en-Provence

Kaye Frances Hawe is Research Fellow, School of Education, University of Nottingham

Talip Kucukcan is Research Fellow, Centre for Research in Ethnic Relations, University of Warwick

Yvonne Mørck is Assistant Professor of Sociology, University of Copenhagen

Marie Parker-Jenkins is Professor of Research in Education, University of Derby

Lars Pedersen is a social anthropologist working with consultative assignments in inter-cultural research projects, Denmark

Alisdair Rogers is College Lecturer in Geography, University of Oxford

Yunas Samad is Lecturer in Sociology, University of Bradford

Thijl Sunier is Research Fellow at the Research Centre for Religion and Society, University of Amsterdam

Steven Vertovec is Research Reader in Social Anthropology, University of Oxford

Lale Yalçin-Heckmann is Resarch Fellow at the Chair of Turkish Studies, University of Bamberg

1   Introduction

Steven Vertovec and Alisdair Rogers

Recently observed in a British city: an Asian man about twenty years old wearing sunglasses, baggy trousers, large trainers loosely laced, and a black T-shirt depicting a photo of the Earth from space under which appear the words '*dar al-Islam*' [the realm of Islam]. Do these trappings merely mark a radical street style? Do they represent a new force of 'fundamentalism'? Do they indicate the retention of an identity across generations and continents, or a new mode of being Muslim that has been forged particularly in the British urban context, or some hybrid form of Islam sweeping Europe?

These possible, wide-ranging interpretations are only a few of many which have been widely rehearsed - by media journalists, academics and Muslim commentators alike - with regard to the myriad expressions of religious identity evident among young Muslims throughout Europe. The best interpretation is probably that such a combination of elements have no single 'message' or 'meaning'. Young European Muslims are increasingly demonstrating that there is no inherent contradiction or cognitive dissonance necessarily associated with having 'street-cred' and hip-hop style, identifying with certain contemporary global orientations within Islam, being for example British and Muslim and Pakistani, and perhaps being at the same time in accord with and at odds with the views and values of one's parents. This Introduction, along with the articles which comprise this volume, explores some of the multiple modes of expression and attachment which young Muslims in Europe are constructing today.

There are at least seven million Muslims currently living in Western Europe (Vertovec and Peach 1997). Although their families' roots may be in South Asia, the Maghreb, or Turkey, a large proportion of Europe's Muslim population - over half in many places (for example, 56% of Bangladeshis in Britain; Jones 1993) - is comprised of persons under twenty years old. They are Muslims who have been born, raised, schooled and who live in various European contexts. 'They are, in a sense,' writes Czarina Wilpert (1989: 6), 'new Europeans searching for a new belongingess and the right to new identities.' Despite their immigrant or 'ethnic' backgrounds, it is therefore fair to describe such persons as Muslim Europeans.

It is particularly the cohort of young Muslim Europeans who are presumed to have a problem with 'identity': yet the 'problem' is far more often in the mind of the non-Muslim (researchers and journalists not least), or the of the Muslim elder, than among the young people themselves. The set of examples below point toward some of the presumptions and complexities surrounding questions of young European Muslims and their 'identity'.

Fundamentalists, apostates or contextualists?

In June 1995, the northern English city of Bradford witnessed several nights of violence which saw police pitted against Asian young men. The police and much of the media put the blame on both a 'cultural gap' and 'generation gap' among the local Asian population: the 'westernized' youths - a generation caught 'between two cultures' - were deemed to be out of the control of their parents and 'Asian community leaders' (Burlet and Reid 1996). Some accounts even pointed to the alleged importance of 'Islamic militancy' in fostering the riots, despite the lack of any kind of evidence of Muslim symbolism surrounding the riot (McLoughlin 1997). It was somehow assumed, and readily accepted by many quarters of British society, that religious extremism must have had something to do with the disturbances, particularly in this city which was context to much of the controversial Satanic Verses protests in 1990.

Just after the riots, it was reported that the avowedly extremist organization Hizb-ut-Tahrir held meetings seeking new recruits from among the disaffected youths in the locale. Over the past few years, Hizb-ut-Tahrir itself has gained a notorious reputation for holding rallies and other activities at British universities at which anti-Jewish and anti-gay messages were propagated. Hence it seems to many that Muslim extremists are emerging both from the unemployed working class Asian youth of inner cities and from the population of intellectuals training at institutes of higher education.

A kind of moral panic concerning the imagined rise of home-grown Muslim extremists has not by any means been limited to Britain. Since the autumn of 1995, when the French police killed Khald Kelkal, the chief suspect in a terrorist bombing campaign, there has ensued a high degree of public debate about whether alienated French Muslim youth in run-down suburbs are turning to violent Islamicist groups and creating a rebel subculture (see Cesari this volume). In Germany a similar debate has followed the publication of Wilhelm Heitmeyer's (1997) *Verlockender Fundamentalismus* ['Enticing Fundamentalism']. In this book, based on arguably spurious research on the connections between German Turkish youth in Hamburg and the Milli Görüs tradition of Islam (associated with the Islamist Refah party in Turkey), Heitmeyer claims there is a dangerous fundamentalist element growing within Germany.

In stark contrast to these stories of emerging Muslim fundamentalisim, many observers have identified what appears to be a wholesale abandonment of Muslim attachments. This is exemplified in France, where Leveau (1997) indicates that 71 per cent of 18-30 year old Maghrebis claim they feel closer to the culture of France than to that of their parents. Hargreaves and Stenhouse (1991) report that between one-fifth and one-third of young people from Muslim backgrounds in France regularly say they are not Islamic believers. Many others profess only a weak allegiance to the religion by way of observing prescribed behaviour and practice. Further, such youths are shown to know little about Islamic doctrines and often react negatively to the dietary, sexual and other restrictions associated with such doctrines. Despite such negativity and low rates of knowledge and observance, the majority of young people nevertheless described themselves as Muslims. This is a new kind of attachment that Hargreaves (1995: 121) describes as 'affective identification with doctrinal detachment'.

A yet different pattern of situational or serial identification is perhaps the most commonplace development among European Muslim youth. This was raised at a 1995 conference in Berlin by Jørgen Bæk Simonsen, who provided a series of illuminating anecdotes concerning the rich multiple lifeworlds of Moroccan youths in Copenhagen. On any Friday night, Simonsen describes, Danish Moroccan youths might go to see a touring Raï (Algerian pop music) group; on such occasions the youths 'are' collective diasporic Maghrebians. On Saturday afternoon, the same youths may go to a meeting of the Union of Muslim Students; then, they 'are' part of a pan-Islamic awakening. On Saturday night, the youths might go to their uncle's place for dinner; there, they 'are' traditional Moroccan youths.

As these contrasting images show, diverse uses and meanings of Islam have emerged among young persons of Muslim upbringing in Europe. The 'problems' so often associated with this cohort lie less with these persons themselves than with observers who attempt to understand the category 'young Muslims in Europe' through conventional concepts of 'culture', 'community' and 'identity'. Clearly there is need to re-think these concepts.

The anti-essentialist critique

There is an increasingly abundant literature critiquing commonplace understandings of the notions 'culture' (see for instance Caglar 1994; Stolcke 1995; Vertovec 1996) and 'community' (see for instance Anthias and Yuval-Davis 1991; Baumann 1996). This gist of such criticism is that both terms are often used to represent integrated and bounded wholes characterized by uniform rules, values, practices and traits - or, as such understanding have come to be portrayed, both terms convey 'essentialist' meanings in which entire groups or categories of people are stereotyped as homogeneously imbued with specific attributes. 'Religion' and 'ethnicity' have also commonly been filled with essentialist connotations as well. More open, fluid, contested and socially constructed understandings of all these terms are now usually advocated instead.

The concept of 'identity' has been focus of comparatively less critique. Whereas 'culture' and 'community' are now often used rather reluctantly by many social scientists, the even more vague concept of 'identity' is still frequently utilized in a range of academic literature. On the whole, attempts to re-think the concept have not moved a great deal from the seminal theorizations of the social dynamics of 'identity' published by researchers such as Erickson (1968), Tajfel (1974) and Jacobson-Widding (1983). While many sociologists use the term uncritically, many social psychologists draw from these earlier works to probe the meaning of 'identity' as 'cognitive-affective consistency'. The latter approach often employs rather formalistic methods and concise sub-categories of identity content in order to get a firm 'fix' on the identity of people. It has therefore followed that the absence of a unitary configuration of measurable characteristics (often determined by the researcher) - in other words, the absence of a single 'identity', itself assumed to be identified with clear attachment to a single 'culture' and a distinct 'community' - was regarded as a serious 'identity problem'.

This kind of formal socio-psychological understanding of 'identity', along with static and bounded notions of 'culture', 'community', 'religion' and 'ethnicity', has long informed sociological work concerning young members of ethnic minorities, who have regularly been deemed 'the second generation'. Hence this cohort has been commonly associated with the concepts of acculturation, deculturation or assimilation, culture conflict, 'between-two-cultures', identity crisis, and bi-culturality (for example Anwar 1976; Abadan-Unat 1985; Singh Ghuman 1994). Despite the emergent anti-essentialist critique, there still appears an abundance of studies that 'measure' identity and its presumed contents through all sorts of quantifiable questionnaires, scales, standard deviations and statistical methods in terms of frequency of cultural practice and extent of cultural distance, degree of attachment to 'home' (pre-migration) countries, degree of integration to 'host' (residence) society, degree of adherence to Islamic principles and other categories themselves based on fixed and bounded notions of 'culture', 'community', 'religion' and 'ethnicity' (see for instance Similä 1988; Liebkind 1989a; Weinreich 1989; Nijsten 1996; van der Lans and Rooijackers 1996).

While these sorts of study continue, the shortcomings of such an approach to 'identity' have become increasingly apparent to many. Indeed, in the final overview of a volume centred around formalistic identity structure analysis, Karmela Liebkind (1989b: 238) concludes that for the majority of second generation youth:

> The number of categories or groups for each individual generating social identities is enormous. Language, gender and political attitudes qualify the impact of ethnicity on one's identity. However, multiple group allegiance is not only a source of strain: cognitive flexibility and the ability to adapt to situational contingencies are acquired in the frequent modulations of social identities that occur when multiple group membership exists. Individuals differ in the extent to which they behave in terms of group membership, and people generally do not identify in an all-or-none fashion with the values and characteristics of various groups and/or individuals. In developing different identity structures, people relate to others and respond to situations in markedly different ways.

Alternative approaches: understanding multiplicity

By way of articulating resistance to essentialist notions, researchers in sociology and cultural studies have invoked a broad new range of concepts to convey better a sense of openness and mutability. This includes notions of translation, creolization, crossover, cut 'n' mix, hyphenated, bricolage, hybridity, syncretism, third space, multiculture, transculturation and diasporic consciousness (see Hannerz 1987; Hebdige 1987; Gilroy 1987, 1993; Ålund 1991; Robins 1991; Bhabha 1990; Back 1996; Kaya 1997; Werbner and Modood 1997).

The terms and approaches certainly mark and advance in conceptualizing emergent forms and modes of expression. However, as Ayse Caglar (1997) points out, we must beware that such terms themselves - especially 'hybridity' - do not become new essentialisms. Alternative blends of cultural backgrounds are certainly being produced on the street celebrated in the literature. Yet an important feature of contemporary socio-cultural dynamics among ethnic minority youth is that many are not just adopting and adapting some (singular) new course which is neither that of their immigrant parents' origin nor that of their ethnic majority peers. Rather, such youths are illustrating their skills at combining, maintaining and serially selecting facets of all of these lifeways. They demonstrate multiple cultural competence (cf. Ålund 1991; Jackson and Nesbitt 1993).

Fredrik Barth (1989: 124) usefully discusses the nature of living in complex societies and complex cultural configurations by asserting that such a way of being entails 'a multiplicity, inconsistency and contentiousness that deflects any critical attempt at characterization.' In such contexts, 'people participate in multiple, more or less discrepant, universes of discourse,' he (*ibid*.: 130) explains, and 'they construct different, partial and simultaneous worlds in which they move; their cultural construction of reality springs not from one source and is not of one place.' Cultural complexity brings about the potential, in every person, for a co-existing multiplicity of worldviews and ways of being.

What is the mechanism of multiplicity? One way of viewing this is through the understanding of culture as a kind of 'toolkit', as advocated by Ann Swidler (1986). Here, cultural attributes drawn from a number of sources throughout one's life are understood as a set of resources from which people can construct diverse strategies of action day-to-day, situation-by-situation. This means, according to Swidler (*ibid*.: 281), that people engage in their everyday activities by 'selecting certain cultural elements (both such tacit culture as attitudes and styles and, sometimes, such explicit cultural materials as rituals and beliefs) and investing them with particular meanings in concrete life circumstances.'

A further way we might better appreciate the nature of multiple cultural competence is via a linguistic metaphor of culture. One such exercise, based on creole linguistics, was undertaken by Lee Drummond (1980). Working in the ethnically plural context of Guyana, Drummond formulated a model of Guyanese society as an intersystem or cultural continuum. Just as creole linguistics posits no clear boundaries between two languages, Drummond saw a wide range of blendings evident between the conceived cultural 'poles' of Guyana's ethnic categories (African, Indian, Amerind, European and others). With such a model, he concluded that:

> Individuals are cognisant of much or all the possible range of behaviour and belief in the continuum, although need not behave or act as the other does, just as speakers of a creole language can generally understand utterances at either extreme of the continuum but rarely control both extremes in their own speech. The reality of the system is, therefore, the set of bridges or transformations required to get from one end to the other. (*ibid.*: 353)

With regard to young Asians in Britain, Roger Ballard (1994) follows Drummond to make an important analogy between cultural and linguistic practice. 'Just as individuals can be bilingual', Ballard (*ibid.*: 31) emphasises, so they can also be multicultural, with the competence to behave appropriately in a number of different arenas, and to switch codes as appropriate.' By adopting such a perspective, Ballard (ibid.) reasons, 'the popular view that young people of South Asian parentage will inevitably suffer from "culture conflict" as a result of the participation in a number of differently structured worlds can be dismissed.'

If we are to probe further the analogy of cultural and linguistic practice, especially surrounding ideas of code-switching and code-mixing, we must recognise that sometimes the process is due to purposeful selection and emphasis, and sometimes it is non-conscious or inadvertent.

Further use of analogies to cultural phenomena and practice is found in Ben Rampton's (1995) detailed sociolinguistic study looking at 'language crossing' among youths in an ethnically mixed neighbourhood. Rampton observes how the everyday uses of Punjabi, 'Stylised Asian English' and Caribbean Creole manifest relationships of 'boundary transgression' as well as affirm participants' claims to membership to certain self-defined groups:

> The ethnolinguistic boundary transgression inherent in code-crossing responded to, or produced, liminal moments and activities, when the ordered flow of habitual social life was loosened and when normal social relations could not be taken for granted. Code crossing occurred at the boundaries of interactional enclosure, in the vicinity of delicts and transgressions, in self-talk and response cries, in games, cross-sex interaction and in the context of performance art. Adolescents used language to cross ethnic boundaries in moments when the constraints of everyday social order were relaxed. (*ibid.*: 281)

Rampton notes that such acts of 'crossing' become ritualised depending on a number of factors: 'the variety selected, the crosser's network relations, ethnic and gender identities, his/her orientation to the socio-ideological horizons indexed by the code, his/her linguistic competence, the presence or absence of inheritors, and the size of the switch itself' (*ibid.* 281). A significant finding throughout was that 'members may alternate between codes without even being consciously aware of it' (*ibid.*: 282) and that problems of cultural/linguistic conflict are met with 'solutions which people improvise together in the arena of intergroup practice itself' (*ibid.*: 296).

Non-conscious acts of 'crossing' were also evident to Bob Jackson and Eleanor Nesbitt (1993) in their research on the reproduction of beliefs and practices among Hindu children in Britain. They conclude that:

> While acknowledging that some practices may reinforce boundaries, our studies suggest that the situation is not clear cut and is becoming less so. Rather than being individuals with a fixed sense of belonging to this groups or that, or feeling comfortable in only one type of cultural situation, it became clear that, in general, the children we were studying could move unselfconsciously from one milieu to another. (*ibid.*:174-5)

Even when the choice of highlighting or blending cultural practices is intentional, Roger Hewitt (1992) suggests, its effects may be unintentional. In the course of hybridization, he writes:

> [N]ot only are new, unholy mixtures of cultural elements compounded -- dress, language, music are most obvious but a much broader spectrum of cultural behaviours is actually encompassed -- but, paradoxically, even the strategic stressing of some clearly defined ethnic culture for political purposes contributes to this process. The reason for this is that the very process of selecting out cultural elements to carry a specialised, symbolic load for instrumental reasons within a contested political sphere, simultaneously has the effect of transforming the bases of selection into a second order. The residue of cultural practices not selected for any role in the symbolic economy become even more susceptible to change and destabilisation. (*ibid.*: 32-3)

'Crossing' and 'milieu-moving' are rather different processes than those usually associated with notions of 'hybridity'. While the latter celebrate new mixtures, the former indicate ways in which individuals not only create syncretic forms, but are competent in - and can improvise from - a number of (in some ways discrete, in some ways overlapping) cultural and linguistic systems. Rather than simply bearing witness to the generation of new hybrid forms and 'third spaces' (Bhabha 1990), an approach recognizing multiplicity and drawing upon a linguistic analogy allows us to appreciate how individuals accumulate, through their own life experiences, and use, for improvising situationally competent action and generating new practices, a kind of repertoire comprised of complex backgrounds and multiple traditions (cf. Bourdieu 1977).

Such an approach was suggested by Ulf Hannerz (1969), in his work on urban Black Americans, who conceived that:

> The repertoire to some measure constitutes adaptive potential. While some of the cultural goods received may be situationally irrelevant, such as most of that picked up at the movies, much of that derived from school, and even some of that encountered within the ghetto community, other components of an individual's repertoire may come in more useful. (*ibid.*: 186)'

Again with reference to culture-as-toolkit, Swidler (1986: 277) noted that 'people may have in readiness cultural capacities they rarely employ; and all people know more culture than they use.' It is an approach appreciating the fact that young people, particularly of ethnic minority background, regularly draw upon their 'multicultural capital' to create new strategies of living (Palmgren et al. 1992).

However, if we are to fully comprehend the dynamics of repertoires, code-switching processes and the like, we must realize that their capacities are not without considerable constraints, as Samad argues in his chapter in this volume. Ayse Caglar (1994: 34) makes this point with reference to German Turks, but with direct relevance to a number of other groups:

> [T]he debris of our past experiences are not immediately usable, since they are already embedded in structures in which they have meanings. These limit their immediate use in producing new arrangements. The ability to take what seems fitting and to leave out the rest is the outcome of a particular set of conditions. To be able to take elements and structures out of their context and create new arrangements with ones from different sources, certain conditions need to be fulfilled. Moreover, these juxtapositions and bricolage are not random, nor do they represent a chaotic jumble of signs. In their hybridity, they still tell a story. They have an organizing principle or principles. The objective is then first to identify the conditions that enable this drastic uprooting of elements and practices from very different sources, and second to explain the organizing principle(s) of their recombination and resetting in light of German Turks' self-images, sense of place in the society, desires and dispositions, which structure and orient their experience and encounters in the FRG [Federal Republic of Germany].

Just as this alternative approach has profound implications for critiquing conventional, essentialist understandings of 'culture', 'community', 'identity', 'religion' and 'ethnicity', so it is also relevant for a significant topic within contemporary sociology: cultural reproduction. Chris Jenks (1993) has provided a useful theoretical overview of the sociology of cultural reproduction. With particular relevance to processes between generations, he concludes that we should underscore the association of cultural reproduction with regeneration and synthesis (implying creativity and innovation) rather than replication or imitation (implying conventionality and constraint) (cf. Williams 1981). For Jenks (ibid.: 1),

> the concept [cultural reproduction] serves to articulate the dynamic process that makes sensible the utter contingency of, on the one hand, the stasis and determinacy of social structures and, on the other, the innovation and agency inherent in the practice of social action. Cultural reproduction allows us to contemplate the necessity and complementarity of continuity and change in social experience.

Indeed, sometimes the result is so innovative and new that, in order to describe the process, the hyphenated qualification 're-production' seems warranted.

With specific regard to young European Muslims, evidence of their multiplicity and complex competences are widespread as the contributions to this volume attest. Following Caglar and Jenks among others, we should examine some of the broad contextual factors that condition or otherwise affect their modes and forms of expression and attachment.

Re-production among young European Muslims: contextual factors

The factors affecting the multiple natures and manifestations of Islamic identification among contemporary Muslim European youth are themselves highly diverse and unevenly distributed. These factors combine create an altogether different context for expression and identification than has prevailed for the generation of Muslims of direct migrant experience in Europe since the 1950s. In brief (and in no implied order of importance), these relatively new factors include:
- socialization within an atmosphere of ethnic/religious mobilization. For at least three decades, Muslim groups across Europe have organized themselves, engaged state institutions and challenged specific policies in order to make a place for themselves within both local and national public spheres (Vertovec and Peach 1997). Many of today's young Muslim

Europeans have grown up in this religiously and politically charged context which has significantly conditioned a sense of organized action. Such struggles have taken place alongside other kinds of anti-racist, anti-discrimination, feminist and human rights campaigns which have informed their political consciousness as well.

- the attraction of Islam as a global symbol of resistance to (variously or even simultaneously) Western political and cultural imperialism, capitalism, racism and white-dominated bureaucratic states. This attraction has gained further appeal as young Muslim Europeans have faced new modes of racist and culturalist discrimination often in conditions of high unemployment. It is because of this kind of symbolic power associated with global Islam that a German-Turkish rap group called themselves Islamic Force: to be subversive, confrontational and controversial - even though they claim no particular adherence to a Muslim identity (Kaya 1997). A similar motivation inspires British rap groups such as Fun^Da^Mental and Kaliphz (Kalra et al. 1996). Many young Muslim women are also turning to Islam as a source of strength and resistance to sexism and patriarchy (both within and outside of their own ethnic group) (cf. Knott and Khokher 1993; Haw 1995).

- a sharpening of self-consciousness, which is especially related to membership of a post-migration religious minority. Jørgen Nielsen (1992: 114-15) writes:

> The circumstances of migration, the situation into which Muslims have settled in European cities, and the adaptations which are being made, especially as the young grow up to be the first European Muslim generation, all impose the need to analyse. The old way has to be analysed into discrete parts so that Islam can be identified. The emphasis of the identification of Islam can be on the Qur'an and Qur'anic principles or it can be on aspects of the Shari'a tradition. In either case, one proceeds to 'reassemble' these Islamic components together with the components arising out of the migration and settlement experience into a new complex whole which functions more successfully in European urban, industrial life.

Among many Muslim European youth there has arisen a desire to analyse religious scriptures for themselves. This embodies reclaiming the concept of *ijtihad* ('interpretation' or 'independent judgement'), which in turn involves both a rejection of authority (of their parents and of the *ulema* or body of Islamic scholars) and a revitalisation of belief and practice.

- the inculcation of implicit values through Western educational systems. In such systems (often contrasted with the education systems in the countries of migrants' origins), there is emphasis on argumentation, critical debate and reflexive questioning. It also contrasts with the modes of learning through repetition sometimes favoured by their parents or instructors in Qur'anic schools. The experience of schooling in the Western system may also been also contribute toward the 'rationalization' of Islam often reported among European Muslim youth. Moreover, the European Islam which is taking shape (Nielsen 1992; Vertovec and Peach 1997) will probably be significantly influenced by the rise of new leadership educated at European universities, such as London, Leiden, Hamburg and Marseilles, where, alongside their formal training, they become well-versed in the language of civil democracy, social justice and equal rights (see also Cesari's chapter in this volume). It is particularly among Muslim university students that use of internet and electronic discussion groups is pushing the frontiers of Muslim values, practice and organization.
- an explicit hardening of the distinction between 'religion' and 'ethnicity' (Knott and Khokher 1993; Jacobson 1997). Many young Muslims in Europe are rejecting their parents' conformity to pre-migration cultural traditions by declaring that particular customs or institutions 'do not belong to Islam' but are merely aspects of, as the case may be, Pakistani, Turkish, or Algerian 'culture'. (This often comes as rather a shock to the parents, who may have always regarded their own national culture as based on Islamic tenets.) Fostering Islamic knowledge, argumentative ability and personal confidence to make such a declaration are some of the key aims of organizations such as Young Muslims UK. Nonetheless, while some cultural values and practices are intentionally disavowed, various forms of conceptual and social linkage with their parents' places of origin are certainly maintained so that some 'identity' as, for example Kashmiri, Turk or Algerian, might continue to be heartfelt. This may involve periodic returns to relatives still living in the country of origin, for both brief visits and longer stays, as Kucukcan's chapter discusses. Although this kind of identification is still held, it represents a decoupling, or at least fundamental re-working, of the attachment to homeland held by their migrant parents or grandparents (see also Sunier, this volume). It is emblematic of many new kinds of diasporic consciousness of belonging both 'here-and-there' being forged among post-migration populations (cf. Clifford 1994).

- the growth of what might be called 'vernacular' Islam in Europe. Increasingly, sermons, literature and public discussions are being conveyed in the local European language. Also grounded in local European languages, there have appeared new journals, newspapers and associations created specifically for young Muslims and addressing the real, everyday problems they face, such as dating and sexuality, conflicts with parents, racism, topics often avoided by parents and imams or hocas. These linguistic changes reflect the fact that Muslim European youths are often entirely fluent in more than one language (complete with specific regional accents in German, English, Dutch or whatever European language they speak locally). Moreover, they are often most comfortable speaking the European language rather than Punjabi, Turkish or Arabic. Youth frustrations with the ignorance of imams and hocas arise here too, since many of such religious figures are from rural backgrounds with little or no knowledge of the local European language or social context.
- variance of religiosity in relation to stage of life. As with members of practically every religion in Western society, one's views on religion fluctuate with age. Many young Muslim Europeans (especially males) claim they are not particularly religious at present, but nonetheless express a desire to be 'a good Muslim' later in life, especially once married with children (see Vertovec in this volume). Indeed youths are often conspicuous by their absence at religious events until such time as they are married and have children.
- a tendency toward compartmentalization and secularization of religion. This means that religious values are not placed at the centre of one's personal orientation to life, but is conceived as a kind of annexe or compartment. Cesari discusses this issue in her chapter in this volume. This tendency within European Islam is parallel to what Kim Knott (1986: 46) has observed among Hindus in Britain. Much as British Christians relate to their own religion, for many believers it is merely something to be remembered during large festivals and at births, marriages and deaths. Certainly for many Muslims, young and old, their religiosity (in terms of consciousness of spiritual issues, observance of scriptural tenets, sense of belonging to a community of faith) increases during Ramadan, and large numbers who never attend the mosque during the year will go on Eid ul fitr. A related pattern affects European Islam, as it does other religions, especially among the young. This is what some sociologists of religion have likened to a kind of consumer attitude

toward religion. People are increasingly choosing which tenets and rules of their religion they will recognize and which they will ignore. There is an associated trend toward the individualization or privatization of religion: people nowadays often choose to keep their religious sentiments and practices to themselves rather than engage in collective worship.

- an immersion in (one might say, bombardment by) American and European youth culture embodied in commodities and consumerism, fashion and other elements of style, modes and expressions of speech, music and other forms of media. School peers are everywhere significant reference points particularly for adolescents and teenagers, and non-Muslim friends and counterparts - as well as Muslim friends - serve these roles for young Muslim Europeans. A desire to 'be like' their peers is often a strong motivating force shaping attitudes, behaviours and social relations, not least with parents. For instance, parental authority might be questioned if a young Muslim demands to know why their Muslim friends are allowed to attend a school function or disco while they are not. Conversely, as Nielsen (1992: 112) observes, Muslim parents in Europe sometimes become more authoritarian because they are no longer authoritative particularly regarding gender roles, sexuality, marriage, (female) dress and modesty, personal and family honour. This is discussed at length by Brouwer's chapter in this volume.

The factors outlined above are but a few of the new contextual features impacting upon the lives of young Muslim Europeans. The socio-religious and identificatory patterns which are emerging out of these conditions (as described earlier in this Introduction) indicate a multiplicity of expressions and attachments, a broad repertoire giving rise to situationally shifting and ever new forms. Rather than a wholesale rejection of the kind of attachment to, or practice of, their religion as enacted by their parents, these forms often amount to a series of negotiations, or (in Drummond's terms) a set of bridges or transformations from pre-migration traditions to an emergent European Islam. The studies which comprise this volume describe several modes of this process of transformation.

The contributions

The contributions to this volume come from five Western European countries: Denmark, France, Germany, the Netherlands and United

Kingdom. They combine national overviews of the position of Muslim youths with detailed and local case studies. The chapters draw upon a range of anthropological and sociological theory, but are united in a scepticism towards, or a rejection of, essentialist ideas along the lines discussed above. Many draw upon ethnographic research with young Muslims and the institutions within which they are often found. These include local government, political and religious associations, hostels and schools, as well as the community and the family.

One of principle themes is that European Muslim youth identities are often forged in reaction to negative and essentialist representations of both Islam and migrants. Certain key events, notably the *Satanic Verses* affair and the Gulf War, seemed to have sparked an intensification of media and academic interest on the one hand, and an occasion for the mobilization of identity on the other. Chapters by Cesari, Samad, Sunier and Pedersen address the significance of the changing national and international context for the development of Muslim organization along religious, ethnic and political lines, either separately or in combination. These may involve new relationships between religion and politics, between public and private spheres and between migrant generations themselves.

Jocelyne Cesari suggests that there are different responses to the novel context in which migrants and their children find themselves. Whereas in Islamic countries fundamentalism may be regarded as an extension of Islam into other social and economic arenas, in the West the so-called 'rise' of Islam is better understood as an intensification of Islamic identity contingent on being a minority community. Within France, she argues, one can distinguish between three responses. For the first generation, many of whom still desire to return to North Africa, Islamic identity is very much bound up with national identification with the homeland. The situation is different for the second generation who grow up among French youth and share many of the conditions relating to their marginal economic position in the suburbs. One group adopt a more secular and individualized approach to religion, confining it more to the private sphere while retaining a symbolic allegiance to the wider Islamic and Arab world. For a second group, Islam is more linked with collective identity and is marked by an increase in piety and religious observance. This fundamentalist response was also shaped by political circumstances, as avowedly Islamic associations filled in the vacuum left by the failings of state-sponsored ethnic organizations. This group is challenging many of the assumptions of French political culture, particularly the equivalence of nationality and citizenship and the separation of religious from secular interests.

On the basis of the French experience, Cesari argues that the kinds of essentialist representations of Islam she terms 'Neo-Orientalist' fail to acknowledge the transformations of Islam among those born in the West and the different ways of being Muslim. Islam and modernity are not diametrically opposed, nor is there some 'clash of civilizations', despite the emergence of more cross-national forms of Islamic identification. She stresses the significance of circumstances within France itself and the fact that the relationship between religion and politics is changing for all, not just for Muslims.

Like the 'Franco-Maghrebis' of which Cesari writes, young Muslims in the Netherlands are also caught up in local, national and international sources of political identification. *Thijl Sunier*'s study of the youth branches of the three main Turkish Islamic organizations in Rotterdam focuses on the development of political organization over time. Family reunification and the birth of a second generation were important factors influencing the second phase of organizational development. The first phase centred on simply establishing spaces for prayer among the newly arrived and mainly male migrants. The second phase, which Sunier terms 'migrantization', was marked by both an internationalization of the political process - making links with Turkish politics - and a greater incorporation into the Dutch institutional structure. During the third phase, in the 1980s, the young generation became more active and began to press their own priorities and needs. As in France, this involved a de-linking of Islamic identity from homeland (in this case Turkish) identity, as well as a greater willingness to relate to the wider society. Sunier therefore argues that such organizations are neither simply migrant organizations nor cultural (i.e. Muslim) organizations, but social movements engaged in rational attempts to address exclusion by mobilising outside formal institutions. He notes that the Rotterdam municipality was relatively open in involving such associations in urban redevelopment and neighbourhood management, but that this permeability of the Dutch political system cannot be taken for granted.

The political organization of young Muslims is therefore shaped by their own needs and interests on the one hand, and the availability of political openings on the other. The lesson of the UK suggests that this is not necessarily a linear process of progressively greater openness. *Yunas Samad* discusses how municipal government provided an institutional framework for the formation of British 'Black' political identities only to have it dismantled by the political New Right. The subsequent political vacuum was filled by the creation of Muslim umbrella organizations which explicitly set out to forge a national British Muslim identification. The problem faced by these organizations was how to unite the many strands of Muslim identity around a number of lowest common denominator themes. Two of these were provided by the Rushdie Affair and the war in Bosnia, while the third revolved around questions of religious discrimination and blasphemy. It was significant that their challenge to the British government was based on an appeal to a notion of human rights. Therefore, Muslim organizations are not only transnational in the sense of funding sources and political support, but also in their strategic use of international issues and discourses. For Samad therefore, British Muslim identity is 'imagined' not in the postmodern sense of a free choice from a repertoire, but is shaped by institutions and by other social identities operating in the same arenas.

As part of his research on new Islamic movements across Europe, *Lars Pedersen* discusses many of these same issues in the case of Denmark. Within institutions, and he refers particularly to schools, there may be a hegemonic politics of representation. While institutions may provide openings for Muslims and their interests, they run the risk of turning migrants into 'problems'. Furthermore, drawing Muslims in may involve struggles over how culture is to be defined and who is to define it. Pedersen gives the example of language teaching. In one case, the kindergarten appointed Alevi Kurds to teach Turkish but Turkish parents objected on the grounds that they were not culturally appropriate. Knowledge of other cultures becomes embedded in institutions and professionals are in a position to become active managers of Turkish cultural heritage. Turkish organizations are therefore faced with the task of defending cultural autonomy and resisting social marginalization. But Pedersen stresses that organizations such as Milli Görüs actually provide a platform for a diversity of views about identity rather than a doctrinal front. Like the other authors, he emphasizes that Muslim political identities are far from monolithic, despite the best attempts by outside agencies to represent them as such.

The remaining contributions are more contextual or local than national in their scope. The significance of geographical context for the negotiation of Muslim identities is explored by *Steven Vertovec*'s chapter on the youth of a small northern British town, Keighley. As with many of the contributors, he is concerned to distance his analysis from the notion that second-generation youths are somehow 'caught between two cultures'. He argues that Muslim youngsters engage with both community and context, which are themselves mutually conditioning. In particular, Vertovec explains the importance of Keighley's relation to the nearby, larger and more well-known Muslim population of Bradford. Many of his informants draw deliberate contrasts between their own 'small town' environment and the more metropolitan Bradford. One observes that the practice of women covering their heads is more common in Keighley. Many of the young people, who form the subjects of Vertovec's ethnography, comment on the enclosed or constraining character of Keighley's Muslim social environment. What is significant about this study is that place or locality - a British place furthermore - is a component of Muslim youth's process of negotiating identity.

Vertovec also picks up on many of the themes which run through all the local and ethnographic studies. Keighley's Muslim youths reside in 'encapsulated social and spatial ambits', with distinct leisure activities and places to the town's other youths. They are more or less alienated from formal religion, making their Muslim identity more a matter of culture than religion. Much of this pride springs from the hostility they perceive from the surrounding society, especially in the wake of the 'Rushdie Affair'. Nonetheless, the young are sometimes aware that when they grow older and have children themselves, they may become more conformist and respectable.

While Vertovec describes a large community in a small town setting, *Talip Kucukcan* surveys a small group in a large metropolis, young Turks in London. He focuses on the differences between 13-18 year olds and their parents on a number of key issues: home; language; the preservation of tradition; and sexuality. Kucukcan surveyed males and females in Turkish supplementary schools, and his findings show some clear gender differences in attitudes and perceptions. Girls feel that they are more controlled than boys, they are less likely to have partners of the opposite sex and are more likely to have disagreements with their parents. But these disputes are related only to certain values and issues. For example, although girls are generally opposed to arranged marriages, like boys they are in favour of maintaining Turkish traditions and values. When asked whether they felt happier in Britain or in their parents' home country, roughly a third expressed a preference for each of these options. In conversation, Kucukcan establishes that many feel that there is more freedom and less hostility in Cyprus than in London. This presents an unusual finding, that the young Turks acquire the values of freedom from British society but often say that their ability to realise these values is greater outside Britain. He concludes that there is no evidence for a wholesale rejection of their parents' values by young Turks, but a desire to negotiate over selected issues and practices.

Two chapters extend these themes through in-depth ethnographies of young Muslims which pay particular attention to gender and sexuality. *Yvonne Mørck* writes about Pakistani and Turkish youth in Copenhagen, Denmark. *Lenie Brouwer* discusses the problems arising among runaway Moroccan and Turkish girls in the Netherlands. Kucukcan found that, although half the boys in his sample approved of pre-marital sex, half the girls did not. He argues that this shows that girls are more likely to accord with their parents' wishes. The ethnographic approach used by both Mørck and Brouwer suggests that there are more complex issues involved. Following Barth's notion of ethnic boundaries and Cohen's idea of symbolic boundaries, Brouwer suggests that virginity is a 'boundary-expressing symbol' for the Muslim community in Dutch society. The quality of a symbol is that it is imprecise enough to allow for a range of interpretations. She therefore argues that girls share the same symbol -- virginity -- as their parents, but do not necessarily share the same meanings or agree with its implications for social behaviour. The girls, even after they have run away from home, value virginity and associate it with being a 'good girl', but do not agree with their parents that this should lead to their confinement in the home or control over their movements. In this respect, running away is less a challenge to their parents' cultural values and more a questioning of parental authority itself.

Mørck indicates that parental control over young Turks and Pakistanis in Denmark is probably greater than it would be in the home country, precisely because of the parental fear of 'losing their children'. By the same token, children worry that they will 'let their parents down'. Invariably, the tension between wanting to be good and wanting greater personal freedom is felt most keenly by young girls. In Brouwer's study, Moroccan and Turkish boys valued female virginity too, but less so for themselves. The power to define symbols, in this case virginity, is therefore mediated by patriarchy as much as by ethnicity or religion.

Brouwer describes a paradoxical situation therefore. In order to maintain cultural boundaries, parents seek to control their daughters' lives and movements. Some of them are driven to run away (although a third of her subjects returned home), which renders them vulnerable to boys and risks damaging their reputation among the community. But Brouwer finds that among these girls, there is often a strengthened awareness of their ethnicity. Exposure to the surrounding society without the support of family or community may increase their feelings of being Turkish or Moroccan. They choose to combine elements of both Dutch society and their own ethnic communities. Mørck interprets this same process in Copenhagen in terms of a 'hybrid culture'. It is a matter of continuous negotiation, mediation or translation between contexts, made all the more pressing by the lack of clear co-ordinates from family, community and nation.

The school is sometimes conceived as a kind of intermediate space between perceived public space of state institutions and the private spaces of families. *Marie Parker-Jenkins* and *Kaye Haw* compare the aims and needs of Islamic education with what is actually provided in two sets of schools: British state schools with large Muslim enrolments and Muslim schools set up by the community to provide a more religiously-based education. The authors carefully set out the range of needs, general, curricular and religious/cultural, found among Muslim children. Their research relates to the ongoing struggle within Britain among Muslims to obtain state funding for denominational schools comparable to that already provided for Christian and Jewish children. They suggest that a key difference between state education and 'Islamic' education is the emphasis placed by the latter on the spiritual dimensions of schooling and by the former on language provision. In general, their survey of schools shows that both kinds meet the needs of dress codes, diet and provision of prayer space. These things are easily achieved with few resources. Where the unmet needs of Muslim education arise is in areas that require greater external funding and this relates directly to the issue of state-financed religious schools. However, they also caution that there may be differences between the needs as voiced by headteachers and those identified by Muslim scholars and writers not directly involved with teaching itself.

Finally, *Lale Yalçin-Heckmann*'s study of Turkish youth in Nürnberg, Germany, uses case studies of four carefully-chosen families. In this research, the tensions and differences between generations are placed within the context of the whole family, as she interviews parents as well as children and youth. The cases are taken from a wider study of religious socialization focusing on how important religion is in everyday life and how religious values are transmitted or negotiated between generations within the family. She reveals how religious education or knowledge is not a single entity or package, but is differentiated between technical, moral and religious forms. She also underlines an important theme which arises in other contributions, that migrant families are often separated for long periods between two countries and in association with grandparents and other kin.

The four families are all Laz Turks: two belong to political organizations of Islam and two do not. Using this paired sampling strategy, Yalçin-Heckmann exposes the variety of beliefs and practices both within and between families occupying similar socio-economic positions. Questions of religion and belief are sometimes negotiated between one child and the next, or between children and their mothers separately from their fathers. Some families are more patriarchal than others. As she suggests, even parents were different and separate individuals before they met and married. Her study emphasizes the potential diversity within the apparently simple labels of first and second generation.

References

Abadan-Unat, N. (1985) 'Identity Crisis of Turkish Migrants, First and Second Generation', in: I. Basggöz and N. Furniss (eds.) *Turkish Workers in Europe*, Bloomington: Indiana University Press: 3-22.

Ålund, A. (1991) 'Modern Youth and Transethnic Identities', *European Journal of Intercultural Studies* 2(2): 49-62.

Anthias, F. and N. Yuval-Davis (1991) *Racialised Boundaries*, London: Routledge.

Anwar, M. (1976) *The Myth of Return*, London: Commission for Racial Equality.

Back, L. (1996) *New Ethnicities and Urban Culture: Racisms and Multiculture in Young Lives*, London: UCL Press.

Ballard, R. (1994) 'Introduction: The Emergence of Desh Pardesh', in: R. Ballard (ed.) *Desh Pardesh: The South Asian Presence in Britain*, London: C. Hurst: 1-34.

Barth, F. (1989) 'The Analysis of Culture in Complex Societies', *Ethnos* 54: 120-42.

Baumann, G. (1996) *Contesting Culture: Discourses of Identity in Multi-Ethnic London*, Cambridge: Cambridge University Press.

Bhabha, H. (1990) 'The third space', in: J. Rutherford (ed.) *Identity, Community, Culture, Difference*, London: Lawrence & Wishart: 207-221.

Bourdieu, P. (1977) *Outline of a Theory of Practice*, Cambridge: Cambridge University Press.

Burlet, S. and H. Reid (1996) 'Riots, Representation and Responsibilities', in: W.A.R. Shahid and P.S. van Koningsveld (eds.) *Political Participation and Identities of Muslims in Non-Muslim States*, Kampen, Netherlands: Kok Pharos: 144-57.

Caglar, A. (1994) German Turks in Berlin: Migration and Their Quest for Social Mobility, Ph.D. Thesis, Anthropology, McGill University.

Caglar, A. (1997) 'Hyphenated Identities and the Limits of "Culture"', in: T. Modood and P. Werbner (eds.) *The Politics of Multiculturalism in the New Europe: Racism, Identity and Community*, London: Zed Books: 169-85.

Clifford, J. (1994) 'Diasporas', *Cultural Anthropology* 9: 302-38.
Drummond, L. (1980) 'The Cultural Continuum: a Theory of Intersystems', *Man* (n.s.) 15: 352-74.
Erickson, E. (1968) *Identity: Youth and Crisis*, London: Faber & Faber.
Gilroy, P. (1987) *There Ain't No Black in the Union Jack: The Cultural Politics of Race and Nation*, London: Hutchinson.
Gilroy, P. (1993) *Small Acts: Thoughts on the Politics of Black Cultures*. London: Serpent's Tail.
Hannerz, U. (1969) *Soulside: Inquiries into Ghetto Culture and Community*, New York: Columbia University Press.
Hannerz, U. (1987) 'The World in Creolisation', *Africa* 57: 546-559.
Hargreaves, A.G. (1995) *Immigration, 'Race' and Ethnicity in Contemporary France*, London: Routledge.
Hargreaves, A.G. and Stenhouse, T.S. (1991) 'Islamic Beliefs Among Youths of North African Origin in France', *Modern and Contemporary France* 45: 27-35.
Haw, K. (1995) 'Why Muslim Girls are More Feminist in Muslim Schools', in: M. Griffiths and B. Troyna (eds.) *Antiracism, Culture and Social Justice in Education*, Stoke-on-Trent: Trentham: 43-60.
Hebdige, D. (1987) *Cut 'n' Mix: Culture, Identity and Caribbean Music*, London: Routledge.
Heitmeyer, W. (1997) *Verlockender Fundamentalismus*, Frankfurt am Main: Edition Suhrkamp.
Hewitt, R. (1992) 'Language, Youth and the Destabilisation of Ethnicity', in: C. Palmgren, K. Lövgren and G. Bolin (eds.) *Ethnicity in Youth Culture*, Stockholm: Youth Culture at Stockholm University: 27-41.
Jackson, R. and E. Nesbitt (1993) *Hindu Children in Britain*, Stoke-on-Trent: Trentham.
Jacobsen-Widding, A. (ed.) (1983) *Identity: Personal and Socio-Cultural*, Stockholm: Alqvist & Wiksell.
Jacobson, J. (1997) 'Religion and Ethnicity: Dual and Alternative Sources of Identity Among Young British Pakistanis', *Ethnic & Racial Studies* 20: 238-56.
Jenks, C. (1993) 'Introduction: the analytic bases of cultural reproduction theory', in: C. Jenks (ed.) *Cultural Reproduction*, London: Routledge: 1-16.
Jones, T. (1993) *Britain's Ethnic Minorities*, London: Policy Studies Institute.
Kalra, V.S., J. Hutnyk and S. Sharma (1996) 'Re-sounding (Anti)Racism, or Concordant Political Revolutionary Antecedents', in: S. Sharma, J. Hutnyk and A. Sharma (eds.) *Dis-Orienting Rhythms: The Politics of the New Asian Dance Music*, London: Zed Books: 127-55.
Kaya, A. (1997) Constructing Diasporas: Turkish Hip-Hop Youth in Berlin, Ph.D. Thesis, Race & Ethnic Studies, University of Warwick.
Knott, K. (1986) *Hinduism in Leeds: A Study of Religious Practice in the Indian Hindu Community and Hindu-Related Groups*, Leeds: Community Religions Project, University of Leeds.

Knott, K. and S. Khokher (1993) 'Religious and Ethnic Identity Among Young Muslim Women in Bradford', *New Community* 19: 593-610.
Leveau, R. (1997) 'The Political Culture of the "Beurs"', in: S. Vertovec and C. Peach (eds.) *Islam in Europe: The Politics of Religion and Community*, Basingstoke: Macmillan: 147-55.
Liebkind, K. (ed.) (1989a) *New Identities in Europe: Immigrant Ancestry and the Ethnic Identity of Youth*, Aldershot: Gower.
Liebkind, K. (1989b) 'Concluding Remarks', in: K. Liebkind (ed.) *New Identities in Europe: Immigrant Ancestry and the Ethnic Identity of Youth*, Aldershot: Gower: 237-43.
McLoughlin, S. (1997) Breaking into Bounded Britain: Discrepant Discourses of Belonging and Muslims in Bradford, Ph.D. Thesis, Social Anthropology, University of Manchester.
Nielsen, J. (1992) *Muslims in Western Europe*, Edinburgh: Edinburgh University Press.
Nijsten, C. (1996) 'Living as a Muslim in a Migration Country: Moroccan Youngsters in the Netherlands', in: W.A.R. Shahid and P.S. van Koningsveld (eds.) *Political Participation and Identities of Muslims in Non-Muslim States*, Kampen, Netherlands: Kok Pharos: 144-57.
Palmgren, C., K. Lövgren and G. Bolin (eds.) *Ethnicity in Youth Culture*, Stockholm: Youth Culture at Stockholm University.
Rampton, B. (1995) *Crossing: Language and Ethnicity among Adolescents*, London: Longman.
Robins, K. (1991) 'Tradition and Translation: National Culture in its Global Context', in: J. Corner and S. Harvey (eds.) *Enterprise and Heritage: Cross-Currents of National Culture*, London: Routledge: 21-44.
Similä, M. (1988) 'The Cultural Identity of Immigrant Youth: a Perspective from Action Theory', *Migration* 3: 61-59.
Singh Ghuman, P.A. (1994) *Coping with Two Cultures: British Asian and Indo-Canadian Adolescents*, Clevedon: Multilingual Matters.
Stolcke, V. (1995) 'Talking Culture', *Current Anthropology* 36: 1-13.
Swidler, A. (1986) 'Culture in Action: Symbols and Strategies', *American Sociological Review* 51: 273-86.
Tajfel, H. (1974) 'Social Identity and Intergroup Behaviour', *Social Science Information* 13: 65-93.
van der Lans, J. and M. Rooijackers (1996) 'Ethnic Identity and Cultural Orientation of Second Generation Turkish Muslim Migrants: Consequences for Minorities Policy', in: W.A.R. Shahid and P.S. van Koningsveld (eds.) *Political Participation and Identities of Muslims in Non-Muslim States*, Kampen, Netherlands: Kok Pharos: 174-89.
Vertovec, S. (1996) 'Multiculturalism, Culturalism and Public Incorporation', *Ethnic & Racial Studies* 19: 49-69.

Vertovec, S. and C. Peach (1997) 'Introduction: Islam in Europe and the Politics of Religion and Community', in: S. Vertovec and C. Peach (eds.) *Islam in Europe: The Politics of Religion and Community*, Basingstoke: Macmillan: 3-47.

Weinreich, P. (1989) 'Variations in Ethnic Identity: Identity Structure Analysis', in: K. Liebkind (ed.) *New Identities in Europe: Immigrant Ancestry and the Ethnic Identity of Youth,* Aldershot: Gower: 41-76.

Werbner, P. and T. Modood (eds.) (1997) *Debating Cultural Hybridity: Multi-Cultural Identities and the Politics of Anti-Racism*, London: Zed Books.

Williams, R. (1981) *Culture*, Glasgow: Fontana.

Wilpert, C. (1989) 'Ethnic and Cultural Identity: Ethnicity and the Second Generation in the Context of European Migration', in: K. Liebkind (ed.) *New Identities in Europe: Immigrant Ancestry and the Ethnic Identity of Youth*, Aldershot: Gower: 6-24.

2 Islam in France: Social Challenge or Challenge of Secularism?

Jocelyne Cesari

To overcome Neo-Orientalism: a new approach to religion

Neo-Orientalism is still alive, as the success of Huntington's thesis on the 'clash of civilizations' proves (Huntington 1993). Without delving too deeply into the complexities of politics and Islam in the Arab and Muslim world, it seems that scholarly analyses of Islamic governance are too often equivalent to a sort of Neo-Orientalism. They are characterized by a rationalized language covering a normative and value-laden approach in which the Muslim world is opposed to the Western one in terms of political moderation, democracy and human rights. Neo-Orientalism refers to a substantialist approach to religion and a linear vision of history in which the politics of the Islamic world cannot be anything other than theocracy and a return to past.[1] With the settlement of Muslims in European countries, the issue of Islamic fundamentalism has been transferred to Western societies in the same inappropriate terms.

Muslims in Europe are also victim of the same substantialist approach. It involves a totalization effect by which Muslims are required to conform to Islamic Law because they are Muslims, or seem to be. It is thereby impossible to take into account the accommodations, faults, mistakes or weaknesses which also characterize their relationship with Islam.

This vision of Islam implies three major misperceptions. First, it neglects the very important transformations in Islamic identity which are going on among the new generations born or educated in the West. These Muslim youths are involved in a quite new secularization process in which Islam is becoming a part of the private sphere. The second consequence of this essentialist vision of Islam is that it pays no attention at all to cultural differences in the various ways of being Muslim. But specificities of cultures and ethnic boundaries do affect the meaning and the content of Muslim identities. They may be more important in certain circumstances than the universal belonging to the 'Umma'. The third problem concerns the artificial and misguided opposition of Islam and modernity. This opposition blocks an understanding of the major changes in the Arab and Muslim world, where references to Islamic Law or to the vocabulary of Islam in general does not signify archaic attitudes but indicates the capacity of this culture to face the issue of social and political modernization (Burgat 1995).

In Europe and especially in France, this antagonism takes place inside a larger debate about the 'return of religion'. But this discussion seems to be at an impasse. It is more constructive to rephrase the question and to consider new forms of relationships between religion and politics even in those societies where the separation between political and religious spheres was initiated. In a period of great doubt concerning the basic values of Western societies, where modernity and Western world are no longer synonymous, there is now an attempt by Third World societies to put the major issues they must face into their own cultural language. The use of Islam in the political arena of Islamic countries thereby becomes more comprehensible. It also explains why the vocabulary of religion is again relevant even in Western societies.

To consider this greater mobility of meanings, it is necessary to devise a new conceptual framework to overcome the separation of politics and religion (Hervieu-Leger 1993; Michel 1996). These two spheres are characterized by similar social and symbolic processes and the emphasis should be placed on the circulation of beliefs from one to another. However, religion remains a particular sort of belief because it needs the legitimation of tradition. This introduces two risks: on the one hand, dogmatic rigidity and on the other, the control of consciousness and behaviour. The propensity to control may be exerted in two opposite directions: *ad extra* as a way of extending religious influence in society or *ad intra* as a way of separating from the rest of society all those who share the same tradition of faith.

The combination of these internal and external dimensions may be extremely diverse. It is possible to distinguish religious groups according to whether they focus on external dimensions (i.e. when the conformity to tradition is a matter of extension) or on internal ones (i.e. when the required conformity to tradition is a matter of intensity). This is what distinguishes the Arab world from the situation of Muslims in Europe. In this view, the so-called fundamentalism of Muslim countries refers to an extension of Islamic references to different social, cultural, economical and political spaces which were formerly secular, at least since independence. By contrast, Islamization in Europe is a way of keeping and reinforcing a belonging to Islam in a non-Muslim context. The other major difference concerns the situation of being a minority in a context of political and cultural pluralism which is a quite new and original experience for the majority of Muslims settled in Europe. They come from countries where Islam is the religion of the State or at least the religion of the majority of the people, and so they are discovering an unaccustomed way of being Muslim which is not analysed by Islamic tradition (Schnapper and Lewis 1992).

Muslims in France: pluralism as an issue

To begin with, the increased visibility of Islam is not the same as a return of Islam. What is generally considered as a return to, or a change in, the intensity of Islamic practices, is in fact a change in the relationship with the host society. Muslims in France, and more generally in Europe, are mainly migrants. Therefore, the construction of mosques since the beginning of the 1980s does not mean a return of Islam or a rise in practice, but is instead a new step in the process of integration. Moreover some Muslims are more visible than others because there is a specific French interest in North African people and particularly Algerians.

Since the 1980s, the question of North African migration has unleashed French passions. The growing number of mosques on the one hand, and on the other, racist murders, riots in suburbs and so on describe the condition of North Africans in French society. There are about four million Muslims in France and half of them are French citizens. Although there are Muslims from Turkey, Senegal, Lebanon and elsewhere, the great majority come from North Africa. This situation is regarded as intolerable by many French people, because of the migration's colonial or postcolonial origins. That is why these migrants have been considered by the host society as only temporary settlers although some have been resident in France for twenty or thirty years. It also explains why French people are very reluctant to accept the visibility of Islam. Their perception is shaped by the colonial past, especially that of Algeria. It should be remembered that during this period, even if Muslims obtained French nationality (Algeria was a French department) they were not considered as citizens unless they renounced

Islamic law. So it is very difficult for a lot of people to accept the settlement of Muslims in France after the Algerian war of independence. To them it looks like history is repeating itself, but this time on the wrong side of the Mediterranean.

Islam and ethnicity

Among Muslim migrants, Islamic identities differ according to ethnic or national origin, gender, age and social class. However it is possible to distinguish the great majority who make no distinction between ethnic and religious ties, from two opposite minorities, one involved in secularization and the other in fundamentalism.

For the first generation of migrants, Islam cannot be dissociated from national membership and refers to the status of Islam in their country of birth. For them Islamic membership is linked with national membership; Islam was an important element of their identity which had to be preserved against French domination. This nationalist memory explains why these migrants denied the consequences of their departure for so long; for instance they refused to let their family come in France during the first decade of their settlement.[2] This resistance continues through their reluctance to get French nationality, which they would regard as a renunciation of their struggle against colonialism. That is why they continue to entertain the hope of a return to their homeland even if their rare attempts to do so are not successful. This attitude towards French society explains why identification with nationalism has now been replaced by identification with Islam as a social referent which enables the struggle against assimilation. The first generation do not want to disappear into French society; they want to be recognised and considered as Muslim. The Islamic referent is a way of evaluating their life and environment by means of a limited number of attributes, especially the distinction between *haram* and *halal*.

This division of their activities and relations between *haram* and *halal* is a way of providing significance to their way of life in France and of establishing the fact that they are not completely lost in their exile. This distinction is materialised through dietary rules, the separation between men and women in public spaces and the creation of mosques. Mosques are not only places of worship but are also communities where ethnic and national networks are strengthened by religious belonging. Social assistance, the education of children and relationships with the countries of origin are all services provided in them. It is not unusual to observe a mosque for North Africans and another for Turks in the same neighbourhood, although there is no difference in their observance. Culture and ethnic identification is a component of Islamic identity. This diversity constitutes a real challenge which can be put in these terms: how can the cultural diversity of Islamic expressions inside the religious community be preserved while avoiding the privileging of ethnicity over religion, especially in the demands concerning the recognition of Islam and the relationships with public powers or political classes (Cesari 1994, 1996)?

There is also diversity caused by the acculturation of new generations to French culture. The second, third or even fourth generation Muslims have specific needs and identifications with Islam. The most important change is the growth of individualization and privatization.

'Islam is my culture'

Among North African migrants the gap between the values of the first generation and those of their children is more pronounced than among other groups of migrants (Malewska-Peyre 1982). Being working class in French society, the parents have struggled to maintain the cultural system of their country of origin, while their children have been more socialised by French institutions such as schools and social workers.

For these young people to define themselves as Arab or Muslim would represent a symbolic assertion which is not always connected with their everyday life, which they share with people of the same age also living in the suburbs. They have adopted some of the most important values of French society such as liberty and equality. They are also very critical about the situation in their family's home country, especially about the way of life and the fact that they are despised by their relatives and considered as too westernized.

So defining themselves in France as Arab or Muslim does not mean that they are homesick but refers to their situation in France. In fact it is a reaction against discrimination. Their relationship with French society is an unequal one because the countries from which their families originate are considered poor. In the case of North Africa, this opposition is also a consequence of colonial history. The more the relations between the groups are unequal the more the migrants are evaluated through pejorative ethnic categories. Even if these new generations automatically obtain French nationality (according to France's liberal laws) they are still defined and considered as Arab or Muslim, i.e. as if they were foreigners.

This negative perception produces different and opposite reactions among North Africans. The majority consider Arab and Muslim identity as positive despite their negative connotations in the French context. In others words, they manage a semantic reversal; the more Islamic and Arab origin is despised the stronger their identification with it is. But this identification with the Muslim or Arab world does not mean that they live as Muslim or Arab: it is more a symbolic allegiance. At the same time, because it is related to cultural values transmitted through their families, it also a very emotional and passionate identity. This identification with the Arab world is not limited to just their parents' country but extends to the worldwide Arab community, especially involving solidarity with, and interest in, struggles such as Palestinian cause, the war in Bosnia or Chechnya. This focus on the Arab world was particularly significant during the Gulf War, during which they felt solidarity with the Iraqi people while also not wishing to be suspected of disloyalty towards France.[3]

Their attachment to their families' cultural values is combined with an affiliation with the French cultural system. This coincidence of values is not hypocritical or deceitful, but an attempt to manage different loyalties. If they really appreciate French political values such as liberty and democracy, identification with the French nation is more difficult. Identification with locality or place is more significant; they consider themselves as members of local collectivities defined as the places in which they are born or educated.

Although the new generations are not always very pious, it does not mean that they do not respect Islamic rules and values. Most define themselves as believers and have a positive perception of Islam. This attests to their desire to remain within their parents' community. Above all, to them Islam relates to the more important episodes of family life such as feasts such as Afd El Kebir. These particular moments are kinds of breaks with the space and time of the dominant social environment.

It is important to note that the second generation has not received a real religious education either inside or outside their family.[4] This lack of religious education within the family can be explained by their parents' attitude towards Islam during the first period of the migration. During this time they neglected Islamic prescriptions because they did not consider themselves to be permanently settled in French society. Moreover, within the traditional rural family in North Africa, religious grandfathers or uncles are more involved in children's religious education than the parents. This cannot be done in France and the migrant family is not able to undertake the responsibility, particularly if it has been separated and then reunited by the process of migration.[5]

These new generations distinguish between practising religion and believing religion to describe their relationship with Islam. It is a part of the cultural legacy within the private sphere, with no direct influence on their social and public behaviour. Especially for those who are upwardly mobile, Islam is an ethic, a source of moral values giving significance to their life but without implication for their practice. Individuals thus demonstrate their autonomy from the group and act as their own mediators between the content and the application of Islamic Law. In this way, they express their inventiveness and liberty. This profound change can be related to new forms of religiosity within modern societies. The believer no longer obeys the norms which are legitimated by tradition or by institutions, but chooses among 'salvation goods' according to preference (Champion and Hervieu-Leger 1990). In this case, the collective dimension of Islamic membership is moderated by an individual logic. This attitude is particularly significant when it comes to the religious education of the next generation i.e., the third generation. A liberal education on religion is preferred, more so among well-educated people.

But this individualization of Islam is constrained by two things: circumcision and the prohibition on intermarriage. They attach great meaning to circumcision. Although this prescription is not yet one of the 'five pillars of Islam', it is considered as a strong obligation shaping the identity of the community. In a non-Muslim society, it acts as the ultimate sign of attachment to their origins. Exogamy constitutes the other prescription which is difficult to break. On this topic distinctions should be made between men and women and also between speech and acts. Although the prohibition affects women, young men are also reluctant to consider mixed marriages for themselves. Their opposition is not justified by religious arguments but by cultural ones; they reason that there would be a cultural incompatibility between husband and wife and the risk of domination of one by the other. Even so, the latest national statistics show that there is a growing number of marriages across religious boundaries among young men (Tribalat 1995). In so far as women are concerned, there is a difference between those who possess financial and individual autonomy and those who do not. Sexual relationships or cohabitation with non-Muslim men is more probable among the former. However it is very difficult for them to legalise such situations since it often means being disowned by their families and ultimately calls their identity into question.[6] Moreover, the fact that there is a growing gap between men and women among the group concerning social behaviour and education explains why a certain number of young women who are aged 25 or over remain unmarried, something which is quite unusual in North African culture.

Most of the people born or educated in France try to find some coherence between their parents' values and those of French society. That explains why, even if they are not always rigorous in their practice of Islam, it does not mean that they are giving up this part of their family legacy. But, for these new generations, the significance of Islam belongs to their private domain and has no consequences for their social behaviour. The priority given to individuality and privacy in their relationship to Islam is an innovation compared with the status of Islam in their parents' countries.

But there is also a quite different relationship to Islam, a more fundamentalist one.

Islamisation of French society

The involvement of the new generations with Islam is a very recent one. Recently, a growing number of young people have become more pious and strict in their respect of Islamic rules, even if they are still a small minority compared with the group described above.

This real practice of Islam often means a separation from their parents' religion. When they decide to become Muslims they distance themselves from the superstitious habits of their parents and choose to learn what they call 'the real Islam'. They learn by themselves or are helped by young students, who come from Arab countries and are often committed to Islamic ideologies. They may represent or belong to organizations such as Muslim Brotherhood, Tabligh wa Jamaat, or Algerian Islamist movements (the Islamic Front but also Hamas). They have brought with them new concepts about community and religious involvement. According to their views, Islam cannot be reduced to ethics or be confined to the private domain. It also affects social behaviour and can even justify social action.

Although some of them are political opponents in their homelands, they do not use Islam as political propaganda for young Muslims in France. Their aim and aspiration is to preserve Islam among the new generations and to prevent their assimilation.

In this regard, Islam is a credible alternative after years during which they experienced unemployment, drugs, alcohol and delinquency. It allows them to recover some personal dignity and project a better image of themselves. But this does not mean that Islamization only concerns marginalized youths. That is why it is necessary to analyse these identities in relationship to the French context. It is impossible to understand the behaviour of these new generations without keeping in mind the fact that they are by now a part of French youth.

In the West in general and in France in particular, there is a questioning of progress and modernity. Some consider these doubts about modernity itself to be a sign of 'ultramodernity'. When the collective landmarks provided by schools, political parties and trade unions are weakened or missing and the economy is insufficient to provide social status, religious membership can provide a collective definition for a part of Muslim youth. This use of religion also concerns young people in other religious groups.

Islamization can also simply be a way to define a collective identity with no real practice. Islam is used to protest against social conditions and can lead to collective action. This is possible after the experiences of other forms of collective action such as the civil rights and antiracist movements of the 1980s. The experience of discrimination and racism can also explain this mobilization, especially when Islam tends to be defined as the new major enemy of Western world.

In the 1980s, the first form of mobilization was one of disorder and violence in reaction to racist murders or police racism. But soon the political support that they found in their struggle contributed to a change in the direction and the meaning of their collective action. This support, especially from socialists, was materialized in the shape of significant public funding given to the associations created by these new political actors. The public aid to these associations was an indirect way of legitimating the permanent settlement of North African migrants in France. But it also helped establish an artificial ethnic elite dependent on political power. This elite was brought about by the creation of jobs in social work for some members of the new generation, giving them opportunities of social mobility.

The Social Action Fund (Fonds d'Action Sociale), a state programme created in 1958 to facilitate the housing and the social integration of Algerian migrants, remains the central institution of this policy. It is the major support for associations and an important partner of municipalities in urban policy. This support encourages young people to develop action which conforms with public priorities in order to receive funding. This explains why they often emphasize their ethnic origin, because it positively influences the allocation of financial resources. But this collective presentation of themselves does not mean that the ethnic referent is significant in daily life or social interaction. Membership of suburbs or of marginalized groups is more decisive in the construction of their political identity.

These associations failed to improve social and economic conditions of suburban youth. Ten years after the struggle for civic rights, nothing has changed. That is why Islam seems to be a better way of action. New associations created by young Muslims are now trying to deal with social action. They are based on religious values, although they do not use proselytizing methods and they appear multicultural to the public. A new form of citizenship is emerging in which priority is given to concrete and local action rather than to voting or involvement with political parties. In others words, the civil dimension seems to be more relevant than the civic one.

In fact, these new actors, either secular or religious, have changed the customary way of doing politics in France. According to the French model, politics is legitimate if it is within the framework of interest groups or public groups which are not based on ethnic or cultural origin. Now leaders of these new particularist associations are trying to mediate between a specific group and the public sphere. For example, during the 1989 local elections, the leaders of an association called FRANCE PLUS managed to place candidates in different electoral rolls or slates. Their justification was that North African-origin people should be elected in order to be considered as a real component of French society. They negotiated this enrolment with the different political parties from left wing to right wing (except the National Front). Other association leaders tried to constitute autonomous electoral lists by combining different minorities (women, various migrant groups) and not only on the basis of North African origin. The leaders of FRANCE PLUS also tried to create autonomous electoral rolls for the parliamentary elections in March 1993 based only on ethnic criteria. But these attempts were not successful because such autonomous lists only win one to two percent of the vote. Although there is a growing number of associations of young Muslims, they are not yet involved in political competition.

The outcome of these different actions was an attempt to legitimate new political actors defined as 'French coming from North Africa' ('Franco-Maghrebins'). They employed an ethnic label to access political and financial resources. But this strategy was not successful and required too many compromises. This explains why young Muslims now prefer to be self-sufficient. In general, this attitude disconnects citizenship from the feeling of national membership. For these actors, citizenship means civic rights, laws and liberties separate from a complete identification with the French nation. To become a national is often considered as an acquisition of French and European citizenship, but it does not mean identification with the memory and history of the national community.[7]

Finally, the forms of mobilization (associations rather than political parties) and the types of demands (housing, improved conditions of life in the suburbs, citizenship for people who are not French nationals) reveal a new conception of citizenship. It emphasizes the different cultural and ethnic groups within civil society, which is quite new in French political life but also tends to appear among other French minority groups. Political life in France is changing because (local and specific boundaries are more visible). Between the State and its citizens there are increasing demands for the recognition of intermediate groups or boundaries. This is not a global process of ethnicization so much as a transfer of participation from the national centralized level to the local level. The main issue concerns the loyalty of all these groups to national community and to common values.

The issue of plural society

Islam implies change not only for Muslims but also for French society, especially the status of religion. The settlement of Muslims in secular European societies has created controversy over religious freedom, tolerance and the limits to the public expression of faith. In France, this debate concerns the content of secularity. The Islamisation of French society demonstrates that secularity (laïcité) is not as universal as it is usually supposed. The main aim of the 1905 law of the separation of State and Church was to exclude Catholicism from the public sphere and limit it social influence. The paradox is that, in order to achieve the unequal balance of power between politics and religion, the law had to establish the equality of all religions. But nobody in France seems to know the content of the law because the cultural vision of secularism is very intolerant towards religious expression. Catholics have accepted this separation and have reduced religion to the private sphere in a context of declining practice. Since 1905, social life has become more and more disconnected from religious references.

However, some demands from different religious authorities have emerged, especially inside the public school system over the introduction of religious education. The 'Islamic headscarf affair' in 1989 reopened the debate on the specificity of French secularism. French girls are still claming their right to wear the hijab in public schools and consider their expulsion as discrimination. Since 1989, the Council of State has always affirmed that a religious symbol does not break the law, whatever it is. But the hijab does not conform to the dominant perception of secularism in which public expressions of religious membership are not legitimate. In this case, the gap between the cultural perception of secularism and the content of the law is evident.

So Islamic membership confuses the boundary between public and private space which had seemed stable since 1905. Islam cannot be confined to the mosques and the private sphere, as Catholicism has been. The social dimensions of Islam are still significant for the majority of French Muslims which is why they refuse to limit the expression of their faith to mosques and maintain many rules intervening in social life, even if this shocks the French majority.

Islam has changed the balance between three major 'pillars' of French political life: unity, respect for religious pluralism and liberty. If pluralism is linked with democracy it no longer refers to the integration of dominated groups or to the representation of the diversity of citizens, but to the balance between multiculturalism and communities. The French political classes and French society are not prepared to deal with this issue.

The question of pluralism in western democracies is also related to transnationalism. In others words, if there are increasing numbers of French citizens who are Muslims, they will continue to maintain solidarities outside the nation state. For example, the major sites of Islamic law are outside Europe and western world in general. The main religious leaders often possess a specific training in the Muslim world but are not prepared to face the specific needs of Muslim minorities. These transnational identities also appear when external events such as Rushdie Affair or the Gulf and Bosnian wars allow French Muslim to show solidarity with their external 'brothers'.

Finally, although Islamic identities help reduce the lack of social ties and collective projects they do not represent a threat to the State as they do in the Maghreb. The major issue at the end of century is not a 'clash of civilizations' but a competition between different claims to universalism.

Notes

1. See Dupret (1994), Norton (1993), Qandil (1993a, b). Ezra Pound once pointed out that it is the habit of democracy to tell two lies (one left wing and one right wing) and then sit back to argue which one is actually true. The 'Ezra Pound effect' has meant quarrelling over whether the so-called Islamic fundamentalists are outright terrorists or just plain anti-secular fanatics. In this dichotomized debate, the third alternative - a political campaign that uses the religious discourse to promote radical social change and oppose government dishonesty and corruption -- has become severely silenced. See also Toth (1996) and Kramer (1994).
2. A comparison between Algerian and Portuguese migrants reveals that Portuguese migrants gathered their families together in less than twenty years whereas Algerians took almost half a century. For a long time, Algerian migration consisted of single men. Only at the beginning of the 1960s did families arrive in France (Hifi 1985).
3. During the Gulf War, this mistrust clearly appeared in the attention paid to them by the French political class and within public opinion because their loyalty to French institutions was questioned (Cesari 1991).
4. For people who are now aged between 25 and 34 years old, there were no Koranic schools when they were children. The situation is now different because the development of Islamic associations in France since the early 1980s was accompanied by the foundation of Koranic courses. The majority of mosques established during this period provided religious education for children.
5. These two stages refer to two periods. In the first the North African migrant came to France alone, he married in his home country and often went back to meet his wife and his first children. In the second period he let his family come to France and new children were born there.
6. Two social circles seem to favour intermarriages: university and associations (Streiff-Fenart 1989). It should be noted that it is impossible to get precise information about mixed marriages in France because official statistics only provide information about marriages between foreigners and nationals. There is no measure of exogamy among the French-born generations because it is illegal to officially differentiate people according to religious or ethnic origin. It is possible to state that between 1974 and 1985 the number of marriages between North Africans and French people doubled, rising from 2703 to 5189 outstripping the marriages between Italian and French or between Portuguese and French (Munoz-Perez and Tribalat 1984).
7. This explains why they also claim the right to vote in local elections for people who are not French nationals. It is a way of preserving their parents' choice of remaining a national of their home countries even if they do not go back there.

References

Burgat, F. (1995) *L'Islamisme en Face*. Paris: La Découverte.
Cesari, J. (1991) 'La Guerre du Golfe et les Arabes de France', *Revue du Monde Musulman et de la Méditerranée* (no hors série): 125-129.
Cesari, J. (1994) *Être Musulman en France, Associations, Militants et Mosquées*. Paris: Karthala.
J. (1996) *La Vie Quotidienne des Musulmans en France*. Paris: Hachette.
Champion, F. and D. Hervieu-Leger (eds) (1990) *De l'Émotion en Religion: Renaissance et Traditions*. Paris: Le Centurion.
Dupret, B. (1994) *Interpreter l'Islamic Politique: une Approche Diachronique de la Matrice Coranique*, Université Catholique de Louvain, CERMAC.
Hervieu-Leger, D. (1993) *La Religion Pour Memoire*. Paris: Du Cerf
Hifi, B. (1985) *L'Immigration Algérienne en France: Origines et Perspectives de Non Retour*. Paris: L'Harmattan/ CIEM.
Huntington, S. (1993) 'The Clash of Civilizations?' *Foreign Affairs* 72: 22-49.
Kramer, M. (1994) 'Islam Versus Democracy', Moshe Dayan Centre, University of Tel Aviv, current issues.
Malewska-Peyre, H. (1982) *Crise d'Identité et Déviance Chez les Jeunes Immigrés*. Paris: La Documentation Française.
Michel, P. (1996) *Politique et Religion, la Grande Mutation*. Paris: Albin Michel.
Munoz-Perez, F. and M. Tribalat (1984) 'Mariages d'Étrangers et Mariages Mixtes en France', *Population* 3: 427-462.
Norton, R. (ed.) (1993) *Civil Society in the Middle East*.
Qandil, A. (1993a) *Le Role des Islamistes dans les Syndicats Égyptiens*, Cairo: Cedej.
Qandil, A. (1993b) 'Le Courant Islamique dans les Organismes de la Société Civile: le Cas des Ordres Professionals', roneo, Cairo.
Schnapper, D. and B. Lewis (1992) *Musulmans en Europe*. Poitiers: Actes Sud.
Streiff-Fenart, J. (1989) *Les Couples Franco-Maghrébins en France*. Paris: L'Harmattan.
Toth, J. (1996) 'Islamic Activism as an Avenue of Radical Social Change', paper presented at the sixth congress of the International Association of Middle Eastern Studies, University of Al-Bayt, Mafraq, Jordan, April 10-14.
Tribalat, M. (1995) *Faire France*. Enquête INED. Paris: La Découverte.

3 Islam and Interest Struggle: Religious Collective Action Among Turkish Muslims in the Netherlands[1]

Thijl Sunier

In recent years the position of Islamic organizations among immigrants in Western-Europe has received increasing attention from social scientists as well as the public. Due to sometimes dramatic events in the Islamic World in the 1980s and 1990s, Islam became a 'hot topic' in public debate. Especially after the so-called 'Rushdie affair' and the second Gulf War, the activities and the attitudes of Muslims and their organizations have been followed and monitored with more attention than before. In general, these events have had a rather negative effect on the image of Islam and Islamic organizations. The visibility of Muslims and their institutions such as mosques and schools has been increasingly linked with discussions about fundamentalism and social integration.

Despite the proliferation of negative images of Islam at this time, it was nevertheless during the 1980s that Islam and Islamic organizations changed their level of organizational structure and gained a foothold in and access to material and political resources in Western European countries (Nielsen 1992; Rath et al. 1996). As a result, Muslims managed to create an infrastructure which gave Islam in Western Europe a public face. The route by which this occurred differed considerably from one country to another due to a variety of reasons deriving from specific policies, attitudes towards Islam, and the characteristics of the various Muslim communities themselves. Although the governments of the various European countries largely determined the terms under which this process of institutionalization took place, the demands put forward by Muslims themselves must be considered as the necessary and initial driving force behind the institutionalization of Islam (Sunier and Meyer 1997). Institutionalization is mainly the result of collective action performed by Muslims and the interests they promote.

Although there is a growing number of publications on Islamic institutions and organizations in Western Europe, organizational development and collective political action among Muslims are rather neglected themes. In public opinion they are often considered extremist. In most social scientific publications, Islamic organizations are approached either as 'migrant organizations', or as 'associations of people with an Islamic background' (a so-called culturalist approach). Although these approaches are relevant to a certain extent, they are inadequate as an analytical tool in attempting to understand why, how, and to what extent Islamic organizations have managed to improve their position. If Islamic organizations are considered solely as migrant organizations, then they will be regarded as only temporary phenomena. This implies, among other things, that the foundation, persistence and development of these organizations is almost entirely based on their function as intermediary between the migrant 'community' and the receiving society. Their *raison-d'être* is supposedly related to the fact that ordinary migrants do not yet fully participate in the new society.

In this approach no fundamental distinction is made between Islamic institutions and organizations and any other organizations founded by migrants. Activities and services performed by these institutions are related to the migrant background of their members. It is assumed that these organizations function as a kind of sanctuary in a strange and sometimes hostile environment. As it is assumed that the process of integration will take place anyhow, it is also supposed that the significance of Islamic organizations as organizations of migrants will gradually diminish.

If they persist however, this is either because migrants are not yet fully integrated or, and this especially the case with Islamic organizations, factors related to religion and culture itself must be looked for. This leads to the second, so-called 'culturalist' approach. The culturalist approach is based on the assumption that Islamic organizations are associations of people with the same religious background. Furthermore, Islamic principles and prescriptions and religio-ideological images and affiliations require specific types of organizational activities. While this may explain their persistence to a certain extent, this approach exhibits the failings of an essentialist perspective. For example, it does not account for the fact that Islamic organizations increasingly perform duties and services which go beyond strictly religious matters. In general this type of approach implicitly fails to distinguish between Muslim community and Muslim organizations. Although the two have much to do with each other, they are certainly not one and the same. In this approach Islam is disconnected from the social context in which it is embedded, and it is assumed that Islamic organizations take on similar shapes, irrespective of the social setting.

Islamic organizations as interest organizations

Although these two approaches encompass elements that are relevant and important in explaining and analysing organizational development, both give inadequate attention to the political processes underlying the dynamics of organizational development. They emphasize *specific* characteristics of the people in question, rather than *general* aspects, characteristic of any form of organization. The analysis of organizational development among Muslims requires, in my view, an alternative approach in which interest struggle, and emancipation are central themes. To a certain extent, Islamic organizations can be characterized as 'interest organizations'. They have been set up in order to attain certain goals and to change political structures. Nielsen (1992: 118) has raised the important fact that Muslims in Europe do not organize themselves because Islam prescribes this, but because they want to achieve certain goals which are related to their circumstances. The interests of Muslims are thus not self evidently based on Islamic principles, as is often assumed. They are contextual and dynamic and change according to altered circumstances. Muslim interest organizations transform the demands and needs of individual Muslims into collective interests. Collective action in defence of collective interests is mainly the result of well-chosen rational strategies by collective actors, bounded by specific societal and political contexts. Therefore, the analysis of organizational development and interest struggle among Muslims can make use of existing general theoretical frameworks rather than develop ones specific to only Muslims or migrants. Although the characteristics of interest struggle among Muslims are specific to a large extent, the mechanisms underlying interest struggle are general and applicable to any interest group. This opens up the possibility of comparison with forms of organization and interest struggle other than those of Muslims or migrants.

The following analysis is based on research I carried out among Turkish Islamic organizations in Rotterdam, a city with a relatively large number of Turkish inhabitants and a larger number of Islamic organizations. In recent years, that is mainly since the end of the 1980s, an important shift seems to have taken place in the strategies, working procedures and in the articulation of interests of Turkish Islamic organizations. These developments have not yet been documented and analyzed until now.

When the way in which Muslims organize themselves to gain access to decision-making processes and defend their collective interests is examined, Islamic organizations can be defined as 'social movements'. They perform activities characteristic of social movements, or more precisely of so-called 'identity movements', as compared to 'instrumental movements'. The main difference between the two variants of social movements is that the former takes a specific cultural, religious or political identity as a starting point, whereas the latter is more concerned with the mobilization of resources for a specific goal. In practise we find elements of both types in every social movement. From among the vast body of literature on social movements the research of McAdam (1982) offers a useful framework, particularly for the analysis of recent developments in the articulation of interest among Turkish Muslims in the Netherlands.

The political process model, as McAdam (1982: 36) describes his approach, rests on the assumption that social movements are political rather than psychological phenomena, and that movements represent a continuous process rather than well-defined, discrete phenomena. His model is based on the fundamental assumption that challengers are excluded from the routine decision-making processes and that wealth and power are concentrated in the hands of a few groups, but that, at the same time, the political power structure is not impermeable. Social movements must be considered as rational attempts by excluded groups to mobilize sufficient political leverage to advance collective interests through non-institutionalized means (*ibid.*: 37). Successful collective action is the result of a favourable interplay of both internal and external factors.

Turkish Islam in the Netherlands: a brief overview

In the Netherlands there are some 550,000 people with an Islamic background, of which 250,000 are Turks. The majority of Muslims live in the western part of the country, mainly in the big cities such as Rotterdam,

The Hague, Amsterdam and Utrecht, although there are considerable numbers elsewhere in the Netherlands. I do not want to label them automatically as 'Muslims'. This is a widely misused concept. Especially since the late 1980s policy-makers and social scientists have tended to use 'Muslim' to describe people from Islamic countries, although only an estimated half are practising believers. The Islamic leadership in their struggle for popular support also use the official statistics.

In my research I confined myself to adherents of the three largest Turkish Islamic organizations operating in the Netherlands. Together they run about 90 percent of the 200 Turkish mosques. About three-quarters of these organizations have separate youth branches. My research particularly focused on the adherents of these youth organizations. Roughly a hundred mosques are controlled by the *Hollanda Diyanet Vakfi*, which represents the so called 'official' Islam in Turkey. About 40 organizations belong to the *Milli Görüs*, adherents of the Turkish Refah Party and another 20 mosques belong to the *Süleymancis*, followers of the sufi sheikh Süleyman Hilmi Tunahan. Both movements play some sort of oppositional role in Turkish politics. The differences between these three organizations have very little to do with religious disputes, however. Their differences in opinion are mainly political.

Local initiatives: the first phase

Taking McAdam's model as an analytical framework and considering the ways in which Turkish Muslims in the Netherlands have defended their collective interests in the past decades as an ongoing organizational process requires that some phases of development be distinguished. I will first describe these phases and will then try to explain them on the basis of three crucial factors McAdam propounds in his model.

The first phase extended roughly from the end of the 1960s until the mid 1970s. During that period, acquiring suitable places for prayer was the main form of collective action among Muslims. At first they were looking for temporary accommodation during important religious occasions, such as ramadan. In this phase Dutch agencies played a crucial role, especially the churches. In fact it was not collective action *by* Muslims but collective action *for* Muslims: Muslims themselves did not even ask for it at the time. Among Dutch agencies however, the idea existed that Muslim 'guestworkers' might need such facilities for the time they stayed here.

It was only some time later that the first co-operation among Muslims developed in order establish places for prayer. Initially Muslims of different nationalities worked together, but later co-operation was mainly between people of the same nationality (Landman 1992). Through collections of money among believers, a house or another location was bought and the first mosques were founded. Religious services were performed by ordinary believers with above average knowledge of Islam, chosen from among the community. It was clear at the time that the need for space in which to prayer among ordinary believers was closely connected to their orientation towards the country of origin. The mosques were not just religious facilities; they functioned as meeting places for people who felt themselves temporary residents and who would soon return to their country of origin.

Most of the associations which were established at that time were very local initiatives and they were far from being professional. This was the time when collective action acquired, for a short time, a more egalitarian character. Dutch agents disappeared more or less to the background. Even so, there were hardly any representatives among the Muslims and organizational means were poorly developed. Not only Muslims themselves, but also the government, policy-makers and Dutch society in general were convinced about the temporary nature of their stay. The creation of religious facilities was thus considered something to be left completely to private initiative. No special policies were needed. As such, both migrants and policy-makers therefore shared the same intentions.

Ideological fragmentation and the 'migrantization' of Muslims: second phase

In the course of the 1970s some important developments occurred. There was a considerable increase in the number of immigrants, especially Turkish ones, due to family reunion. These families settled in the old quarters of the inner cities. The vast majority of the Muslims, however, still intended returning to the country of origin. The actual return was postponed, due to family reunification. In addition, many migrants had no other alternative than to stay in the Netherlands because of financial problems. For a variety of reasons, Muslims were increasingly confronted with all kinds of dilemmas and problems, prompted by living in a non-Islamic country and by all kinds of intra-familial developments. As a consequence the need for religious facilities increased, as did the need for qualified religious personnel. At the same time organizational structures improved and the variation of activities increased. Many mosque organizations became real centres for migrants. There were teahouses, shops and other facilities. Also in this period the first coordinative structures came into being among Turkish Muslims.

Organizational development among Turkish Muslims reached a new dimension when several religio-ideological movements started to operate among Turkish Muslims in Europe. The origin of these movements was related to the political situation in Turkey, where Islam is very significant politically (Sunar and Toprak 1983). These movements were partly opposed to the Turkish state and its official version of Islam in which all political statements inspired by Islam are forbidden. They could not only act more freely in Western Europe, but they also considered the thousands of Turkish migrants as a means of developing their movement. For the leadership it was of crucial importance to build up rank-and-file support from among Turkish migrants.

The development of religious institutions, which were still scarce throughout the country, became an important activity of these movements. As there was a need for religious accommodation, founding them became an important means by which these movements sought to enlarge their influence among ordinary Muslims. The foundation of mosques and other religious institutions now became also an expression of the competition between movements.

Although this organizational development was a clear extension of the political climate in Turkey, there was also a break with the past. The various movements found themselves in a very different context. Not only were they located a different position in society as compared with Turkey, the ordinary membership also occupied a different position and came from a different background as compared with their Turkish counterparts. Whereas the political struggle in Turkey mainly takes place in the more urban areas, in Europe the potential rank-and-file has a largely rural background. This meant that the movements had to adapt their discourse, strategy and operational modes to the worldview and experiences of the Muslim population. As a consequence, once in Europe the movements 'ruralized' in relation to the characteristics of their members.

Apart from these internal aspects important developments took place, which were also related to the socio-political context in the Netherlands and which influenced the position of Islamic organizations and migrant organizations in general. At the beginning of the 1980s the Dutch government changed its policies towards migrants. Permanent residence became the central focus. Migrant organizations became more significant in the process of social integration. They were politically and ideologically incorporated into the government's policies. Islamic organizations were considered important migrant institutions, and their activities were assessed according to their functions in the process of integration. I call this the 'migrantization' of Islamic organizations.

As a result of this migrantization a new type of leadership appeared on the scene. These leaders had lived in the Netherlands for a relatively long time, knew the society quite well and acted as intermediaries between Muslim migrants and Dutch society. They were entrepreneurs, rather than 'ideologues', and they were oriented towards mobilizing as many resources as possible. They made successful use of their contacts with Dutch policy-makers and institutions and emphasized that Islamic organizations must be considered as the main forms of 'self-organization' among migrants. These leaders increasingly took part in public discussions on the position of migrants and as opinion leaders they gained influence over the 'definition of the situation'. That meant that they represented the Muslim population to Dutch society, and they articulated what needs existed among them and what it meant to be Muslim in a non-Islamic society.

By stressing the 'foreign' character of Islam i.e., as something which is part of the cultural heritage of a specific group of migrants, they were able to convince policy-makers that certain facilities were necessary. These leaders emphasized the unique character of this cultural and religious heritage and claimed that they were the only ones able to gain access to these communities. Schierup (1992: 20) has called this the 'enclavization of culture'.

These organizations gradually gained more influence in decision-making procedures concerning migrant issues, because the government considered them as the main representatives of the migrant populations. Whereas in the 1970s leftist migrant organizations where the principal interlocutors with the government, now this role was increasingly taken over by Islamic associations. Because these leaders were at the head of the umbrella organizations the initiative in interest struggle shifted gradually from the local towards the national level.

As far as Muslims themselves were concerned, most were still very much orientated towards their countries of origin. They still considered their stay in the Netherlands as a temporary one.

Orientation towards the Netherlands

New developments occurred in the course of the 1980s which not only made the above mentioned strategy increasingly obsolete, they also put the legitimacy of the leaders under pressure. Three issues in particular were advanced by leaders who were inclined to change the organizations' strategy: greater focus on the position of Muslims *in* Dutch society; the position of youth within Islamic organizations; and the relation between local and national umbrella organizations.

External relations

Towards the end of the 1980s, at least a part of the leadership of Turkish Islamic organizations realized that establishing enduring relations and co-operation with Dutch institutions such as welfare organizations and local politics and paying more attention to all kinds of societal issues, was crucial for their future. Those leaders willing to change the strategy thought that Islamic organizations had been adopting a position of weakness vis-à-vis Dutch society. This strategy had proved to be beneficial in the past, but it was turning out to be increasingly counter-productive.

These leaders wanted to correct the image that Muslims were not willing to participate in neighbourhood development and other important societal issues. Some of the younger cadres of the organizations considered good relations with the surrounding society more important than strong ties with the countries of origin. Relatively more energy had to be put into establishing good relations, especially by local level organizations. Two issues were at stake: first, the recognition that Islamic organizations form a part of the local neighbourhood community; and second, that Muslims were very capable of adapting themselves to new circumstances without giving up their religion. They wanted to be acknowledged as equal citizens of society.

The articulation of interests is gradually shifting towards matters concerning recognition. A growing number of young Muslims feel that Islam's foreign connotations and the image of Islamic organizations as comprising of foreigners or migrants, perpetuate rather than improve their position. It hinders them in their efforts to participate in society. Recognition is thus linked with the question of whether and to what extent Muslims can be considered a part of the Dutch 'imagined community' (Anderson 1991).

While the 'migrantization' of Muslims was an important and effective strategy of integration in the 1980s, a new strategy now seems to be necessary. According to these young leaders opting for change, policies concerning Islamic organizations should be disengaged from policies on migrants, and a discussion must take place about the question how Dutch society should be defined. According to them, full integration will only be accomplished when this redefinition has taken place. We must, however, realize that these kinds of strategic considerations are still in a very early phase. There is not yet a definite shift as far as organizational structures and power relations are concerned, not least because the Dutch government still considers Islam something which is closely connected to migrants. Nevertheless, we must not ignore the significant signs and developments which are taking place.

Internal relations

A shift in strategy not only concerns the position of Islamic organizations in Dutch society, but internal changes have also occurred. In recent years, the number of young people in Islamic organizations has increased rapidly and their influence has grown. As a consequence the activities offered by the organizations have changed. Young people have also recently gained more say in the administration of Islamic organizations. This is not only because the intensified negotiations with Dutch institutions require more qualified personnel than before, but also because the increase of young people within the organizations influences the balance of power. In short, Nielsen's (1992: 125) hypothesis that a shift occurs from achieved to earned leadership within Islamic organizations, seems to have actually happened.

Of course, these developments have not occurred without serious discussions, controversies and power struggles. In a large number of organizations power is still firmly in the hands of the first generation of Muslims. But, as already stated, the legitimacy of their power is increasingly questioned.

One important aspect of this power struggle is the role and influence of umbrella organizations. The initiative in negotiations and interest struggles with Dutch society shifted towards these national bodies in the 1980s. In addition, Turkish Islam is organized along religio-ideological lines. According to many young leaders, both this centralized decision-making structure and the ideological fragmentation impede the successful establishment of local contacts and co-operation between all types of institutions. The young leaders want to return the initiative to the local level. I saw many examples of young and active members of Turkish Islamic organizations from different ideological backgrounds working together at the neighbourhood level, while at the same time their national leaders were fighting each other for influence.

In short, it seems to me that religio-ideological conflicts are increasingly being replaced by conflicts between two generations of migrants. The young generation within Islamic organizations is trying to alter them from organizations *for* into organizations *of* Muslims. Until the late 1980s organizational development and interest struggle was a matter of representatives and managers. A cleavage existed between the leaders and the rank and file membership. In recent years this unbalanced situation seems to have gradually altered. Young people want to be members of an Islamic organization out of conviction and not just out of tradition.

Factors in organizational development

How should these developments be understood? As stated above, I used McAdam's work on Black insurgency in the USA as an analytical guide. His perspective provides an alternative way of analyzing organizational development to the immigration and culturalist perspectives. McAdam (1982: 40-51) distinguishes three crucial factors which account for the development of social movements: indigenous organizational strength, the structure of political opportunities and the raising of consciousness among the aggrieved population. These three crucial factors can be applied to the situation of Turkish Islamic organizations.

Indigenous organizational strength

According to McAdam, indigenous organizational strength can be considered as an important resource for collective activists. He gives some intriguing examples of Black activists drawing on church communities to fuel their organization (*ibid.*: 150). As far as Turkish Islamic organizations are concerned, it is certain that those young leaders opting for change also make effective use of existing structures, networks and communication channels among the Turkish population. Since we do not deal here with *new* social movements, but with existing organizations within which changes are taking place, it is clear that existing networks and power relations are also hampering change. As I mentioned earlier, established power relations are a controversial matter within Turkish Islamic organizations. This mainly manifests itself as an inter-generational conflict, i.e. between two generations of migrants, or rather between migrants and 'post-migrants'. Debates within Islamic organizations resolve into a change in perspectives on the future of Islam in Dutch society.

These changes manifest themselves, firstly within the organizations as a struggle over strategy, and secondly in changing attitudes towards the host society. Paradoxical as it may seem, the internal struggle is far from being concluded, whereas changes in strategy towards Dutch society have already been rather successful in some cases. In many organizations older people still are in power whereas young people are increasingly representing them to the outside world. Contrary to what is often assumed, I do not consider this situation as an inherent characteristic of Islamic organizations based on religious authority. It is a transitional phase in organizational development, and it is closely linked to the second crucial analytical factor, namely the structure of political opportunities.

Structure of political opportunities

The reason that changes occur in the strategy towards the surrounding society is closely related to both the structural and the ideological contexts in which Turkish Islamic organizations operate (Rath et al. 1991). Both can be considered as either 'openings' or impediments for Muslims in their actions. The political opportunity structure consists partly of previously formulated government policies, but partly also of the result of current struggles and negotiations between two or more parties.

In general, the above-mentioned recent developments are closely related to changes in the political and ideological context in which Islamic organizations operate. These changes became evident at the end of the 1980s when the Dutch government realized that the position of migrants in the so-called 'hard' sectors such as education, employment and housing, was far weaker than among native Dutch people (see WRR 1989). Emphasis was put on integration into these sectors. The preservation of cultural specificities among migrants was tolerated so long as it did not impede structural integration. These policies were sometimes so phrased as to imply that cultural preservation inhibits full-fledged participation in the central institutions of society.

The ideological climate towards Muslims and Islam also changed at that time and the 'Rushdie affair' functioned as a kind catalyst. The media paid exaggerated interest in the occasionally extreme statements of some Islamic leaders. The image of Muslims seemed to shift from 'unintegrated migrants' to a 'fifth column'. This alteration in the ideological climate led many young Muslims to reconsider their position in Dutch society. To a certain extent this may explain why so many young Islamic leaders insist on an orientation towards societal issues ('vermaatschappelijking') by their organizations.

Apart from these more general contextual developments, the main changes in the structure of political opportunities are to be found at the local level. In general, local governments have to carry out policies formulated by the national government, but in big cities where the municipal administration is subdivided into local 'borough' administrations, the local level becomes all the more relevant for Islamic organizations. Previous research has showed that there exists a great variation in actual policies between municipalities (Rath et al. 1996). I carried out my research in Rotterdam, partly because this city has adopted rather new and, by Dutch standards, unique policies on Islam and Islamic organizations in recent years. It is the first and as yet the only Dutch city which has developed a specific 'mosque' policy. It is also the only city with a subsidized council of Islamic organizations (SPIOR). Although the situation in Rotterdam is far from being ideal, it is nevertheless beyond doubt that Muslims gained greater access to political decision-making procedures there than elsewhere in the Netherlands.

At least one very important factor relating to these new policies must be mentioned here, namely the very extensive renovation of the city. Rotterdam has been almost entirely rebuilt in the past twenty years. This renovation occurred at the same time as the number of migrants grew rapidly. The most thorough renovation activities took place precisely in those areas where most of the migrants live. In order to involve them in the process, and to open communication channels to the several migrants communities, the municipality needed Islamic organizations, being the largest migrant associations. Some of the Islamic organizations' younger leaders understood quite well that this offered them a unique opportunity to gain greater access to decision-making circles.

By the mid 1990s urban renovation was almost accomplished, and the attention of policy-makers and local institutions shifted towards matters like neighbourhood management and the development of safe and clean urban environments. This is precisely the moment in which those Islamic leaders opting for change clearly see a perspective for their organizations' future. They emphasize the local function of their organizations and understand the necessity of turning their attention from purely internal affairs to matters concerning their place in the urban neighbourhood. One of my informants, a young chairman of a local Turkish mosque, put it as follows:

> For the older generation it is enough when the street in front of the mosque is clean. They do not bother about our position in the neighbourhood. They think that a mosque is just a prayerhouse, period. If we do not take part in discussions about community development and neighbourhood management, we as Muslims will stay outside this society till in eternity.

Cognitive shift

The most crucial factor in explaining the recent developments in the interest struggle among Muslims is, in my view, the changing perspective among young Muslims. It is important because it can be considered as the ultimate cause, or even the initial motive for recent organizational development and change. I call this factor a cognitive shift. Young Muslims increasingly realize that they have to orientate towards Dutch society and break away from the status of their parents. It is the typical rupture in future perspectives between migrants and post-migrants which is also seen elsewhere.

The focus in Islamic organizations had already shifted towards the young generation in the 1980s. Activities for young people increased considerably. Young members made it clear that the leadership of the organizations must accept the fact that their societal position is completely different from that of their parents. They must be approached in a different way, with different means. As the research found, most young people in Islamic organizations had completely different motives for participating in their activities as compared with older Muslims.

For the majority of first-generation members pre-migration circumstances and their own community form the single most important points of reference in the formation of their Islamic identity: Dutch society hardly plays a role. Ethnic and religious categories seem to merge. For a growing number of young people, however, the receiving - i.e. Dutch society - forms an important point of reference. This is especially the case with those who have a relatively good position in society. Many have moved away from their parents' socio-economic position. Returning to the country of origin is not a viable option for them anymore. Their future is situated in the Netherlands and not in Turkey, not only practically but increasingly also mentally. It seems to me that the psychological effects of the 'myth of return' option have been underestimated in literature. The practical feasibility of returning does not have to coincide with the psychological function it can perform. For many first-generation migrants, returning is still an essential aspect of their future perspective, although the actual decision is postponed again and again. Even when they accept that their children will stay in the Netherlands, they think of returning when the children are grown up. To a certain extent it functions as a survival strategy. It makes them more or less immune to stigmatization and discrimination.

For a growing number of young people these psychological functions have disappeared. Because returning to the country of origin can no longer function as release, their orientation towards Dutch society becomes stronger and their expectations towards society become higher. This can make them more aware of mechanisms of real or perceived exclusion and they are ready to challenge them.

This changing perspective influences the way in which they interpret Islam. Those who have lived in the Netherlands for quite a long time, speak Dutch well, have mastered social skills, and interact intensively with Dutch people at school, work or in leisure, attach a clearly different meaning to Islam as compared with those who do not posses these qualities. They tend to emphasize the dynamic or changeable aspects of Islam. In doing so they more or less move away from the 'traditional' Islam of the older generation. Due to their long stay in the Netherlands, the significance of their own ethnic and regional background has diminished in the construction of Islamic identity among some young Muslims. This does not mean of course that their own community and the country of origin are not important anymore. Rather, the Netherlands have become the main point of reference in constructing Islamic identity. Many have the feeling that they treat Islam more consciously and that they are able to formulate more clearly what it means to be Muslim in the Netherlands. For them, Islam is an alternative rather than something which is self evident. The fact that Islam is just one of the religious denominations in the Netherlands is not simply something which has to be accepted. It must instead play a role in the development of their identity, provided that Dutch society accepts Muslims as being equal to other people. Among this category, I met the most 'converts' i.e. young men who stated that they had long neglected Islam, but now thought better of it and embraced Islam on new terms.

Although I undertook the research among Turkish males, there is enough evidence that a similar cognitive shift is taking place among females. This will of course work out differently due to differences in experience between males and females. For example, young Muslim women are much more active in setting up organizations which cut across ethnic boundaries than young men.

A typical characteristic of this cognitive shift is that the boys wanted to 'rewrite history' and to give a new interpretation of Islam, of which the gradual disassociation of Islam from its ethnic connotations was the main aspect. The concepts of 'Turk' and 'Muslim' as important identity-markers seem to be disconnected. Although most of the young males considered their Turkish background an important part of their identity, they thought it 'complete nonsense' to single out the Turks as a specific category in Islamic history. Consequently, every society could finally become an Islamic society, provided certain conditions had been fulfilled. Although the history of Islam was related to the history of specific countries and peoples, Islam itself was considered a universalist and inclusive religion. The message was directed toward every living soul, and there were no countries and no peoples for whom Islam was more suitable or appropriate than for others. For Turks it is as difficult or as easy as for any other person to become a good Muslim. Every view of Islam as a kind of national ideology was an assault to the very nature and message of Islam itself. Islam thus renders a more inclusive meaning (Sunier 1995: 63).

According to these young Muslims, reconciling an Islamic way of living with permanent residence in the Netherlands is not simply a matter of compromising between the principles of Islam and those of Dutch society. This changing significance manifests itself primarily as a shift from Islam as a tradition to Islam as a conviction. Religious 'community' does not necessarily run parallel with other social ties anymore and Islam becomes a matter of individual choice. Islam becomes significant as an ethic system in which fragmented life experiences are symbolically linked together in a new discourse. Religious 'community' is constantly being reproduced within the context of changing circumstances.

This tendency manifests itself clearly, among other things, in the increasing number of 'multi-national' or rather 'non-national' Islamic organizations in the Netherlands. This does not imply that 'being Turkish' becomes irrelevant for them. What these young Muslims in fact say is that 'being Turkish' belongs to another realm than 'being Muslim' in the Dutch context. It should be borne in mind that ideas of this kind are still only expressed and articulated in such an elaborated way by a small more or less intellectual elite. Nevertheless, among the majority of my informants I could trace similar, though not always well-articulated, sentiments.

Conclusion

In this chapter I have tried to show under what conditions development and change among Turkish Islamic organizations takes place. The crucial factors accounting for this development, namely indigenous organizational strength, political opportunities and cognitive shift, have their own separate effects, but they must also be constantly analyzed in relation to each other. Both the idea that Dutch society is anti-Islamic and mainly impedes organizational development, and the idea that formal constitutional equality of religion guarantees equal treatment, are too narrow and too simple.

As to the influence of indigenous organizations and networks, it turns out that they constitute an important factor, but we should be very careful of overstating their influence. In most publications on Turkish Islam, religious fragmentation (between for example Milli Görüs, Süleymanci, and Diyanet) is usually given as the most important factor explaining the attitude and the ideas of Turkish Islamic organizations. Although these ideological movements certainly do have influence, they do not explain everything. I deliberately did not elaborate on these movements in this chapter therefore. The recent developments described above were apparent in *all* Turkish Islamic organizations to a greater or lesser degree.

The relative influence of each of the three factors is not fixed, but constantly changing according to circumstances. Although there are some clear tendencies discernible in organizational development and the articulation of interests, from which very careful predictions can be made, these processes nevertheless remain largely unpredictable. The 'Rushdie affair' was, after all, an unexpected event. As a consequence, organizational development, articulation of interests and the process of institutionalization of Islam itself do not appear the same everywhere. They do not develop the same way in Rotterdam, Tilburg or Enschede, and certainly not in the same way as in Germany or the UK. In other words, we must always include the local context in our analysis and not concentrate on large scale national and international developments alone.

The discussion here has only touched on certain dimensions in the development of relations between Islamic organizations and Dutch society. I have tried to show that these organizations act collectively and defend their interests by entering the ordinary political arena. Although the characteristics of this political struggle and negotiation is specific, it is a process which does not differ from other types of collective action in its basics.

By promoting their interests, Islamic organizations alter the surrounding situation, which in turn generates new circumstances. Ultimately it can be anticipated that this process will affect not only the position of Islamic organizations vis-à-vis society, but also Islamic discourse itself. How this discourse changes will of course depend on very specific circumstances, but there are at least two crucial factors which can be expected to influence any such change. As has been demonstrated, a growing number of young Muslims engaged in Islamic organizations are increasingly oriented towards Dutch society. This implies that they expect more from this society, especially with regard to their position within it. Combined with an 'open' and permeable structure of political opportunities, this expectation is likely to produce an Islamic discourse which, rather than rejecting the host society, emphasizes that Islam can become an integral part of it. If such a strong orientation towards Dutch society is combined with a 'closed' and impermeable structure of political opportunities, however, it is likely to produce a separatist and more radical discourse.

Notes

1 This article is based on my PhD thesis *Islam in Beweging: Turkse Jongeren en Islamitsche Organisaties* ('Islam in Motion: Turkish Youths and Islamic Organization') published as Sunier (1996). An English translation is under preparation.

References

Anderson, B. (1991) *Imagined Communities. Reflections on the Origin and Spread of Nationalism*, (second edition). London: Verso.

Landman, N. (1992) *Van mat tot minaret. De institutionalisering van de Islam in Nederland*. Amsterdam: VU Uitgeverij.

McAdam, D. (1982) *Political Process and the Development of Black Insurgency 1930-1970*. Chicago: University of Chicago Press.

Nielsen, J.S. (1992) *Muslims in Western Europe*. Edinburgh: Edinburgh University Press.

Rath, J., K. Groenendijk & R. Penninx (1991) 'The Recognition and Institutionalisation of Islam in Belgium, Great Britain and the Netherlands', *New Community*, 18(1): 101-114.

Rath, J., R. Penninx, K. Groenendijk & A. Meyer (1996) *Nederland en zijn Islam*. Amsterdam: Het Spinhuis.

Schierup, C. (1992) *Multiculturalism, Neo-racism, and Vicissitudes of Contemporary Democracy*, paper for Nordic Seminar for Migration Research, Esbjerg.

Sunar, I & B. Toprak (1983) 'Islam in Politics: The Case of Turkey', *Government and Opposition*, 18(4): 421-441.

Sunier, T. (1995) 'Disconnecting Religion and Ethnicity: Young Turkish Muslims in the Netherlands', in: G. Baumann & T. Sunier (eds.), *Post-Migration Ethnicity. Cohesion, Commitments, Comparison*. Amsterdam: Het Spinhuis: 58-77.

Sunier, T. (1996) *Islam in Beweging: Turkse Jongeren en Islamitische Organisaties*. Amsterdam: Het Spinhuis.

Sunier, T. & A. Meyer (1997) 'Religie', in: H. Vermeulen (ed.), *Immigrantenbeleid voor de multiculturele samenleving. Integratie-, taal- en religiebeleid voor immigranten in vijf West-Europese landen.* (TWCM voorstudie no.9). Amsterdam: Het Spinhuis: 95-126.

Wetenschappelijke Raad voor het Regeringsbeleid (WRR) (1989) *Allochtonenbeleid*. Rapporten aan de regering Nr. 36. Den Haag: SDU.

4 Imagining a British Muslim Identification

Yunas Samad

In Britain, Muslims have come to the public's attention with their opposition to *The Satanic Verses*, the war in the Gulf, the controversy over the Muslim Parliament and the demand for state-aided Muslim schools. These political manifestations have been symptomatic of a deeper process, the imagining of a British Muslim identification. This has been a categorisation that combines belonging to the global Muslim community (the *Ummah*) with being British. This move towards constructing an Islamic identity differs from what has been loosely called 'fundamentalism'. The development was not about religious fervour or revivalism but the fashioning of a Muslim community by subordinating national, linguistic and regional affiliations to Islam. This reductive process projects religious classification as the primary identification. However the imagining of a British Muslim identity takes place in contestation with other nomenclatures such as British\Pakistani, British\Bengali, Asian or 'black', etc. The attempt to reduce culturally, ethnically and linguistically diverse groups to Islamic essentials has been explicitly expressed by the activities of various umbrella organisations, with varying degree of success, claiming to represent Muslim opinion on the national level. The United Kingdom Action Committee on Islamic Affairs (UKACIA), formed during the Rushdie controversy, was an exemplar of this imagining process. This paper examines the context in which, and the process by which, this organisation actively tried to establish a political constituency based on British Muslim identification.

Construction of identity

In exploring the link between culture, identity and political action, past orthodoxies, both the left and the right, saw culture and identity as fixed qualities unmediated by time or context. It was precisely in countering 'primordialism' that Hobsbawm and Ranger's *The Invention of Tradition* (1983) became so popular. The appeal was not just the focus on the fact that essential categories were invented, but also on the role that colonialism played in the reconstruction process. In 'The Invention of Tradition Revisited' Terence Ranger (1993) subsequently refined the idea of inventing tradition. This was in response to the criticism that there was a danger of ahistorical dualism (i.e. that once the colonial invention had been stripped away an authentic other would emerge) which could allow the reassertion of essentialist categories. In order to avoid these pitfalls he suggested that the 'imagining of tradition' might be a more appropriate term, whereby tradition - whether religion, custom, ethnicity or nationalism - is imagined and remains in a constant historical process. The flexibility of this term is perhaps closer to reality and helps to explain how identification is being contested in the migratory process.

The Muslim population in Britain is overwhelmingly South Asian in origin (HMSO 1991, Runnymede Bulletin March 1992). Out of a total of one million recorded in the Labour Force Survey 1990-1991, 485,000 originate from Pakistan, 127,000 from Bangladesh and smaller numbers from India, Africa, Malaya, Iran, Cyprus and from Arab countries. Muslims have multiple identifications which, as a broad generalisation, can be conceptualised as consisting of several intersecting strands (Yinger 1986).

Some of the basic features which influence the construction of identity are nationality, region of origin, language, religion, and social strata. These strands break down into sub-categories, overlap and intermesh, thus allowing new permutations to emerge. Identity is malleable in character - i.e. shaped and reshaped by internal and external forces. One strand of identity which has been presented to wider society is national identification such as Indian, Pakistani and Bangladeshi. Such national identifications are, however, internally differentiated along cultural lines based on locality. The various populations come from specific parts of western Punjab, Azad Kashmir, Sylhet, Gujarat or particular cities such as Karachi, Nairobi and Mombasa. These cultural variations, reflecting the locality of origin, are grounded in village-kin networks, *biraderi* and extended family relations which are reinforced by chain migration, arranged marriage patterns etc.. These specific cultural configurations are reinforced by the strand based on language, more precisely dialects, such as Mirpuri, Sylheti, Kutchi etc. Social stratifications based on caste are another factor reinforcing these cultural features. The majority are of low status with a dash of high caste groups. Class characteristics are also influential, as most Muslims are working class with a sprinkling of middle-class business people and professionals mainly from India and Africa. Islam is an overarching characteristic subsuming, national, regional, kin, linguistic, caste and class affiliations. It is, however, also divided along doctrinal lines such as Sunni and Shiah, as well as by denominations such as Deobandi, Barelvi, etc..

These various 'primordial' authenticities are reformulated in the British context and alienation plays a role in how they are reimagined. Thus local manifestations of the various classifications emerge. Syncretic developments such as Muslim\Brummie or Bengali\East Ender intermingle with other hybrid identifications such as Asian and 'black'. The reformulation of these categories in the British context, however, has not been a purely voluntarist exercise, as suggested by some post-modernists (Rose 1991: 4). The postmodernists' decentered approach, in which identifications are continuously slipping and sliding, is useful in so much as it rejects essentialism. But to argue that there are endless multiple identities from which to choose freely is a grotesque caricature. Ethnic minorities are stereotyped and their cultural heritage becomes a valuable resource in turning difficult (and at times intolerable) situations to their advantage. However, what and how they chose to project themselves is heavily dependent on their relationship with state and civil society. The question of state power and domination in the Foucauldian sense (where power is related to knowledge) has to be considered (Eade 1996). The options available are circumscribed by wider arenas.

Institutionalisation of identity

In Britain national policies concerning ethnic minorities are implemented by local authorities. This development has had a profound impact on the way identity has been constructed by ethnic minorities and where they have become located in the hierarchy. The Race Relations Act, the Commission for Racial Equality (CRE) and its local network of Community Race Council (CRC) and Race Equality Councils (REC) legitimated 'secular' identifications based on ethnicity and race at the expense of others such as religion. In the case of Sikhs and Jews, the courts' interpretation of the legislation brought them within the ambit of the Race Relations Act by treating them as ethnic and not religious minorities.

For a variety of reasons including the response to the 1981 riots, the emergence of a 'black' electorate and the rise of the left in the Labour Party, muncipal authorities implemented various multi-cultural and anti-racist strategies. In anti-racism, the emphasis was on racism itself and the focus was on policies designed to introduce institutional change. Multi-culturalism, by contrast, focused on self-identity, ethnic culture and family background. Despite their differences the two were not mutually exclusive. The administration of these policies by anti-racist activists and the Labour left also reinforced secular identifications. Thus 'black' as well as ethnic identities were legitimated by fund holders such as the Greater London Council (GLC) (Fitzgerald 1984: 35-36; Ouseley 1990: 141). An example of this development was the propagation of 'black' identification as a homogeneous category representing Afro-Caribbeans and South Asians. As long as resources were distributed on this basis, some Bangladeshis and Pakistanis were prepared to accept this nomenclature. Internally, however, they identified themselves specifically as Sylheti, Mirpuri or Punjabi and these identifications coexisted in a pragmatic relationship with being 'black'.

Identifications adopted by activists were ultimately dependent on the politics of 'ins' and 'outs' that operated in local arenas. In the case of the Bangladeshis in Tower Hamlets, many of whom were Labour Party members, they were quite prepared to accept a 'black' identity as it was perceived to be the idiom of multi-cultural, anti-racist and equal opportunity initiatives financed by the GLC and the Inner London Education Authority (ILEA). Within the 'black' paradigm, linguistic and even religious needs were also accommodated. Supposedly secular community projects for mother-tongue education had Koran classes tacked on. The eventual abolition of the GLC and ILEA made being 'black' redundant and Asian identity, first suggested by African Asians, became an alternative vehicle for attracting funding: but this turned out to be unsatisfactory. Bangladeshis lacked the professional and academic qualifications to compete effectively with Sikhs, Gujaratis and African Asians for limited resources. As a consequence, they needed to differentiate themselves from being Asian by asserting their Bangladeshi characteristics. Their weakness relative to other groups led them to assert identifications which would benefit the Bangladeshi community. The balance of power was a significant feature which influenced the way identities were being constructed. In the case of Bradford, Labour Party activists adopted 'black' identity even though they felt disgruntled by the fact that it had not rewarded them with Members of Parliament as it had done for Afro-Caribbeans. Within the Asian community however, the general perception was that the notion of being 'black' had led to Pakistanis becoming dominant. In reaction to this development, Indians rejected this identification and asserted their Hindu characteristics as an alternative. The subscription to 'black', Asian, Pakistani, Bangladeshi etc. was a highly instrumental feature and intimately associated with the fate of local authorities whose powers were denuded by Tory legislations.

The other impact of implementing polices on ethnic minorities by municipalities has been to restrict their politics to the local level. Municipal-level activists on race issues were co-opted to the CRC\REC, equal opportunity units in the councils and anti-racist projects. Given that many were also politically motivated, they naturally eased into politics. Pakistanis and Bangladeshis became councillors, mayors and justice of the peace but only a few Indians and Afro-Caribbeans were elevated to the national stage. There is clearly a gulf between local and national politics, but the combination of discrimination, sheer competition and intra-party rivalry has blocked the advance of Muslim candidates. There were claims suggesting that racism within the Labour Party in Bradford, blocked the nomination of a prominent Pakistani councillor as the Parliamentary candidate. In Small Heath in Birmingham, the union block vote was used to impose an unwanted Parliamentary candidate against wishes of the local Labour constituency (Back and Solomos 1992). Generally speaking, the competition in all parties for a safe seat has been so intense that ethnic minorities and Muslims in particular are sidelined. They are similarly underrepresented in the judiciary, the civil service and the police, where they represent barely over one per cent of the total force and hardly present at all in the higher echelons of these institutions (Anwar 1991: 5).

New Racism and Thatcherism

To understand the emergence of British Muslim identification it has to be contextualised in terms of the structural shifts in British politics since 1980 and how these changes have affected ethnic minorities. It is not intended here to enter into a detailed analysis of the discourse on 'New Racism' or its relationship with the Conservative government, but only with its impact on multi-culturalism and anti-racism. The Thatcher government's policies affecting ethnic minorities contained elements of continuity and change. While immigration and asylum laws and granting of refugee status were tightened up the race legislation remained intact. Mainly in response to the urban upheavals of 1981, the subsequent Scarman Report on these events and political pressure, Tory commitment to the Race Relations Act, Commission for Racial Equality (CRE), CRCs and Section 11 continued. However in the government's statement of Autumn 1992 on Public Expenditure substantial cuts were envisaged in Section 11 funding (All-Party Parliamentary Group on Race and Community 1993).

The 1980s witnessed new developments affecting ethnic minorities in general and Muslims in particular. Two contradictory views within the New Right gained influence within government circles. The neo-conservatives emphasised strong government, hierarchical stratification and authoritarianism on social issues. The other current, neo-liberalism, reversed the order of priorities emphasising right of the individual, laissez-faire and minimal government. The political practice of Thatcherism combined selectively elements from both sides of the New Right (Kavanagh 1987: 107). Their influence was felt in the question of local democracy and race.

John Rex (1991) has described multi-culturalism and equal opportunities in Britain as a doctrine of two cultural domains within an inclusive British national identity. Cultural diversity was the preserve of the private domain while equality of citizenship was declared a part of the public domain. Whether one accepts or rejects this definition is not important, however. What is significant was that all concepts of multi-culturalism and anti-racism were located within a pluralist conception of national identity. This notion of British culture and national identity was attacked by the discourse on new racism. It should be noted that there is nothing new in this phenomenon, merely being a redefinition of an existing exclusiveness which previously was expressed as anti-Irish, anti-Semitic and anti-Chinese sentiments. The neo-conservative combination of social authoritarianism with race, national identity and patriotism leads them to redefine biological racism to one based on culture and being British. A monolithic, ethnically undifferentiated British identity based on Christian culture and family is constructed, which is then threatened by alien cultures and values (Solomos 1988: 228-230). New racism wanted to replace multi-culturalism with a pluralism in which separatism would prevent cultural contamination. This virulent brand of cultural exclusivity was the progeny of Enoch Powell, propagated by the Peterhouse Group including Roger Scruton and Sir Alfred Sherman and others such as Ray Honeyford. However, what widened the appeal of their ideas from the limited readership of *The Salisbury Review*, was the dissemination of New Right race-thinking among a growing body of journalists found both in the quality and tabloid press. They led the New

Right media onslaught which undermined the legitimacy of anti-racist initiatives (Mitchell and Russell 1990: 186-7).

One area in which their influence was found was the Education Reform Act. The National Curriculum introduced three 'core' subjects (English, mathematics and science) and seven other 'foundation' subjects, while religious education (RE) remained a statutory requirement as a 'basic' subject for everyone in county and voluntary schools (unless their parents wished otherwise). The legislation required that RE and assemblies should be explicitly Christian in character. In addition, the brief of the History Curriculum Group and English Working Group was Anglo-centric and patriotic. Moreover the Education Reform Act reconstituted the relationship between central government and the Local Education Authorities (LEAs). It reduced the LEAs to operating as functionaries of the centre and undermined them by providing for both opting out from LEAs and the local management of schools. The Act ushered in a fragmented school system run by individual governing bodies by-passing the LEAs. Token commitment to multi-culturalism was retained by central government but the anti-racists strategies emanating from the LEAs were made redundant (Troyna and Carrington 1990: 99-104).

The neo-liberals' influence in the Tory party increased after 1975 with the support of Sir Keith Joseph, Milton Friedman, the Institute of Economic Affairs and the Centre for Policy Studies. They wanted to control inflation by keeping a tight grip on the money supply, reducing state ownership and spending and favouring free market policies, while they took an authoritarian line on law and order and social issues. This strategy led them into conflict with local government over high spending and high local taxes or rates. Many Labour-run boroughs resisted attempts by the centre to restrict local democracy. The attack on municipal authorities was disguised as an offensive against the 'loony left'.

Multi-culturalism and anti-racism were the principal victims of this assault but not the real target. The New Right collapsed the two together, which was not difficult as they did overlap, and initiated a media offensive. The tabloid press ridiculed local government's attempts to combat racism. Anti-racism was portrayed as 'left loonyism' and anti-racists were labelled as the real racists because they were involved in witch hunts against tolerant, reasonable people such as Ray Honeyford. The debate eventually turned to the allegedly negative effect of diluting British culture and identity (Mitchell and Russell 1990: 187). The assault against anti-racism legitimated the centralisation of power and the subversion of local democracy. The need to control the 'loony left' became the justification for greater centralisation of power. A series of steps were initiated, beginning with the Local Government Planning and Land Act, designed to curtail the spending targets of local councils. Labour councils remained defiant and in 1982 the Local Government Finance Act abolished the right of local authorities to set supplementary rates. In 1985 it was followed by the abolition of the Greater London Council and the Metropolitan Councils (Kavanagh 1987: 282-5).

Because the leadership of ethnic minorities was mainly situated in local government they were highly vulnerable to the changes introduced by the Thatcher government. The internal dynamics of Afro-Caribbeans and Asians on the one hand and within the various Asian groups on the other, were different, as were the specific responses. But there was a recognisable drift towards reification of cultural categories. Paul Gilroy (1990) has pointed out that the new racism's emphasis on culture and absolutist conceptions of ethnicity has been complemented by the anti-racist orthodoxy of the left and by essentialists ('black', Asian or Muslim, etc.) who needed no prompting to observe a narcissistic celebration of culture and identity. The destruction of local government combined with the socio-economic hardship associated with post-industrialisation has only entrenched the feeling of radical powerlessness and frustration, turning ethnic minorities inwards. This has even led some 'black' cultural nationalists to celebrate Thatcher's enterprise culture because it forced them to become self-reliant and dependent solely on the 'black' community (Gilroy 1990: 77-79). For Pakistanis and Bangladeshis the new racism's influence on the Education Reform Act confronted them directly with the potential threat of religious assimilation. These cultural assaults left the 'secular' leadership vulnerable to Islamic activism and simultaneously exposed their weakness at the centre. The centralisation of education and the traumatising of local government where past gains had been concentrated, left them with no voice in Parliament or Whitehall. It was precisely into this political vacuum that explicitly Muslim organisations became active.

Muslim umbrella organisations

This changing political context provided the opportunities for Islamic organisations to exploit. Islam, however, is not a monolithic entity. There is a division between Shiah and Sunni and, as Nielsen (1992) points out, there are three overlapping categories to be found within the Sunni presence.

Doctrinal rivalry, however, divides them into traditionalist Barelvis and revivalist trends. Thus, while on one hand the *Islamic Times* - a Barelvi paper - calls for Islamic unity, it simultaneously castigates Whabbism and the danger it presents (*Islamic Times* 1992). Most mosques belong to the Barelvi persuasion and there are several currents within the Barelvi network based around individual *pirs*. There is also a nebulous development of the Sufi *tariqas* which are difficult to detect because they overlapping with Barelvis. But the Naqshbandi, Qadiri and Chisti orders are active mainly among the youth and British converts. Within the revivalist current there are several strands such as the Tablighi Jamat, Deobandi and Ahl-i-Hadith. There is also another category which consists of elite organisations which aspire for national status. Some of them have been associated with the World Muslim League (Rabita) based in Mecca. Organisations such as the UK Islamic Mission and the Islamic Foundation are based in the Jamat-i-Islami which originated from the Indian sub-continent. Moreover, there are also a number of Muslim organisations of non-South Asian origin: the oldest is the Alawi Sufi order among the Yemenis. There are also Turkish Cypriots.

The emergence of umbrella organisations was a conscious attempt, only partially successful at best, to construct a British Muslim identification and present a common position to the authorities on the national level. The fact that these organisations were multi-ethnic, multi-linguistic in character as well as multi-denominational meant that they had to search for lowest common denominators to forge unity. In practice, the sectarian and personal rivalries which were so common among the various mosques and organisations were only partially overcome when they joined these organisations. A number of federations developed and it was common for their constituents to hold membership of several bodies. The first development was the Union of Muslim Organisations (UMO), which was established in the late 1970s. By the 1980s it was reduced to one of many organisation vying to represent Muslim interests and its influence was restricted to the fringes of the main theological currents. The Council of Imams and Mosques was influential among the Barelvi currents. The Council of Mosques had support among the revivalist currents (Nielsen 1992: 43-8).

The advantage that the Islamic leadership had over their 'secular' counterparts was that they were able to fill the political vacuum at the centre with the financial support they received from Middle Eastern and North African powers. The funding of the UMO came from the Saudi Arabian and Iraqi governments. The Imam and Mosques Council was associated with the

Islamic Call Society of Libya, while the now-defunct Council of Mosques was a pro-Saudi federation. The Saudis intervened directly through the London office of the World Muslim League, closely associated with the Saudi government, and via the director of the Islamic Cultural Centre at Regents Park, who was a Saudi diplomat. It was financially dependent on the House of Saud and when its funding was cut, due to the financial squeeze implemented by the Saudi government in the late 1980s, it collapsed.

The Muslim Institute also was initially funded by Saudi Arabia and then indirectly by Iran. Generally speaking their dependence on Middle Eastern resources should not be misconstrued to suggest that they are agents of foreign powers or that these countries are gaining influence among Muslims in Britain. The financial support can be best described as seed corn funding to encourage like-minded thinkers. Certainly there is evidence to suggest such organisations actually mitigate the external influence and are more sensitive to their constituency than patrons. For instance Zaki Badawi of the Imam and Mosques Council was quite independent from his Libyan patronage and when the Saudis attempted to cash in on their investment during the Gulf War many rejected their exhortations to support them and instead backed the opposition to the war (Samad 1992: 515-6).

Islamic solidarity was issue-based and only those issues that could be dealt on the central level proved effective. The Honeyford affair, education (including the Swann Report and the Education Reform Act), *The Satanic Verses* issue and the Gulf War were all examples where various umbrella organisations thrived, if only briefly. Despite these indications that they had some influence on the national level with the authorities they only had nominal influence within the Muslim community. They were in effect trying to work from the top downwards to establish popular roots.

British Muslim identification is a contested category, which attempts to subsume the multi-ethnic, multi-linguistic and multi-denominational features of the community. But it only does this thorough contestation and with partial success. The Rushdie affair resulted in greater unity than at any other moment in the community's history. There was unequivocal unanimity in the opposition to *The Satanic Verses*. The United Kingdom Action Committee on Islamic Affairs emerged as a loosely structured confederation incorporating nearly all the various currents, the only exceptions being the Imam and Mosques Council and the Muslim Institute. It was also the first time such umbrella organisations established a presence on the ground. There were several reasons accounting for this success. The most significant factor was that the issue drew 'sociological' Muslims into the fray. Islamic identity became the metaphor and idiom for social discontent, particularly among the youth of Bradford. The intermeshing of identification resulted in a reimagining which drew in secular leadership. There are cases of councillors in Bradford who claimed to be socialists, yet became passionate campaigners against Rushdie. Another factor was the ascription of Muslim identity by civil society. It imposed a religious identity and forced groups to close ranks. In the case of the Bangladeshis of Tower Hamlets the ascribing of identity, particularly by the media, resulted in the community rallying around the religious leadership and participating in a massive demonstration in Hyde Park. The fact that sections of the media orchestrated a vitriolic campaign against Islam forced the secular leadership to show solidarity even if they did not agree with the aims of campaign (Samad 1992).

The Rushdie campaign spearheaded by UKACIA was a unique demonstration of Islamic unity, a phenomenon which has not been repeated on other issues. Aware of the fragile nature of Muslim unity, the UKACIA has tried to avoid contentious issues and concentrate on those where there is unanimity. Besides the Rushdie affair, it has only focused on religious discrimination and Bosnia. The Gulf War exposed some of the limitations of this organisation. Their silence on the issue reflected internal divisions. The fact that Dr Mughram al-Ghamidi, Director of the Islamic Cultural Centre, was the Chair of UKACIA and that there was a strong presence of pro-Saudi groups meant that the organisation would have split wide open if either a neutral or pro-Iraqi line had been adopted. Sympathetic observers point out that its ambivalence was also due to the fact that it had little say in the matter. There was, however, a current led by the Bradford Council of Mosques which opposed this approach and in their personal capacity went on a fact-finding mission to Iraq. On their return they made an equivocal statement partially expressing sympathy for Iraq (*The Muslim News* 31/9/90). This enabled them to avoid a split in the organisation and yet simultaneously fend off the criticism emanating from the Muslim Institute. At that time, Kalim Siddiqui's virulent anti-Saudi campaign was beginning to bite and needed to be checked. Thus the intermediate position adopted by elements within the UKACIA was designed to retain unity and grassroot support.

Long term unity is a real problem and is one of the major issues that has yet to be successfully addressed. Thus when suggestions were made that UKACIA should officially constitute itself as national representative of British Muslims it was rejected because of the leadership aspirations of its many components. A unity group has been established to look into how the transition to a properly constituted organisation can be made.

When one turns to the local associations and their constituents it not clear whether they have been given any other mandate other than the opposition to Rushdie. Their fragility was exposed by differences over sighting of the moon for Eid-ul-Fithr. The South London Mosque Association recoiled at the unilateral announcement by the Islamic Cultural Centre, that Eid would be held on Tuesday 23 March 1993 (*Q News* 26/3-2/4/93). More out of pride than ideological differences, the Association decided that Eid would be on the following day. But two of their members followed the Cultural Centre. Anyone familiar with the politics of Eid knows that this is a regular, but not insurmountable, controversy. What is significant for our purpose was that this dispute showed how tenuous solidarity was among the constituent members of the Action Committee.

It becomes apparent that British Muslim identification is a contested category which is only successful in subsuming a variety of cleavages as long as it is mobilising the community against exclusionism. Of course if the central authorities institutionalise a Muslim leadership it would consolidate religious identification. The resulting legitimacy would attract support and consolidate such a development. The estimations of this development occurring vary. Pessimists among the leadership feel that this may happen in the early 21st century but those optimists close to the Home Office Minister feel that such developments could possibly occur sooner. This may be over optimistic as there are significant elements within the Tory Party and the New Right who would fight such a development tooth and nail.

Furthermore, any organisation aspiring to official recognition has to demonstrate that it represents a significant body of Muslim opinion. Partly to reinforce the view that UKACIA represents the greatest range of Muslim opinion and is the only serious candidates for official recognition and to prevent the rival Muslim Parliament undermining their support, new issues have been taken up. Great care has been taken on what issue should be adopted. The obvious choice is education, which was targeted by the Muslim Parliament and was the hobby horse of Yusaf Islam, the driving force behind the Muslim Education Forum (MEF). Many of those associated with the MEF are also members of the UKACIA and a move in that direction could lead to divided loyalties and friction within UKACIA.

In many ways the taking up of the issue of discrimination on the basis of religion and sacrilege against Islam were logical corollaries of the Rushdie agitation. A document, officially presented to the Home Office in April

1993, argued that Britain was in contravention of its international treaty obligations on human rights. Article 20.1 of the International Covenant on Civil and Political Rights specifically refers to the prohibition by law of religious discrimination and to the incitement of religious hatred and violence. Thus the UKACIA argues that the British government's commitment to a multi-cultural and multi-faith society remains unfilled as long as there is no legislation declaring it illegal to discriminate against Muslims and as long as the blasphemy laws do not include Islam in their remit (UKACIA 1993). The document coincided with the CRE's review of the Race Relations Act which wanted its remit altered so that religious discrimination could tackled as a form of indirect discrimination (CRE 1991: 61). There were important differences between the two approaches. The former wanted a level playing field for Islam, while the latter wanted to turn Muslim groups into an ethnic category and protect them in the same way as Jews and Sikhs. Irrespective of the alternatives mooted there are clear grounds to argue that Islam is not covered by the law and reform is necessary. If the Home Office accepts these recommendations it will have strong implications for the UKACIA, since it would be considered as giving them tacit recognition.

The efforts by UKACIA to influence central government policy have in effect brought the argument to a full circle. In acting as a pressure group lobbying Parliament and campaigning against government policy, it has been increasingly drawing into secular environments. UKACIA lacks the necessary public relations expertise to effectively lobby the central arenas of power. That does not mean that they have not been effective so far, but without support from within these institutions their task has been made more difficult. The missing piece in the jigsaw is the cultural Muslim leadership. They need to break out from the local level and penetrate the highest echelons of power. Their presence is required in the House of Commons and in the higher civil service and judiciary to facilitate the accommodation of Muslims in a truly multi-cultural and multi-faith Britain and Europe. Although there is a possibility that such representatives may not really be representative of the community and they may not be in a position of any real influence (Fitzgerald 1990: 19-29), their voice should be heard in the corridors of power. The role of mediators is clearly vital as was exemplified by the supportive part played by Keith Vaz and Max Madden in the Rushdie controversy or by Bernie Grant in organising the Peace Committee's opposition to the Gulf War.

David Coleman has argued that the greatest challenge to social stability in Europe in the next century will come from migration from the collateral states of the EC. He specifically sees difficulties in integrating Muslims due to their religious attitudes (*Guardian* 16/11/93). This seems to be an exercise in blaming the victim. British Muslim identification, intermittent and oscillating in intensity, is emerging out of a process of contestation with other identifications. This imagining of a British Muslim identity has been partly in reaction to the politics of exclusion, influenced in turn by the New Right. It has been argued that accommodation of Muslim demands in terms of human rights would perhaps lay the matter to rest. But this would lead to the kind of multi-religious, multi-ethnic and multi-cultural Britain and Europe which is so vehemently rejected by the New Right. As a consequence, the imagining of a British Muslim identification has increasingly become part of a much wider debate over developing an inclusive hybrid European identity.

Conclusion

Religion, ethnicity, tradition, custom and nationalism are imagined and reimagined in a constant historical process. Identity is therefore a malleable construction that is shaped and reshaped by internal and external influences depending on time and context. By giving identity non-essentialist qualities it becomes possible to deconstruct the process that leads to the emergence of a British Muslim identification. It is clear that this development has taken place in contestation with other identifications such as British\Pakistani, Bengali\East Ender, 'black', Asian etc.. These developments are not a-historical inventions plucked out of thin air, but constructions which emerge out of specific historical, political and social contexts.

In Britain, race policies were transferred to the local domain and this has had two consequences for ethnic minorities. Through the provisions of legislation and through local initiatives in implementing multi-cultural, anti-racist and equal opportunites policies, secular identifications were recognised and institutionalised. The ultimate mark of legitimacy was the receipt of grants and funds which resulted in a highly instrumental approach by groups and organisations to which identification they highlighted. Thus the subscription to Pakistani, Indian, Asian or 'black' identifications were dependent on the politics of 'ins' and 'outs'. The other consequence was that the various community activists were co-opted into the local hierarchy. They became councillors, mayors and members of the local bureaucracy. Muslims were not successful in projecting themselves on to the national level for a variety of reasons.

The emergence of new racism and the influence it had on the Tory administration changed the political context which had nurtured the secular leadership. It did this by redefining biological racism to one based on a monolithic, ethnically, undifferentiated British identity based on Christian culture and family values. The New Right influenced the media which then castigated and ridiculed the various multi-cultural and anti-racist initiatives emanating from municipal authorities. It also influenced the Education Reform Act by introducing in different aspects of the curriculum explicitly Christian, Eurocentric and patriotic features. The Act neutered the LEAs and made their anti-racist strategies irrelevant. The Thatcher government's other impact was that, in order to control the money supply, it became involved in a struggle with Labour-controlled local authorities. It concealed its attack against local authorities by targeting the 'loony left'. Although they were not the real target, the prime victim of the centralisation of power was multi-culturalism and anti-racism. The reduction of municipal power was a major set back for the secular leadership who were concentrated in that arena. The emphasis on culture by new racism dovetailed with developments within the ethnic minorities encouraging 'authentic' notions of identity. Moreover, the centralisation process and ERA exposed their lack of influence on central government.

In this shifting political context, Muslims organisations began to make an impact. Doctrinal divisions impeded early efforts to establish a common Muslim position on the national level. However they did receive assistance from Middle Eastern and North African powers without compromising their independence, which helped in the initial phase. Islamic solidarity, however, was galvanised by contestations with central authority. The Honeyford affair, the education debates, the Rushdie controversy and the Gulf War were issues which created a favourable climate for Muslim umbrella organisations. British Muslim identification is a contested category. The UKACIA only successfully subsumed the multi-ethnic, mutli-linguistic and multi-denominational characteristics of the Muslim community during *The Satanic Verses* dispute. The affair fused the secular with the sacred on the grassroot level and gave UKACIA, and for that matter any umbrella organisation, a following on the ground for the first time. Unity was fragile and differences which were papered over during the Gulf War emerged with vengeance over the dispute over Eid-ul-Fithr.

In order to sustain the momentum and retain the degree of recognition received from the Home Office, the UKACIA searched for alternative agendas. The Action Committee's new thrust was to argue that the British government has failed to meet its international commitments on human rights by not introducing legislation which would make illegal religious discrimination and profaning Islam. It is becoming clear that UKACIA has begun to act more as a pressure group and its activities will only be more successful if there are secular Muslim MPs who could argue their case within the Establishment. There are no illusions as to what influence or power they may have, but they would act as mediators as some MPs from the ethnic minorities have already done.

Finally, Islamic organisations have only become significant as consequence of the rise of exclusionary influence emanating from the New Right. Their claim that organisation reflects an unwillingness to integrate is blaming the victim. The emergence of British Muslim identification raises profound questions concerning the construction of a hybrid European identification and whether the New Right would allow ethnic minorities to participate in this process.

Acknowledgements

I want to thank Marion Fitzgerald, John Rex and Terence Ranger for their comments and the Wingate and Nuffield Foundations for their financial support.

References

All-Party Parliamentary Group on Race and Community (1993) *Section 11: The Future of Funding for Race Equality.*

Anwar, M. (1991) *Race Relations Policies in Britain an Agenda for the 1990s,* Coventry: Centre for Research in Ethnic Relations, Warwick University.

Back, L. and Solomos, J. (1992) *Who Represents Us?: Racialised Politics and Candidate Selection,* Department of Politics and Sociology, Birbeck College, University of London.

Commission for Racial Equality (1991) *Second Review of the Race Relations Act 1976: A Consultative Paper,* London.

Eade, J. (1996) 'Ethnicity and the Politics of Cultural Difference: An Agenda for the 1990s', in: T. Ranger, Y. Samad and O. Stewart (eds.) *Culture, Identity and Politics: Ethnic Minorities in Britain,* Aldershot: Avebury: 57-66.

Fitzgerald, M. (1984) *Political Parties and Black People: Participation, Representation and Exploitation,* London: Runnymede Trust.

Fitzgerald, M. (1990) 'The Emergence of Black Councillors and MPs in Britain: Some Underlying Questions', in: H. Goulbourne (ed.) *Black People and British Politics,* Aldershot: Avebury.

Gilroy, P. (1990) 'The End of Anti-Racism', *New Community,* 17: 71-84.

HMSO (1991) *Labour Force Survey 1990-1991.* London: HMSO.

Hobsbawn, E.J. and Ranger, T. (eds.) (1983) *The Invention of Tradition,* Cambridge: Cambridge University Press.

Islamic Times (1992) 7(9) July.

Kavanagh, D. (1987) *Thatcherism and British Politics,* Oxford: Oxford University Press.

Mitchell, M. and Russell, D. (1990) 'Race, the New Right and State Policy in Britain', in: T. Khushner and K. Lunn (eds.) *The Politics of Marginality: Race, the Radical Right and Minorities in Twentieth Century Britain,* London: Frank Cass.

Nielsen, J. (1992) *Muslims in Western Europe,* Edinburgh: Edinburgh University Press.

Ouseley, H. (1990) 'Resisting Institutional Change', in: W. Ball and J. Solomos (eds.) *Race and Local Politics,* Basingstoke: Macmillan: 132-152.

Ranger, T. (1993) 'The Invention of Tradition Revisited: The case of Colonial Africa', in: T. Ranger and O. Vaughan (eds.) *Legitimacy and the State in Twentieth Century Africa,* Basingstoke: Macmillan.

Rex, J. (1991) 'The Political Sociology of a Multi-Cultural Society', *European Journal of Intercultural Studies* 2(1): 7-19.

Rose, M. (1991) *The Post-Modern & the Post-Industrial,* Cambridge: Cambridge University Press.

The Runnymede Bulletin, March 1992.

Samad, Y. (1992) 'Book Burning and Race Relations: Political Mobilisation of Bradford Muslims', *New Community* 18(4): 507-519.

Samad, Y. (1996) 'The Politics of Islamic Identity Among: Bangladeshis and Pakistanis in Britain', in: T. Ranger, Y. Samad and O. Stewart (eds.) *Culture, Identity and Politics: Ethnic Minorities in Britain,* Aldershot: Avebury: 90-98.

Solomos, J. (1988) *Black, Youth, Racism and the State: the Politics of Ideology and Policy,* Cambridge: Cambridge University Press.

Troyna, B. and Carrington, B. (1990) *Education, Racism and Reform,* London:Routledge.

United Kingdom Action Committee on Islamic Affairs (1993) *Muslims and the Law in Multi-Faith Britain: The Need For Reform,* London, February.

Yinger, M. (1986) 'Intersecting Strands in the Theorisation of Race and Ethnic Relations', in: J. Rex and D. Mason (eds.) *Theories of Race and Race Relations,* Cambridge: Cambridge University Press: 20-41.

5 Islam and Socialization Among Turkish Minorities in Denmark: Between Culturalism and Cultural Complexity

Lars Pedersen

When immigrant cultures are subjects of discussion they are also made into objects of politics. The politicization of immigrants and Islam that has issued from Denmark's political community and Danish society makes Muslim immigrant culture a political issue.

Racism, in the form of physical and verbal attacks is part of the reality faced by immigrants. But I maintain that racism also plays a much larger role as a point of reference. The political power and the political interests that are found in controlling immigrants is being legitimated with reference to racism. The argument goes as follows: 'if we don't limit the numbers of immigrants in Denmark, in municipal districts, housing societies, buildings, floors, schools and kindergartens, then racism will arise.' There is a paradox therefore, in that racist laws are introduced to prevent racism, and democracy is restricted in order to defend it.

I further maintain that *culturalism*, particularly as it is institutionalized, is of central importance to the immigrants in question. Mention the suppression of women, religious fanaticism, forced marriages, culture conflict, language problems, ghettoes or high birth rates and nobody doubts that immigrants and Muslims are being discussed. It is in this Western mental landscape that Muslim immigrants must find their place to live. In the media Islam and Muslims are always represented in connection with conflicts. The implicit explanation is that Islam is the cause and the prevailing assumption is that

Islam is a conservative, reactionary cultural form. In this line of reasoning, once present in the West as an immigrant, Muslims have a problem: they cannot be true Muslim believers in a modern, democratic welfare state. If they want to be modern, they must betray their Muslim identity, with the consequent loss of culture. If they want to be a Muslim they cannot enjoy the fruits of modernity.

This representation of Muslims is not confined to the media. It also dominates Western academic discourse. Helma Lutz (1986) has, for example, critically examined studies of Muslim immigrant women and concludes that they are viewed through the lens of theories of underdevelopment, in which Islam is the dominant force of oppression. The assumption of such research is that changing the conditions of reproduction will have a negligible effect on women's traditional status so long as they are under influence of Islam. Islam is, in other words, opposed to modernization and regarded as a homogeneous and anti-modern influence. In this perspective 'Islam' is the *cause* of socialization and identity. To label something 'Muslim' is to initiate a project of reduction. The line of argument goes something like this: The Qur'an (and the holy texts) creates an 'Islamic identity', which then produces 'Islamic societies', 'Islamic wars' and 'Islamic histories'. The classic work *The Cambridge History of Islam* (1970) is based on this idea.

The public schools are faced with sceptical Muslim parents. They are frustrated by the limitations imposed upon Muslim children by their parents, especially upon girls. This is particularly evident in the area of sexuality, where Muslim girls are subject to a social code which, compared to Danish girls, is seen as limiting social experience and thus personal development. Social control is intensified from early puberty onwards. Various social anthropological accounts indicate that such restrictions seem stronger in Europe than in Turkey, Pakistan or North Africa. Since a common normative framework is reduced by migration, Turkish parents are obliged to emphasize social control. It cannot be assumed that common norms have been internalized. Social anthropological literature reveals that family roles and structures of authority are changing. Andezian and Streiff (1982) show that the social position and status of younger women are growing within the immigrant community, not because they are the guarantors of tradition but because of their significance to new, host-society relationships. As Andezian and Streiff argue, 'social control based on status conferred by age and family hierachy is replaced by joint control shared between the women of the same generation' (*ibid.* 309). The stress in recent studies is on 'resourcefulness' in the host country rather than on traditional roles.

There are therefore new answers to new questions. Modern society is, in this respect, the source of social and cultural discontinuity. This does not mean that heritage is now just a reminiscense of 'the good old days'. My previous research shows that heritage is of central significance; for example, 'tradition' is followed in arranging marriages (Pedersen and Selmer 1991). The connection with the place of origin and the family is reproduced through marriages and by economic activities. Important events in the life cycle such as marriages, funerals and male circumcision are still conducted in area of origin to a large extent.

Although Turkish minorities are found in the same social institutions as the Danes, the two groups exist side-by-side rather than together. This is the case whether in role games in kindergartens or football played in the school yard. The experience within institutions is seen as different and immigrants are often regarded as problems from the point of view of the institutions (Pedersen and Selmer 1991).

The 'immigrant problem' may be regarded as the hegemonic representation of the communicative action between immigrant and institution. The 'problem' arises in the relation between institution and immigrant, but it also takes the form of hegemonic politics in institutional representation (*ibid.*; see also Grillo 1985). As long as there is a consensus that the cultural values of these institutions are universal, there is also a consensus that the clients themselves are the problem and not the institutions. It therefore appears obvious to reduce immigrant cultures to problem cultures. From this critical point the cultural dimension is actualized and from this perspective professionals become active managers of the cultural heritage of Turkish minorities, whereby Islam becomes a social problem. This argument has been dealt with at length by Pedersen and Selmer (1991).

A case study: bilingual teaching

The reaction of immigrants to the organization of teaching in the mother tongue at schools and to the use of bilingual staff in kindergartens shows how the cultural field is treated with great seriousness. Turkish parents perceive it as a beginning of a process of cultural dialogue or bargaining. They think that it is important exactly who is to represent Turkish culture for the children. In some cases they have organized support for their own candidates as an alternative to those chosen from the institutions, although this has not been successful. While Turkish parents employ cultural values as the criteria for selection, the schools refer to formal criteria such as language and argue that parents' criticisms are simply reflections of political discussions and rivalries imported from Turkey.

A conflict between Turkish families and a local public administration that arose over the employment of Alevi Kurds as bi-lingual personnel in kindergartens with children of Sunni Muslim Turks illustrates these points (see Pedersen and Selmer 1991). A group of Turkish families protested against having Alevi Kurds employed in a kindergarten. One of the arguments they raised was their dissatisfaction with Alevi Kurds as multi-cultural personnel in an institution with Turkish Sunni Muslim children. They argued that they could not adequately represent Turkish culture.

The local administration responded that the challenge was irrelevant since the relevant criterion was knowledge of Danish and not cultural background. While nobody doubted that the Alevi Kurds were well qualified in *language*, it did not meet the parents' demand for a *cultural* representative. The local administration viewed bi-lingual personel as kinds of 'cultural translaters', helping Danish professionals in their daily communication with the children and communicating the goals of the institutions to the Turkish children and their parents. The administration claimed that the parents 'did not understand' this and wanted not only a translator but also a representative of Turkish culture in the institutions. There were different reactions among Turkish immigrant organisations to this case. Those characterized as possessing a Turkish national-cultural discourse backed the Turkish parents while the left wing secular groups critizised the initiative. In the event, the former eventually withdrew their initial support from the parents.

No matter what pedagogical strategy is chosen, it will relate directly to the administration of the cultural heritage of immigrants. The development of so-called 'bi-cultural', 'multi-cultural' or 'anti-racist' strategies shows a critical awareness of this role, which is the first step. But this initial step does not produce solutions because new problems arise, for instance an awareness of 'culture' as a technique of management. Some writers, including Sivanandan (1983), criticize this cultural crisis management as a response to the anticipated revolt of the 'second generation' for being no more than an adjustment to a racist society. Institutional hegemony will then rest on the superior knowledge of other cultures. In this way, culturalism, ethno-racism, ethnicism or new-racism will make it impossible for the immigrants to promote their own political alternatives.

But in my view it could also be a new point of departure in negotiating culture. It is central to my understanding that the development of migrant cultures as minority cultures depends on the dominant social institutions as administrators of cultural heritage, but that such cultures do not accept assimilationist strategies but instead engage in cultural resistance.

The state, the life world and Islamic organizations

I have argued that significant ideological and conceptual problems arise when discussing Islam in Danish society. But the concepts involved are not pure - they are materially linked to the larger context of international capital and the consequent global integration process that has led to extensive structural changes in the international division of labour and an expansion of the European State Apparatus. The role of the State Apparatus has been to secure priorities linked to this rationality and to establish social stability through new institutions. Following Habermas (1981), the *system world* organizes new areas of the *life world*.

The State organizes ever larger areas of the life world. During the last 10 to 15 years the imperative of decentralizing and minimizing the State has been articulated in public debate. These ideas might imply that the *life world* would expand its area, but the actual outcome has been privatization and cuts in welfare services. So the ideological stress on rebuilding self reliance and networking actually means administrative control over the clients' intimate life world rather than an enlargement of local autonomy and community responsibility (Schierup 1988). If this is true for the Danish population in general, it is certainly true for Turkish and Muslim minorities. They are defined as specific problems by the various levels of public administration. The social and economic vulnerability and marginalization of the immigrant ethnic minorities is also extensively documented in the rest of Europe (Castles 1984; Cross 1986).

The management of cultural heritage is an important element of socialization and is of course too important to be left to Danish educational authorities alone. The immigrants have their own methods. Socialization within the family is supplemented by self-help organizations which circulate their own cultural values. These organizations discuss and formulate their own demands towards society, but they are also places for redefining a new collective identity. The social and cultural interests that these independent organizations express is a result of the system world's colonization of the life world. These interests cannot be articulated sufficiently through pre-existing Danish associations because they have been an integral part of the historical development of Danish society (Pedersen 1993).

When immigrants organize themselves independently in relation to life world relations it is because they are linked to contradictory social and economic processes, in particular within migration. Firstly, they form a new social category, created through the development of a socio-economic demand in the economic centre. The history of Islam in Denmark is linked to labour migration. In 1970 there were about 6,000 Turks, 2,000 Pakistanis and 1,000 Moroccans, mainly men, in the country. The 1970s was the decade of family re-union, such that by 1980 the Turkish population numbered 14,000, rising to over 30,000 by 1990. The total Muslim population is estimated to be somewhere around 70-80,000 which makes Islam the second largest religious community in Denmark, outnumbering the estimated 40,000 Catholics.

Secondly, their numbers are still growing and they have simultaneously lost their dependence on traditional life world relations. Thirdly, their relation to labour market is weak in every respect. With such a basis of identity, ambivalence and sensivity towards conflicts are created, unique cultural identifications are developed and cultural roots are radically reevaluated. The new social actors express themselves by crossing the accepted hegemonic system of representation, i.e. they are crossing the 'imagined'. In so doing they challenge the discourse and praxis of public institutions. It is against this background that the former 'Fremdarbeiter' has been transformed into a 'Muslim minority'.

If one can speak of the creation of an Islamic structure of socialization, then it is this specific socio-economic history that has relegated Turkish immigrants to the cultural periphery, left them without hegemonic power and given these particular life world processes their dynamics and meaning as 'Islamic'. The Turkish minorities have been caught in a historical economic trap that shapes a 'local public' (Schierup 1984) and is totally different from that of the rest of Danish society. Social communities and networks that relate to descent, ethnicity and/or Islam are now the answer to the threats of disintegration and the fragmentation posed by the system world. The strategy is, in other words, to produce symbols and institutions to defend cultural autonomy. The development of a cultural syncretism redefining social identity cannot stem from the continuous transformation of life world from system world. It simply does not have the potential to do so. It must come from the life world itself, perhaps from music (see Paul Gilroy (1987) on hip-hop-music for example).

During the last 15 years there has been a complete change in the leadership of religious institutions. The first *hocas* (imams) were individuals without formal religious education i.e. lay *hocas* who came as labour migrants. Nowadays the *hocas* possess religious education, usually from one of the Turkish theological faculties. They are employed as *hocas*. Furthermore, since 1985 the Turkish government has financed the majority of them, through the department for religious affairs, Diyanet Isleri Baskanligi. An agreement made between Denmark and Turkey in 1989 gives the Diyanet *hocas* the right to stay in Denmark for up to four years. This agreement also means that independent *hocas*, who might have connections with the Islamist movement in Turkey find it very difficult to enter the country.

In Western society, religious relations do not overlap with other social relations. Religious praxis is an integral part of society in the traditional Turkish village, but in a modern society religion changes its value. The symbolic structural totality is broken and religion has become an individual matter (Schiffauer 1988). Social relations can now be defined as strictly religious e.g., one can choose to become a believer as one possibility among others. For many 'Muslims' Islam only plays a marginal role in social identity and so it is not an important part of their lives. They may take part in prayers twice a year at most, Ramazan Bayrami (Id al-Fitr) and Kurban Bayram (Id al-Adha). Nevertheless they identify with Islam and feel responsible for defending it against what they regard as false interpretations made by non-Muslim Danes. As one informant told me, 'in Islam we find equality between the sexes', and he continued, 'what the Danes think of as Islam is tradition'. This group of people typically organize themselves (formally or informally) along ethnic lines in secular and even anti-religious associations.

It is rare to meet young Turks who are able to get on with their peers in two separate ethnic environments. Those who are able to do so also distinguish sharply between two cultural realities. Separated worlds give separate possibilities and separate limits: a Danish world and a Turkish world. Where they relate to different cultural codes, some can keep these possibilities flowing. A nice, polite and respectful Turkish boy paying regards to his family can quickly turn into a stylish conversationalist among Danish youth. The posters in a young man's bedroom might juxtapose the actor and martial arts champion Bruce Lee with religious signs. When they marry, they may well choose 'a quite normal girl with long black hair and light, brown eyes' because the time has come to be a full-time Muslim. In other words, there is a time to be young and a time to be Muslim.

For other Turks of the younger generation, Islam is the central point of identification. As such, Islam involves key authentic values. For these youngsters, often of the second generation, Islam makes it possible to simultaneously criticize tradition and the social stigma of immigration. Islam provides a position for self-assertion, from which the world can be engaged and even conquered with self-respect.

The dramatic changes in social conditions experienced by immigrants places them in a kind of permanent state of crises. Of course not all Muslim immigrants channel this experience into the activities of immigrant organizations. Those who do can, for the time being, relate to organizations with quite different ideological profiles: secular, a-religious even anti-religious; national-cultural oriented; and Islamist organizations.

One such Islamist organization among Turks is Milli Görüs. Since 1986 Milli Görüs *cemaats* (religious communities) have developed in Denmark in an organized but low profile manner. Denmark constitutes one so called *bölge* (region) in the European wing of the organization.[1] Besides organizing Mosques, Qur'anic courses, study circles on Islam's role in the world (using video and cassette tapes as sources of inspiration and information), they also organize sports such as football and taekwon-do. They attempt to learn more about Danish society by involving outsiders, such as trade union representatives. Separate women's circles are also set up.

Milli Görüs attacks the processes of social marginalization found among immigrant societies in Western Europe. The movement's dominant outlook might well appear problematic, since it displaces the locus of social conflict from the social realm towards the individual's relation to God. This becomes central to closing the gap between utopian and actual social initiatives. But its strength is that it aims to install Islam at the centre of social identity as an alternative to the labour market, in which the possibilities of establishing a positive identity are lacking. Social reality reveals that there are good reasons for Islamists to organize their life world relations, threatened both socially and economically as they are, as a defence against a Christian civilisation.

The key motivations for participating in Islamic movements seem to be firstly, resistance to the deprivation of autonomy and its consequent loss of authority, and secondly reaction against the loss of control within personal or close social relations. At first sight it might be argued that the perspectives of Milli Görüs and the Islamic movements in relation to social change are negative. This view is, however, incorrect and needs to be modified. There is not necessarily a total correspondance between world view and the local and individual social action, which tends to exceed the limits of the community. The different *cemaat* religious communities constitutes *a community of interpretation* (Said 1981). Within the community, certain views on Islam are circulated and create the basis for individual and collective action. But the involvement of the participants is flexible and differs in intensity. In other words, Milli Görüs deserves merit for establishing an alternative platform, one that can serve as a point of departure for autonomous reevaluations of collective heritage and identity.

Against this background social and cultural strategies are created that demonstrate, that it is possible to be socially active. Similar to other immigrant movements, the Islamists thereby establish a position far from the centre of power, one that insists on its own presence. It refers to existing local communities, whose social and cultural interests lack representation. It is about processes of marginalization and the struggle over the representation of social and cultural interests in the life world. Here we can see tendencies among immigrant Muslim minorities, not least among the Islamists, to formulate demands and to be considered as valid citizens.

Notes

1 I have completed a research project on the new Islamic movements in Western Europe (Pedersen 1994).

References

Andizian, S. and J. Streiff (1982) 'Transpositions and Reinterpretations of the Traditional Female Role in an Immigration Situation', in: *Living in Two Cultures: The Socio-Cultural Situation of Migrant Workers and their Families*. Aldershot: Gower.

Castles, S. (1984) *Here for Good. Western Europe's New Ethnic Minorities*, London: Pluto Press.

Cross, M. (1986) 'Migrant Workers in European Cities: Forms of Inequality and Strategies for Policy', Proceedings from an International Seminar on Migration

Research. The Migration Initiative of the Danish Social Science Research Council.
Gilroy, P. (1987) *There Ain't No Black in the Union Jack*, London: Hucthinson.
Grillo, R. (1985) *Ideologies and Institutions in Urban France: The Representation of Immigrants*, Cambridge: Cambridge University Press.
Habermas, J. (1981) *Theorie des Kommunikative*, Handelns: Frankfurt am Main: Suhrkamp.
Holt, P., A. Lambton and B. Lewis (eds) (1970) *The Cambridge History of Islam*, Cambridge: Cambridge University Press.
Lutz, H. (1986) 'Migrantinnen aus der Türkei: Eine Kritik des gegenwärtigen Forschungsstandes', *Migration & Ethnizität* 0/86. Berlin.
Pedersen, L. (1993) 'Newer Islamic Movements in Western Europe: An Analysis of the New Cultural Trend Represented by Islamist Movements Among Immigrant Muslim Minorities in Western Europe'. Dept. of Ethnography and Social Anthropology, Aarhus University. (In Danish).
Pedersen, L. and B. Selmer (1991) *Young Muslim Immigrants. Cultural Identity and Migration*, Aarhus: Aarhus Universitetsforlag. (In Danish).
Said, E. (1981) *Covering Islam*, London: RKP.
Schierup, C.-U. (1984) 'Do They Dance to Keep up Tradition? Analysis of a Social Situation among Yugoslav Immigrants in Scandinavia,' Research Report no. 81. University of Umeå, Sweden.
Schierup, C.-U. (1988) *Immigrants and the Nordic Welfare States*. Uppsala: Maktutredningen.
Schiffauer, W. (1988) 'Migration and Religiousness', in: T. Gerholm and Y.G. Lithman (eds), *The New Islamic Presence in Western Europe*, London: Mansell: 146-158.
Sivanandan, A. (1983) 'Challenging Racism: Strategies for the 80s', *Race and Class* 25(2): 1-12.

6 Young Muslims in Keighley, West Yorkshire: Cultural Identity, Context and 'Community'

Steven Vertovec

Among many young British Muslims of Asian descent, day-to-day life involves engaging two identifiable sets of factors which condition values, activity and identity. One concerns the strong conceptual frameworks, social networks and emotional bonds associated with 'community' - a notion which has been locally constructed by the youths' elders who have, over decades, involved themselves with a variety of processes surrounding settlement (forging a livelihood and a lifestyle in a new social and economic arena) and religious-cultural institutionalisation (formally establishing as authoritative and representative certain roles, relationships and practices). The other concerns aspects of basic context including local geography (social, cultural, economic and physical), state structures, the education system, employment and unemployment patterns, leisure activities, class dynamics, and racism.

Such a view is not the same as the 'between two cultures' perspective which saw Asian youth as schizophrenically suspended between the presumed 'ethnic culture' of their parents' homeland and the equally presumed 'British' way of life. Instead, it should be recognised that young Asians carry out their lives engaging both 'community' and 'context', and that 'community' itself has been continually defined and redefined vis-à-vis contextual features. These are not to be understood as discrete spheres, but overlapping, or better, mutually conditioning, ones. Social, cultural and religious ideas, beliefs and practices among Asians of all generations are the culmination of interactions with both, complex and interrelated spheres.

The following is a brief ethnographic account regarding the Asian population of Keighley, West Yorkshire,[1] which indicates some of the ways in which these issues have manifested and affected the situation of young Muslims.

Context: Keighley and its Asian population

Although now it is officially part of Bradford Metropolitan District, Keighley (set in a valley about eleven miles northwest of central Bradford) has remained an autonomous geographic and economic space in which inhabitants have staunchly maintained a separate identity. Long independent with its own Borough Council, however, Keighley was subsumed into Bradford Metropolitan Council during the local government reorganisation of 1974; subsequently, there was much resentment coupled with heightened local identity in Keighley. A feeling of autonomy and local identity, which has proved strong enough in the face of outsiders from Bradford, has had no little effect on race relations: since their coming, Asians have faced hostility from many in the town.

During the 1950s and 1960s, Keighley received a large influx of Asian migrants during a time when the town's total population was declining and its economic base, the textile industry, was shrinking. As throughout Yorkshire, the industry was able to maintain itself in the face of increasing international competition by installing machinery that required continuous running, and by hiring workers such as Asian migrants who were willing to undertake the consequent round-the-clock shift work, and to receive wages which were unattractive to indigenous labourers. In the late 1950s and early 1960s, only a relatively small number of Asians actually settled in Keighley; many lived in Bradford or other nearby urban areas, only commuting to Keighley for work. As time passed and more Asians arrived in Yorkshire through chain migration networks, settlement in Keighley increased. This changing pattern was observed in the mid 1960s by Butterworth (1967: 4), who wrote:

> Although the concentration of migrants in the larger towns in West Yorkshire is apparent there has been movement to towns such as Keighley in the west and to smaller centres within the ring formed by the larger towns. The characteristic of the ring, and the situations which develop from it, are in part determined by the structure of the migrant groups and their cultures.

In 1966 there were 1,200 Asians in Keighley, all of whom were Pakistanis (yet one must bear in mind that these included 'East Pakistanis', known as Bangladeshis after 1971). As with Asian migrants throughout Britain at this period, most were men between the ages of 25-45 who originally came intending to work for a number of years, to accumulate a given amount of money, and to return to their families and villages of origin. Eventually, personal motivations and family strategies among the migrants changed (usually in light of greater legal restrictions regarding immigration), and more women migrated to join their husbands. In 1961 only 10 percent of West Yorkshire's Pakistani population was comprised of women, rising to 25 percent by 1966-7; Butterworth (1967: 5) noted that the process of family reunification was much later in Keighley due to the comparatively more recent settlement of male migrants there. Although in Keighley reunion continued throughout the 1970s and 1980s and sometimes up to the present, the number of males born in (West) Pakistan is still considerably higher than the number of females. This is even more marked for Bangladeshis, among whom settlement and family reunion has taken place at a later stage (see below).

In the 1960s, 94 percent of Keighley's Asian migrants were employed in the textile industry. Although this fact is no different from elsewhere in Yorkshire, Keighley exhibited a greater tendency toward racial exclusion in employment. A survey of 55 firms conducted by the Junior Chamber of Commerce at this time showed that only 31 percent would employ Pakistanis, while 22 percent were ambiguous or wouldn't state their view and no less than 47 percent said they would not (*ibid.*: 51). Further, of six West Yorkshire areas covered in a PEP Report in the mid 1960s, 'Keighley ... was shown to be the only area in which there were no white collar workers who were immigrants, although 470 immigrants were employed as manual workers in the firms in Keighley providing information' (*ibid.*: 52). There was also evidence of 'fewer immigrants with higher education qualifications in places such as Keighley, where settlement is relatively recent, than in the main and continuing centres of immigrant settlement such as Bradford and Leeds,' and in Keighley, 'the question of immigrants getting less money than local workers has arisen on a number of occasions.' Housing among Asians in Keighley was also shown to be poor and overcrowded.

In addition to having a distinct economic sphere and to harbouring perceptions of community independence and resentments toward the Council, Keighley also stands out in the region for its notorious record of racial incidents. Despite having only 9.5 percent of the Metropolitan area's

Black/Asian population, Keighley had 41.6 percent of the area's reported racial incidents in 1988. In 1987 and 1989, in fact, Keighley was said to have the worst such record in the country (*Keighley News* 27/3/87; *Keighley News* 2/6/89). With regard to this appalling reputation, the Council wrote:

> There have been a number of major incidents which have led to serious injury and large scale arrests. The issue of racial harassment may be the major social issue facing Keighley in the coming years. ... The geography of Keighley is important. A small poor black population living in the town centre and a poor white population living on the outer estates. The two communities seldom interact except in school. There is good reason to believe that extreme racist political parties have in the past tried to exploit this situation
> (Bradford Metropolitan Council 1988: 35-36).

Several of the above characteristics of Keighley - especially its declining industrial base, nature and pattern of immigration, quite separate structures and sentiments within a larger regional socio-economic and political framework, and atmosphere of racial discrimination, tension and violence - are key to understanding features of community development among Muslims.

Keighley is rather remarkable in that its non-'White' ethnic minority population is almost entirely Asian, and virtually all Muslim. Within a 1991 total population of 45,121 persons in Keighley, 'Asians' (including the census categories 'Indian,' 'Pakistani,' 'Bangladeshi' and 'Other Asian') numbered 5,859 or 12.9 percent. The bulk of the Asian population, however, is concentrated in specific parts of inner Keighley, and in some neighbourhoods or streets Asians comprise a large majority. Pakistanis account for 4,674 inhabitants or 79.7 percent of the town's Asian population, Bangladeshis 993 or 16.9 percent of all Asians, Indians 131 or 2.2 percent of all Asians and 'Other Asians' 61 or 1 percent of all Asians.

The rather late reunion of Asian families in Keighley - most women and children joining their husbands and fathers during the course of the 1970s and 1980s (with Bangladeshis undergoing the process most recently) - has naturally affected the gender ratio over the years, although a high fertility rate has begun to correct the imbalance particularly among the Pakistanis and Bangladeshis. In 1991 no less than 52.4 percent of Keighley's Asians were under 16 years old, while only 1.5 percent were of pensionable age.

Housing conditions among Keighley Asians have remained poor since the earliest days of settlement by unaccompanied male migrants. In the 1960s Butterworth (1967: 53-54) observed that Asian migrants had moved into depopulated parts of the town, into housing often designated for slum clearance adjacent to industrial works. A 1967 PEP Report found that in Keighley, local authority housing was generally easy to obtain for migrants (a letter from an employer was all that was needed). However,

> Very few had in fact been housed through this arrangement, and this reflected on the one hand the desire to own property and, on the other, the continued concentration of men without their families in multi-occupied houses. 97% of the immigrant respondents from the Keighley area said that they hadn't considered local authority accommodation. This also reflects the relatively high cost of this, which is also a feature for local people in view of the lower wage rates that prevail in Keighley and in most of West Yorkshire.
>
> (*ibid.*: 53)

Today, Asians in Keighley tend overwhelmingly to own their houses, with only negligible numbers applying for Council housing. Still:

> There is a particularly acute housing need in the older central part of Keighley where for the most part the Asian Community lives mainly in owner-occupied nineteenth century stone built housing often back to back. Two thirds of the houses are considered to be over-crowded with 12% lacking basic amenities. In this area there is a shortage of larger family houses at a price families can afford. A typical case is a family with five or six children living in an average terraced house of two bedrooms and an attic, where one of the bedrooms has already been reduced in size to form a bathroom. Families often include other adult relatives and/or more than five children.
>
> (Bradford Metropolitan Council 1988: 37)

Keighley Asians are also faring poorly with respect to jobs. The situation is bluntly described by the Council, and worth quoting in full:

> People of Pakistani and Bangladeshi origin - 95% of Keighley's Asian population - are three and a half times as likely as whites to be unemployed. For 16 to 24 years olds of Pakistani and Bangladeshi origin, the national unemployment rate was 43%. Although no comparable figures are available for Keighley (The Dept. of Employment stopped collecting them in 1982), the local picture is likely to be very similar. This is confirmed by Bradford Council's Careers Service statistics, which show that in 1987 only 20% of the 64 Asian 16 year olds who left school to look for a job were successful, compared to 45% for white school leavers. ... It seems almost certain that, as a group, Keighley's young Asians are still bearing the brunt of unemployment in the town.

But it is not just young Asians who are suffering from unemployment: Although no figures are available, it seems that many of Keighley's long-term unemployed are Asians who emigrated to Britain in the 1960s, lured by the promise of plentiful jobs in the town's textile mills. Most of these jobs have now gone: the skills learned have become largely redundant. Many of those who lost their jobs are poorly educated, sometimes with a limited command of English, and are poorly equipped to compete for the new jobs available.

Asian unemployment is a major issue for all of Keighley.

(*ibid.*: 21-22)

It has been suggested that perhaps only 30 percent of Keighley's Asians are fully employed (*Keighley Target* 16/1/91). Lack of needed work skills and poor English language competence are considered to be the greatest hindrances for middle aged and older Asians. Young Asian males in Keighley, though unemployed, seek to learn a variety of skills and trades, especially through the Youth Training Scheme (although their rate of success in finding a job following a YTS programme is far below that of whites; *ibid.*).

Young Asian females, on the other hand, are not exhibiting such range in desire or choice with regard to employment. While a very small number engage in higher education, a few Asian female school-leavers in Keighley pursue career courses such as nursing; others become helpers in nursery schools, perhaps leading eventually to a teaching profession. But it seems the bulk of young Asian females do not become employed; most of those who do undertake sewing work on a somewhat temporary basis in one of the textile mills. This work is considered by many Keighley Asian parents to be appropriate for young women since sewing is considered a useful woman's skill, the work environment is one mainly comprised of other Asian women (and therefore culturally and sexually 'safe'), and parents hope their daughters will soon marry and therefore move to somewhere else in Britain or to Pakistan, in either place solely to become a housewife and mother. Increasingly, however, it seems parental views toward 'appropriate' kinds and spheres of female work in and around Keighley are being contested - or at least are not being fully shared - by the young Asian women themselves, many of whom harbour desires and aspirations to engage in further education or a career. Yet, in many ways the situation in Keighley reflects (even perhaps accentuates) that of elsewhere in West Yorkshire where, Afshar (1989: 224) describes,

The acceptance of familial obligation, both to parents and to children, makes Asian women particularly vulnerable to the control of the moral economy of kin. At the same time the sharpened experience of racism by the youngest generation of Muslim women amongst the middle and working class families appears to have resulted in a further tightening of familial bonds, an acceptance of segregated and home-based work and, in some cases, even a deliberate, though reluctant, return to arranged marriages in Pakistan.

Asians in Keighley live and work in rather encapsulated social and spatial ambits - Asian women even more so. Keighley Asians have recently come to face a growing kind of discrimination specifically against them as Muslims. Muslim workers in factories of Keighley (as well as in Huddersfield, Dewsbury, Batley and throughout Yorkshire) have complained to the Commission for Racial Equality that employers are singling out Muslims and treating them worse, especially with regard to work practices and time off (particularly to celebrate Eid) than their white, non-Muslim co-workers (*The Guardian* 15/3/93).

There are other ways in which Keighley Asians are excluded or segregated from Keighley whites. Many Asians in the town, including a surprising number of young people, lack full competence in English. In years past, this was to be expected due to relatively recent settlement (a survey in 1976, when many families were undergoing reunion, found that over 63 percent of Asian children in Keighley could not speak English; *Keighley News* 29/10/76). The persistence of this trait today may in many ways be attributed to a kind of social encapsulation among Asians in the town, including Asian youth. Firstly, mobility within parts of Keighley and between Keighley and other towns is said to be low among most residents and among Asians in particular: most tend to engage in work or social life within their own locality among their own ethnic group. The Keighley Detached Youthwork Project (Youthlink) has identified discrete leisure patterns among white and Asian young people, as well as specific parts of town frequented by each - or places, in the case of many Asians, avoided for fear of racist abuse. In schools, too, one can observe separate friendship and socialising patterns among pupils which very largely reflect race and ethnicity (such patterns are not only observable between white and Asian pupils, but often between Pakistani and Bangladeshi too: this includes close friendship networks within each of these kinds of groups on the one hand, and often conflict between them).

The Keighley context has therefore affected Asians such that they comprise a quite distinct population segment in terms of both structural and social features. Yet it is cultural features - especially ones surrounding areas of origin, kinship networks and importantly, Islam - which usually account for their own, most significant, criteria of 'community' distinction.

'Community': Muslim Keighley

Processes of formal social organisation among Asians in Keighley have resulted mainly in the establishment of Muslim associations. In the early stages of settlement, men would gather in private accommodations to pray collectively. By the mid 1960s, the men pooled resources to remodel a house into a basic mosque. Soon after, they rallied to campaign successfully for the establishment of Muslim slaughtering facilities in the town (see Butterworth 1967: 53). Throughout this period, when the Muslim population of Keighley was overwhelmingly male, such organised religious activity was nonetheless rather loose-knit and *ad hoc*.

It was with the increasing reunification of families in Keighley through the end of the 1960s and into the early 1970s which stimulated a greater degree of institutionalisation among Muslims. Larger facilities for congregational prayer led by an Imam, Islamic teaching facilities for children, and proper burial facilities quickly arose as matters necessitating formal organisation among a growing, male and female, multi-generational Muslim community.

A Muslim Association was established by 1968, comprised of both Mirpuris and Sylhetis, and linked to Tabligh ul Islam, a Barelvi organisation based in Bradford. Eventually, however, the Sylhetis split to form their own organisation (following the war over the creation of Bangladesh), and both associations distanced themselves from Tabligh ul Islam. Eventually, the two created their own large mosques and Quranic schools (see Vertovec 1994). Keighley Asians are therefore currently divided into two 'communities', each proudly autonomous, formally organised, and inherently Muslim.

Young Muslims in Keighley

While in many ways both associations have succeeded in uniting and providing for their respective communities, they have not, arguably, succeeded in supporting or integrating the desires, needs and energies of the large number of Keighley's young Muslims. Although youths (for the most part, male) are seen in number at association-run events - for instance, at Friday prayer, in annual processions through the town marking the Prophet's birthday (see *Keighley News* 12/10/90) - many youths attest to feeling alienated from the associations and their decision-making elders. There is no youth wing or sub-group for young people - nor, for that matter, is there a women's group or any other sub-group. Despite their sometimes rather lax participation in collective prayer and other mosque activities, and their general exclusion from the main Muslim organisational activities, these factors have not diminished sentiments surrounding Muslim cultural - if not religious - identity.

For instance, Muslim young males were present in force at a town square demonstration in protest over *The Satanic Verses* (*Keighley News* 10/3/89). Although many - both Asian and white - feared trouble (possibly caused by radical Muslims or the National Front), the demonstration passed with little incident or backlash, and was even praised by a Keighley police inspector as 'peaceful and well organised'. (This was probably due to the fact it was held at noon on a Sunday, and police were present in large number.) The demonstration, which entailed the co-operation of both the Keighley Muslim Association and the Bangladesh Islamic Association, entailed a march by well over 1,000 Muslims (many with 'Kill Rushdie' placards) from the Jamia mosque to the Town Square. There, speeches were made castigating the book and calling for its withdrawal from bookshops and libraries. A drawing of Rushdie was burned. The event not surprisingly drew letters to the local newspaper, protesting not only about death threats and the need to preserve freedom of the press, but also, in two cases, about 'the spectacle of a thousand Muslims swarming over our War Memorial' (a statement which is significantly indicative of the existence, among Keighleyites, of a common complex of underlying feelings or understandings surrounding notions of people and locality/nation and history/religion and culture - amounting to an identity assumed to be threatened by the presence of [dark-skinned] Muslims; see *Keighley News* 3/3/89, 10/3/89, 17/3/89).

The Rushdie Affair in Keighley, like elsewhere, did much to fortify Muslim identity and pride, especially among Muslim youth. Even in casual discussions among three teenage Muslim women and me, when the Rushdie Affair was raised, the women became quite agitated. Though none attended the demonstration, they agreed that Rushdie 'said something bad about the Prophet [which was] the worse thing you could do'; 'he just wrote what he wanted to write - he knew nothing, that's why we were all so mad.' There was a pervasive feeling that an insult to their collective identity had occurred, affecting all Muslims no matter how lapsed or devout. They pointed out that among the many youths attended the demonstration, 'even those who don't do their prayers still went.' Some, they said, went without really knowing why they were doing it. For example, a group of teenage males recounted racist incidents in Keighley where '"Rushdie" was a swear word': the name was written on the doors of some Muslim homes, and one of the group tells (with laughs) of a white man who approached him and some friends, saying 'Rushdie' while pulling down his own trousers as an obscene gesture. The Rushdie Affair, and particularly the increased modern communications surrounding it, made an important impact on Keighley Muslims: before, the community 'was not aware of Muslim identity [but] are now aware that there are Muslims [all over the country].'

A great many young Muslims in Keighley are quite devout, or at least firmly believing in their faith. Almost regardless of degree of practice and intensity of faith, however, most are staunch in their Muslim identity. For example, at one of the public youth clubs frequented by Asians, the teenage members of two football teams insisted - despite considerable protest by the (himself Asian but atheist) Co-ordinator of the club - that the teams should be called the 'Keighley Young Muslims' and 'Keighley Muslims'. This kind of identity manifestation seems indicative of a growing kind of 'cultural Muslim identity' among young Muslims: as described below, many are the first to acknowledge their negligence of religious proscriptions and lack of religious knowledge - but this in no way mitigates their pride in being of Muslim heritage, nor their current desire to be associated with perceived Muslim causes.

The lack of religious knowledge is embarrassing to some. Practically all young Muslims in Keighley have all been to madrassah, yet many claim to have gained little from the rote learning and recitation characteristic of religious instruction there. Instead, they would like to have learned, or be taught, Islamic values which have 'relevance' to their lives here and now in Keighley. This fairly negative experience of, and alienation from, madrassahs and Muslim Associations - combined nonetheless with a desire to know more about Islam and its potential for their lives - seems to be even deeper among young women in Keighley, especially since they were taken out of madrassah at puberty, and rarely if ever go to mosque or any kind of association-sponsored meeting.

A range of other perceptions and opinions were conveyed in interviews, several of which are related below under separate headings.

On Asian Keighley

Young Asians' self-perceptions of their own community centre on the small size, compact spatial distribution, and social concentration of Keighley's Asian (mainly Pakistani) population, especially in comparison to nearby Bradford. These are particularly expressed in ways which underline the fact that there is a considerable proportion of people who are related to one another, and that there exists a dense communication network through which certain behaviours are collectively reinforced or reproved. An Asian school liaison officer sums up the situation by way of an anecdote concerning a young Asian woman in Keighley who went out to a neighbourhood shop, stopped to talk to someone, and by the time she reached home again, her parents had already been informed of, and disapproved of, her impromptu meeting.

For young people, this situation is especially perceived in terms of restrictions on their actions. Almost invariably, in response to questions concerning ways in which they foresee raising their own children, answers accorded with notions of 'just the same as we were [because] you must know your culture ... but more freedom.' In the meantime, most seemed to feel that they lived within a closed, controlled, and prescriptive social sphere, as these excerpts indicate:

> We all know each other. Everybody knows each other here and they start talking, then the parents say 'Oh no, you can't do this because everyone will start talking about you,' you see?
> Those who misbehave get shipped off to Pakistan or Bangladesh.
> In Keighley, in order to keep your family honour, you keep yourself to yourself.
> People have to be really, really careful because cause they are under the spotlight all the time. In that respect, Bradford is about is about ten or fifteen years ahead.

Certain other observations comparing Keighley to Bradford, which some make, are revealing of ways in which such dense networks and behavioural feed-back have bolstered in Keighley a more 'tradition-oriented' community than elsewhere. For instance, the co-ordinator of the Asian Women's Centre - who moved to Keighley upon marriage some years ago - notices a number of features unique to the Asian community here as opposed to Bradford or to her native Manchester. She says for instance that, in other such communities these days, no one really expects women to cover their heads in public any more, but in Keighley even young women 'do it instinctively'. She also points out that in Keighley one never sees other young Asian women or girls wearing blue jeans or other Western casual dress. When I posed this observation to a teenage girl, she replied: 'Keighley's a smaller town, right, and community, so if one girl starts wearing jeans all the other Pakistani families start talking and say she's right bad. It's just so small.' And in a discussion with three young women about such issues - especially in comparison to their counterparts in Bradford (again, just around eleven miles away) - they concurred that in Keighley 'we're not westernized.'

On learning to be Muslim

Practically every young Muslim in Keighley receives some form of formal religious instruction, mainly consisting of training in Quranic recitation (either at one of the four madrassahs or at one of the many private homes were individual parents tutor neighbourhood children; it seems the majority of Muslim children in Keighley attend such instruction in private homes, thereby making for a great variety of experience with regard to teaching styles and methods, levels of linguistic competence, and understandings of Islam and Muslim practice). Informal religious nurture at their own homes appears negligible: informants claim they knew very little about Islam and Islamic practice before undertaking religious instruction at about the age of five. Prior to that, at best parents might simply say to small children, 'come stand by me and do what I do' during prayer. In Pakistan and Bangladesh, many facets of religious nurture are in the hands of grandparents who see the children daily; here, relatively young parents often lack the religious knowledge which such grandparents, who are not present in this country, would normally impart. Thus the great interest, among such parents, in establishing and supporting madrassahs.

Attitudes to experience in religious instruction at madrassah vary considerably. Most found it boring, but admit they did learn quite a bit, especially how to recite and pray. For most attending was merely routine: 'you just rush to get there on time ... you don't think about it.' The main purpose of madrassah, according to one teenage male, is to learn to recite chapters of the Quran and 'learn to keep them in your mind'. Children are also taught different prayers, are told to 'be courteous, helpful, give salaam', and ultimately learn 'a way of living'. Instructors are very strict, most agree. But many children nonetheless have some fun attending madrassah since they know everyone, and they manage to get away with much horseplay because the groups are very large and therefore somewhat unmanageable by one or two often elderly instructors.

The young women see great disparity in the religious teaching provided to girls and boys. Girls are only taught a basic set of recitations, and are taken out of instruction around the age of twelve. Boys, on the other hand, learn a larger set of recitations, receive more teaching on expected forms of behaviour and religious observance, and stay on into their teens.

Although most appreciate the importance of Islamic religious instruction (informants all affirmed they would send their own future children to madrassah), certain negative images and impressions were voiced: the perspective offered in madrassah and mosque is 'very tunnel vision'; 'they only talk about the "evil" aspects of women', and do not mention the good; the people doing the teaching are themselves 'not very learned'; and there is still very much in Islam which they don't understand or would like to know more about. Perhaps typical of young people anywhere, they dislike being told to do something 'because it says so'; 'that's not good enough', one woman says with reference to the kind of teaching currently offered. In the Quran 'it's all there, it just needs interpretation, that's all. ... It's not just reciting. I think you have to explain the principle behind it.' But instead, at present children are 'like sheep herded into the mosque, told to recite this. They come out learning how to read really well, and to recite the Quran, but they're not understanding what's behind this, why are they doing this.' This kind of dissatisfaction with regard to ideal and real in religious instruction is also reflected in more general opinions concerning the present practice and future plight of Islam and Muslims.

On Islam and being Muslim

Elders, it is suggested, look on the young Muslims of Keighley and 'tend to think we're getting a bit slack.' But one seventeen-year-old male expresses a widely held view among youth:

> You're not going to tell an eighteen-year old, like 'do this, do that' - he's not going to do it. It's up to him at the end of the day. They sort of like drift out of it when they're eighteen, nineteen. When they're into their thirties, they're back into it. [Until then, they] tend to mess around, take life like a joke.

His friend, aged nineteen, agrees that people in their teens and twenties do little with regard to Islam, but later - particularly with the advent of a family - they come back to it. He reasons,

When you're married, and you got kids and responsibilities, you think twice. You think, 'my parents told me this about this' - it's my duty as a parent to teach my children the same way. The older you get, you tend to, you know, change a bit. With yourself, you start going to mosque, to teach your kid.

Young women also attested that there was a kind of accepted, prevailing attitude among many youths to the effect that 'I'll be a proper Muslim when I'm old.' Teenagers, they say, 'don't want to know'. This lack of interest and practice among many youths (and, for that matter, among many throughout the Muslim community), however, has little bearing on the maintenance of a strong Muslim identity.

All are proud to be Muslims, of that there is no doubt. However, some are critical of current aspects of identity: one teenage woman says 'we think we're Muslim, but we're not proper Muslims.' Another adds, 'some people born in a Muslim family [are] proud to be Muslim, but don't know anything about Islam. ... Proper Muslim is something different: you've got to obey all those rules, right, and then you're Muslim.' Yet another gives an opinion generally about her young peers in Keighley (reflecting a sense of sincere identity and doubtless interest in Islam, but also, a conflict with their parent's generation), saying that 'we are Muslims, but we need freedom.'

With regard to the future of Islam in Keighley and in Britain generally, informants were confident of its sustained presence. 'Islam is always strong' stated a sixteen-year-old woman. 'It's going to go on,' a seventeen-year-old male says, 'and it's not going to get affected. There may be less people at the mosque, but it's not going to get affected.' A youth worker foresees Islam's perpetuation in Britain because it is 'ingrained into a child from such an early age'. 'Things should all get better for Muslims in the future,' another woman says, 'but people shouldn't be forced into it.' Regarding elders' fears of the threat to Islam posed by Westernization among youth, a teenage male insists that 'if they really want to be Westernized and Muslim, they can do it.'

Conclusion

Local context, and not just the fact of living in Britain, has much to do with the development of young Muslims' cultural identities. Incidents of racism (anti-Muslim as well as anti-'immigrant'), employment and education opportunities, leisure activities, and other key areas of young Muslims' lives are determined by aspects of local context, and any attempt to understand their needs and desires must take into account this fact. Similarly, facets of 'community' - including kinship patterns, the nature and history of Muslim associations, and leadership contests - also strongly affect ways in which young Muslims see themselves and react to their parents and others of their parents generation. This too is a largely local phenomenon all too often overlooked in attempts to understand young Muslims throughout Britain.

Many young Muslims in Britain are currently adopting a strong 'Muslim' identity, although as we have seen, this often does not necessarily entail an enhanced knowledge of Islam nor an increased participation in religious activity. Adoption of this kind of 'cultural Muslim' identity often is as much, or more, undertaken as a kind of resistance: there is doubtless at present growing anti-Muslim sentiment in many quarters of Britain, particularly expressed in local spheres: many youths consequently take up a publicly expressed 'Muslim' identity purposefully 'to fly in the face' of such a growing kind of racism. Other young Muslims, of course, do indeed maintain a more religiously oriented identity. What kind of Islamic communities and Muslim identities develop among this generation in the future will be conditioned strongly by what happens to attitudes among non-Muslims in local contexts throughout Britain.

Acknowledgements

Ethnographic research was carried out under the auspices of a grant (No. F697) from the Leverhulme Trust. The article was written while the author was a Visiting Fellow at the Institute of Ethnology, Free University Berlin, under the auspices of the Alexander von Humboldt Foundation.

References

Afshar, H. (1989) 'Gender roles and the "moral economy of kin" among Pakistani women in West Yorkshire' *New Community* 15: 211-225.
Bradford Metropolitan Council, City of (1988) *The Future - A Report from Keighley.*
Butterworth, E. (1967) *Immigrants in West Yorkshire: Social Conditions and the Lives of Pakistanis, Indians and West Indians,* London: Institute of Race Relations.

7 Continuity and Change: Young Turks in London

Talip Kucukcan

This chapter analyses the continuity and change among the young Turkish generation's attitudes towards cultural and traditional values in London. My usage of the term, 'young generation', includes not only children who were born in the country of immigration but also those who were born in the country of origin but joined their parents, or migrated with them, at an early age and participated in social and educational life in the receiving country.

Young generation and socialisation

Young generations of immigrant origin are exposed to a different socialisation than that of their parents in the new setting. Their socialisation is characterised by different social and cultural values. In the case of the Turkish immigrant community in London, the first generation was socialised in Turkey or Cyprus where they grew up in a social and cultural environment surrounded by family, tradition and religion from an early age. The content of Turkish-Muslim identity is transmitted by the readily-found structural forces and agencies in the society which passed on its values to the children and therefore, helped in the construction of their identity.

Turkish parents who were born and raised in the country of origin did not experience most of what their children experienced in the country of immigration, where different social and cultural forces determine the contents and boundaries of identity. Among the structural forces and agencies in the country of origin, are included linguistic unity within the society, the traditional family structure and educational institutions that aim to create a national Turkish identity. Religious influences of the mosques, mystical orders and Qur'an courses teaching the traditional Islamic way of life may also be added to this list. In contrast to their parents, the young generation in the Turkish diaspora lack the influence of many of these institutions during the process of their socialisation while developing a sense of identity and belonging. Although some of the above factors exert their influence on the young, they are not only less persistent but also less firmly rooted compared with Turkey and Cyprus. It should also be pointed out here that the influence of traditional Turkish and Islamic agents are countered and contested by the establishments of the host society.

The young Turkish generation therefore experiences continuity and change in the face of their upbringing in British society. The changes they experience are largely rooted in their socialisation and exposure to contextual factors. This means that the identity development 'is not simply an intrapsychic process, but also an interpersonal process, embedded in a social context'[1] (Phinney 1993a: 47). The sociocultural context is recognised 'as a determining factor in the process of ego-identity formation' (Watermann 1992: 54). Markston-Adam's (1992: 174) findings also lend support to my argument that 'social-contextual factors' are influential in identity formation of the young generation.

In the following sections I focus on the development of ethnic identity among the young Turkish generation. The process of continuity and change will be analysed in the formation of their identity. Since identity construction is a dynamic process, the young Turkish generation is constantly renegotiating and redefining their identity.

A number of studies have already been published on the Turkish young generation, focusing on several aspects of their life such as identity conflict, cultural clash, changes in their socialisation, educational problems, generational differences and transmission of traditional values and attitudes.[2] With one exception,[3] they are not based on Britain. Whereas there is a lack of literature on young Turks in Britain, there is an increasing number of publications on the young generation of other ethnic minorities in Britain. Such literature helps us to understand the experiences of young Turks from a comparative perspective. Studies by Anwar (1976, 1994), Ballard (1979), and Weinreich (1986) among others[4] are good examples of such efforts, providing an overview of other ethnic youth in Britain.

Characteristics of the sample

The following findings are based on a survey, in-depth interviews and participant observation that took place in London and Berlin. The survey however, was only carried out at supplementary schools for Turkish students in London. Some of these students - 21 males, 15 females - were interviewed at length. The questionnaires were distributed among almost an equal number of both sexes to assess gender differences in relation to several variables (religion, culture, sexuality and birth control etc.). When the completed questionnaires were analysed, I discovered that there were 42 males and 51 females in the sample.

Since most of the earlier studies of identity formation focused on young people aged between 13 and 18 years old (Patterson et al. 1992: 15), I looked for a similar sample. The reason for choosing such an age cohort is the contention that adolescence, and the years following are the formative period of identity acquisition (Phinney 1993b: 75). Therefore, I chose supplementary schools for the survey. However, depth-interviews included young people outside the school. A targeted sample of young Turks was achieved (Table 1). Of the male respondents, 57 per cent come from the 12 to 15 age cohort whereas 43 per cent come from the 16 to 18 age cohort. As for the female sample, the 12 to 15 age cohort includes 71 per cent and the 16 to 18 age cohort includes 29 per cent of the female sample.

Table 1: Age distribution of respondents

	Male	%	Female	%
12-15	24	57	36	71
16-18	18	43	15	29
Total	42	100	51	100

There is an increasing tendency among researchers to use concepts such as British-Pakistanis, British-Caribbeans, British-Muslims, French-Muslims and Dutch-Muslims. This suggests that the country of settlement creates an hyphenated identity structure. As Table 2 shows, the majority of the respondents (68%) were born and brought up in London. Therefore, it may be suggested that young Turks in Britain will also develop hyphenated identity.

Among the male respondents, 41 per cent stated that they were born in Turkey and had moved to London with their parents or joined them at a later stage. Fourteen per cent were born in Cyprus and 45 per cent in London. The birthplaces of the female respondents was different. The overwhelming majority of the female respondents (86%) were born in London. Only six per cent said that their birthplace was Turkey and eight per cent said that they were born in Cyprus. The major part of the respondents' upbringing and socialisation is taking place in British society. It is plausible to argue that the children of ethnic communities have to deal with multiple identities within a multicultural society where they are likely to adopt several aspects of different value systems. The young generation is influenced by the social forces and civic culture of the birthplace to which they develop an allegiance and sense of belonging. It is likely that the terms such as British-Turks, German-Turks, Dutch-Turks, French-Turks, will soon appear in sociological literature.

Table 2: Birthplace of respondents

	Male	%	Female	%
Turkey	17	41	3	6
Cyprus	6	14	4	8
London	19	45	44	86
Total	42	100	51	100

It could be argued that the symbolic meaning and influence of the birthplace are increased by the length of stay. A prolonged period in a multicultural society means a longer process of socialisation and acculturation of the immigrants' children in terms of educational processes, peer group relations and media influences. A greater proportion of the females compared with the males had grown up in London (Table 3). Forty-five per cent of male and 86 per cent of female respondents had lived in London since their birth.

This research included people with origins in both mainland Turkey and Turkish Cyprus. Therefore it was expected that the respondents had different parental origins.

It appears that more than half of the male respondents (55%) came to London at a later stage. Of these, 36 per cent who came with their families or joined them later had been living in London for 6 to 10 years. A smaller number of the male sample (19%) had lived here for 1 to 5 years. Only fourteen per cent of females had not lived in London since being born.

Table 3: Length of living in London

	Male	%	Female	%
Since birth	19	45	44	86
1-5 years	8	19	4	8
6-10 years	15	36	3	6
Total	42	100	51	100

Table 4: Parental origins of the respondents

	Mother	%	Father	%
Turkey	28	30	32	34
Cyprus	53	56	51	54
Other	4	5	2	3
No reply	8	9	8	9
Total	93	100	93	100

The majority of the sample's parents came from Turkey and Cyprus (Table 4). Among both mothers and fathers, the majority (56% and 54% respectively) came from Cyprus. Around a third migrated from Turkey. Among the parents of non-Turkish/Cypriot origin, there were one American and three English mothers, and one British-Italian father. The marriage pattern among Turkish community is largely confined to the country of origin. Although there are some marriages between Turks from mainland Turkey and Turks from Cyprus, it seems that the marriages of the first generation primarily took place in their own countries. Because the majority of the mothers (88%) and fathers (90%) came from Cyprus or Turkey, the parents are constitute the first generation, while the respondents themselves comprise the first young generation of the Turkish community in Britain.

Young generation and family

The family is the first context of a child's socialisation. This section analyses the attitudes of the young generation towards living with family, parental control and generational differences. All the respondents were living with their parents at the time of my research. Being young people aged between 12 and 18 they were not expected to leave home at an early age. Nevertheless, as Table 5 shows, some of the respondents expressed their wish to live on their own rather than with their parents.

Table 5: Attitudes towards living with parents

	Male	%	Female	%
Want to live with parents	22	52	32	63
Want to live on their own	11	26	19	37
No reply	9	22	-	-
Total	41	100	52	100

A majority (52% of the male and 63% of the female respondents) said that they would like to live with their family, whereas only 26 per cent of the males and 37 per cent of the females said that they wanted to live on their own. For the combined sample this represented 58 per cent of the sample wanted to continue living with their parents as opposed to 32 per cent who did not.

When asked to explain why they wanted to live with their parents, a variety of replies were given. 'Love' and 'attachment' towards parents, 'being loved' by them, the 'need to be protected', 'lack of confidence' in living on their own at this very young age, were frequently mentioned as reasons for living with parents. One female (aged 14) said, 'I love my parents and at the moment I do not have any problem with them. I know they love me as well. We have really a good relationship and I do not see any reason to leave them even if I become older.' Another respondent (a male aged 17) said:

> We have strong family relationships nurtured by respect and sacrifice for the family. My parents are both working and they are doing it for us, to provide us with good education and good future. And I am aware of this. Time to time trivial problems occur as to when and where to go, but I do not think that I would like to live on my own for such simple matters.

The 'need for protection' is another reason for living with parents as one respondent (female aged 16) said, 'I am only sixteen and I would like to continue my education. I need my family to support me in that without which I would not be able to finish my education. This is also their wish and expectation.' A similar pragmatic reason was voiced by another female respondent (aged 17) who said, 'I cannot live on my own yet. I need my family and their protection until I establish myself.'

Those who expressed their wish to live on their own instead of with their families mostly gave reasons such as 'lack of independence', 'to have more freedom' and 'proving their self'. One 17-year-old male, for example, mentioned 'responsibility', saying that 'I want to be responsible for my life and I want to prove to my parents that I can manage looking after myself.' Similar replies came from others of both sexes. This suggests that some young people are trying to show that they have attained maturity which would justify their claim for more freedom and responsibility. But the more common reason to live on their own appeared to be the 'constraints' exercised by the parents on the behaviour of young people. An 18-year-old girl summed up her feelings in a paradoxical expression. She said:

> To be honest, I do not have big problems with my family except that they are overprotective which sometimes becomes unbearable and limits my social activities. I would like to have more freedom. I want them to trust me. On the other hand, I understand that they want to protect me and I respect it, but when it becomes too constraining I wish that I was living on my own.

Another female respondent (aged 16) who thought that she was more confined to domestic activities compared with her brother and wanted to have equal freedom said: 'my parents allow my brother to go out and he wears whatever he likes. When it comes to me, they always interfere. If I lived on my own I could do what I wanted and when I wanted.' As this reply shows, some of the girls do not want to be accountable for whatever they do and wish to receive equal treatment with boys. These findings suggest that the girls in Turkish families are more strictly controlled than the boys. It appears that the reputation of the girls is more central than that of the boys. If a boy is seen with a girl this is usually regarded as a matter of temporary enjoyment for the boys and most of the families, except those religious families who believe that chastity must be equally observed by both sexes, tolerate such forms of behaviour as the community does not condemn these acts. However, when it comes to girls, the preservation of chastity suddenly becomes a centrally important issue and therefore girls' behaviour is more closely watched over since any act of wrong doing, such as going out with unrelated boys, would bring shame and damage the reputation of the family.[5]

Parental control is further documented by the findings in Table 6 which show that 33 per cent of the male and 73 per cent of the female respondents felt that their parents exercised 'too much' control over them.

Table 6: Parental control as perceived by the respondents

	Male	%	Female	%
Too much	14	33	37	73
Not too much	19	45	14	27
No reply	9	22	-	-
Total	42	100	51	100

Overall, more than half of the respondents (55%) found parental control 'too much' whereas 35 per cent of the respondents felt that their parents did not have too much control over their behaviour. The figures confirm my earlier observation that parents place stricter control on the girls.

The children of minority ethnic communities within a multicultural society face different sets of cultural values. The young generation may sometimes adopt the culture of the larger society which might conflict with the parental culture. The existence of multiple identities may lead to disagreements between parents and the young generation. As presented in Table 7, differences emerged between Turkish parents and the young. This suggests that the Turkish young generation are developing different attitudes against the wishes of their parents, giving rise to tensions and disagreements.

The great majority of the respondents have some kind of disagreements with their parents. Eighty one per cent of the total sample were experiencing disagreements whereas only 11 per cent of them seemed to give in to parental demands. The majority of the male (69%) and female (90%) respondents said that they had disagreements. Only 12 per cent of the males and 10 per cent of the females felt that they had none. When asked what kind of issues were at the centre of disagreements, respondents mentioned several points of conflict most of which may be directly related to the parental culture. Among the frequently mentioned issues were the 'type of clothing', 'make-up', 'meeting and socialising' with the opposite sex, 'spending time outside' the house, 'restriction of freedom', 'friendship with non-Muslims and non-Turks', 'schooling', 'plans for the future', and the ways in which their 'marriages' would be arranged. Generational differences and conflicts rooted in cultural and religious values of the parents appear to be a common feature of Muslim communities. Anwar (1976: 20-35), for example, explored cultural and religious attitudes of parents and children in a survey of Hindus, Sikhs and Muslims in Britain. He also found differences between the generations on several issues. In a later research carried out on the Pakistani Muslims, he reported (1985: 60) that at least three issues (wearing western clothes, arranged marriages and limitation of freedom) emerged as areas of disagreement which affected the relations between Pakistani parents and their children.

Table 7: Disagreements between respondents and parents

	Male	%	Female	%
Have disagreements	29	69	46	90
Have no disagreements	5	12	5	10
No reply	8	19	-	-
Total	42	100	51	100

When the content of the disagreements and conflicts between young Turks and their parents were analysed, two facts emerged: firstly, most of the issues of conflict are rooted in the traditional and cultural values of the parents; secondly, the young generation are distancing themselves from some of the values of parental culture by internalising social attitudes of the wider society. These observations suggest that a process of change and deeper integration in the surrounding society are becoming influential forces shaping the identity of the Turkish young generation in Britain.

Turkish families try to keep their honour intact. The reputation and chastity of a girl is very important for the honour of the family. Therefore parents watch their daughters' behaviour more closely and limit their actions if they feel it necessary for the protection of family reputation and honour. The young generation, especially girls, feel that their parents are overprotective and have too much control over them (Tables 6 and 7). Therefore they have disagreements with their parents. One of the frequently-mentioned issues of conflict for girls was parental disapproval of friendship choices. A sharp contrast emerged between parental approval/disapproval of girl/boy friendships for boys and girls, as perceived by the respondents (Table 8).

Table 8: Parental attitudes towards girl/boyfriend relationships as perceived by the respondents

	Male	%	Female	%
Approve	27	64	6	12
Do not approve	6	14	45	88
No reply	9	22	-	-
Total	42	100	51	100

When asked 'do you think that your parents would approve of your having a girl/boy friend if they knew?', 64 per cent of the male respondents said that their parents would approve of them having a girl friend. As opposed to the males, only 12 per cent of the girls thought that their parents would tolerate such a relationship.

Findings on parental attitudes towards boy/girl friendship among their children confirm the pattern I have proposed earlier that allows boys to have more freedom whereas it presupposes stricter control over the girls. These figures clearly indicate that boys were raised more freely and enjoyed a wider toleration, whereas moral codes relating to boy/girl friendships were more strictly applied to the behaviour of the girls. When asked what might be the reasons behind the disapproval of their parents, respondents generally used value-laden terminology such as: 'they are strict' (15-year-old female); 'they are typical Turks' (13-year-old female); 'they do not expect us to do such things' (14-year-old female); 'because of religion' (male aged 16); 'they are not open minded' (female aged 14); 'they are old-fashioned and do not trust boys' (female aged 18); 'they think I am too young' (15-year-old male); 'it is not right until you get married' (male aged 17); 'they do not want me to go behind their back' (female aged 17); 'they do not want me to get harmed' (female aged 15); 'they want me to concentrate on my education and career' (17-year-old male). When the same question was asked to a mature female university student she said:

> Problem of honour was the central issue for my parents when I was 15-16 years old. At times, I felt apart, dealing with conflicting family values. I was mixing up

with other young people who had different attitudes towards sexuality. With the passage of time, excessive protection of my parents subsided and since we did not have immediate family who might talk behind us, my parents came to accept my choice. But this was a difficult and painful experience.

Parents who were interviewed were more concerned with the chastity of their daughters than their sons. According to parents, girls are more vulnerable and need more protection. One mother who has two daughters and one son argued that 'girls need more control'. When asked, she said 'streets are full of danger for our children, especially for girls. Drugs, sex and prostitution are increasing. These are threatening our children. We must protect them, especially girls, because they can be easily deceived.' While conversation was taking place the father intervened and said: 'I do not want my daughters to go around with boys and sleep with them. This is totally unacceptable. And if we allow them to go out with boys and tolerate such loose behaviour, one day they will harm themselves and us both. As you know, girls are the *namus* (honour, reputation) of the family and *namus* must be protected.' This is a typical reply of most parents who, more or less, used identical words and concepts when referring to differences between boys and girls and explaining why girls should be more closely watched over.

One can observe in the statement of parents that boys are not thought to damage the *namus* and reputation of the family. In order to find the grounds for parental justification of their different approach to boys, some parents were asked why they treated boys and girls differently. But before asking this question I reminded them that religious values discourage both sexes from going out with the opposite sex, and male chastity is considered as important as female chastity. The responses of parents led me to conclude that differing attitudes towards girls have much to do with cultural practices, not necessarily rooted in Islamic beliefs. Therefore, the justification of parents cannot be based totally on religious grounds. Had it been so, they should have developed the same attitudes spontaneously towards their sons because religious principles apply equally to both sexes.

Language and culture

It is argued that language is one of the first elements of immigrant culture to disappear over the generations (Waters 1990: 116). In order to counterbalance this trend, one of the main concerns of the Turkish families has always been teaching of the mother tongue to their children as language is regarded as an indispensable part of Turkish culture. Turkish parents feel that teaching the mother tongue will enable children to learn more about Turkish society, its history and customs. More importantly, Turkish is regarded as a key to establishing effective communication between the generations. Many parents feel that not being able to communicate in Turkish is a strong sign of a loss of identity. In order to prevent this, supplementary weekend classes were organised by the Turkish organisations and a number of teachers were invited from Turkey and Cyprus. Mosques were also involved in teaching Turkish language in addition to religious subjects. To what extent these efforts have borne fruit is shown in Table 9.

Table 9: Language fluency of respondents

	No.	%
English/Turkish	67	72
English	12	13
Turkish	6	6
No reply	8	9
Total	93	100

When asked 'in which language(s) are you fluent?', 13 per cent of the respondents stated that they were fluent 'only' in English and six per cent said that they were fluent 'only' in Turkish. As shown in the above table, a great majority (72%) of the respondents claimed that they were fluent in 'both' English and Turkish. Nevertheless, these figures should be treated with some caution for several reasons. First of all, the survey was carried out in supplementary schools where children are taught Turkish. Therefore, the findings on language represent the situation of young people who were taking Turkish education. It is difficult to generalise these findings for those who have not received such an education. The second reason is directly related to the sample under question. Although 72 per cent of the respondents claimed to be fluent in Turkish, none of them asked for a questionnaire prepared in Turkish. All of the participants asked to have forms prepared in English. Therefore, it can be argued that the young generation might be fluent in spoken Turkish but they are not fluent in written Turkish. This argument is supported by the fact that children learn Turkish mostly at home through conversations within the family. Therefore their Turkish language skills are not attained through a formal education in reading and writing. Therefore, children may not be expected to be as fluent in reading and writing as they would be in spoken Turkish. The third reason for caution in looking at these figures is the fieldwork observation recorded during the research and after the interviews.

Before the start of the in-depth interviews with young informants they were asked whether they wanted to conduct the conversation in Turkish or in English. As it happened, many started conversing in Turkish, but when complex questions were asked on culture, religion and identity most of them switched to English. Then interviews continued in both languages. Questions that required straightforward replies were answered in Turkish, whereas questions such as what religion meant to them were answered in English. That led me to believe that in simple daily conversations most of the respondents were fluent in Turkish but in the exploration of ideas and expression of feelings they seemed to be more comfortable using English.

Families who are concerned about the language education of their children speak Turkish at home to encourage the younger members of the family to improve their Turkish. In order to find out the extent to which the use of Turkish and English dominates the family atmosphere, young people were asked which languages they spoke at home. As Table 10 shows, a very small number (only two per cent) of the respondents speak 'only' English at home, and 12 per cent speak 'only' Turkish.

Table 10: Languages spoken at home

	No.	%
Turkish/English	71	76
Only Turkish	11	12
Only English	2	2
No reply	9	10
Total	93	100

Table 10 also shows that both languages are spoken in most of the Turkish households. Seventy six per cent of the respondents said that bilingual usage of language was taking place within their families. Van der Lans and Rooijackers (1996: 181) reported contrasting findings over the use of languages at home among young Turks in the Netherlands. They found that among Turkish youth with 'exclusive Turkish ethnic identity', almost all preferred speaking Turkish at home, whereas 37.5 per cent of the subjects with 'dual ethnic identity' indicated that Dutch and Turkish were used equally.

As mentioned earlier, young Turks seem to be fluent in both languages in daily conversations. They are able to deal with using both languages in the family context where parents and the older generation prefer speaking Turkish. Nevertheless, drawing upon my findings, I suggest that there is an increasing concern among the Turkish community about the language fluency and communication between generations. The case of a Turkish-Cypriot family typifies this growing problem among many families. The parents in this family knew only a little English when they came to London. As the father explained, there had not been a great deal of improvement in his English since he was working in a car-repair shop owned by a Turkish person where everybody spoke Turkish. He only improved his English to the level he needed at work. His wife's case was much worse in terms of learning English, as she was mostly confined to their public housing flat. At the time of interview this informant had four children, two of whom were at the school age, of which one was on the threshold of adolescence. During a visit to their flat I noticed that English was the only language of communication within the family, but neither the father nor the mother was articulate in using English. Similarly, the children were not able to converse in Turkish. When asked how they communicated and resolved problems, the informant said:

> Well, this is our main problem. My English in not enough to explain my opinions on matters such as their education, our culture, religion and traditions. Neither can they understand Turkish properly. There is certainly a lack of communication which is growing. And that worries me quite a lot.

Some families send their children to Turkish classes at supplementary schools to overcome this problem. The number of young people at supplementary classes is steadily increasing. According to a recent estimate by the Turkish Educational Attaché in London, there are more than 2,500 students them. The first young generation seem to have gained knowledge of Turkish. At least they have fluency in daily conversations. But it remains a question whether subsequent generations will acquire adequate language skills in Turkish.

The young generation were bilingual and they used both languages in conversing within their families. However, when they were asked which language they would 'prefer' in their daily conversations with their family and Turkish friends, a different pattern of attitudes towards the use of Turkish emerged, which suggests that the young generation feel more comfortable and fluent in using English. As presented in Table 11, 27 per cent of the respondents said that they would prefer speaking Turkish whereas 63 per cent of them said that they prefer using English as a medium of communication in their conversations.

Table 11: Preference of language during daily conversations with family and Turkish friends

	No.	%
English	59	63
turkish	25	27
No reply	9	10
Total	93	100

When asked why they would prefer a particular language with family members and Turkish friends, similar replies were given which revolved around the issues of 'speaking and understanding better', 'feeling more comfortable', 'being more fluent', 'expressing oneself better', 'natural and spontaneous reaction', and 'one's own language'. A fifteen-year-old female informant said, 'well I know English better than Turkish. If it is convenient I prefer speaking in English.' A typical reply came from a 17-year-old male who said 'I can speak English better and it comes naturally. When it comes to Turkish, I can speak it too, but not as natural as my English'. Another seventeen-year-old also made a remark that can be generalised for other young people. She said: 'although I can speak both languages fluently, I can express myself better in English. I think our education, television, films and books all contribute to that. When I want to say something, English comes naturally and I feel more comfortable when I use it instead of Turkish.'

As shown in Table 11, 27 per cent of the respondents stated their preference for Turkish. One respondent (male aged 16) gave the following reason for his preference: 'well this is our language and I want to improve it by practising.' Another one (male aged 17) said: 'we are Turkish and we must learn it. Look at Greeks and Pakistanis for example. They all know their language. Why then should not we learn and use it in our daily conversations.' The high rate (63%) of preference to use English by the Turkish young generation suggests that, the mother tongue is gradually loosing its value as a medium of communication.

It is a widely observed phenomenon that immigrants and their children face acculturation and assimilation as a consequence of living in a different society where they are exposed to cultural influences. The Turkish community in London is trying to reproduce Turkish traditions and values on the one hand, and attempting to transmit these values to the young generation on the other, who have to deal with the cultural values of the Turkish community and with the influence of British society. The identification of the young generation with Turkish traditions and values can be seen as one of the indices of cultural assimilation. To find out the young generation's attitude towards their own cultural values, the following question was asked: 'do you think that Turkish traditions and values should be preserved while living in Britain?'. As Table 12 shows, a significant number (76%) of the respondents said that Turkish traditions and values should be preserved.

Table 12: Attitudes towards the preservation of Turkish traditions and values while living in England

	No.	%
Should be preserved	71	76
Should not be preserved	10	11
No reply	12	13
Total	93	100

The question did not specify what Turkish 'traditions' and 'values' were. This allowed the young people to express their views on what these things meant for them. The terms 'tradition' and 'culture' were understood to include 'religion', 'Islam', 'language', 'chastity', 'family', 'religious and national festivals', 'respect', 'identity', 'marriage' and 'origin/roots'. These words were most frequently mentioned by the respondents when they wanted to explain what they understood by Turkish traditions and values, and why they thought that they should be preserved. One male (aged 18) referred directly to Islam when this question was asked to him and said 'Islam is our religion, a way of life and a source of identity which is deteriorating. We should keep our identity.' For some young Turks there was a direct correlation between tradition, religion and identity as a 17-year-old male explained: 'you cannot be a proper Turk without being a Muslim. Look at the Jewish people in this country. They stick to their religion which keeps their identity strong. Therefore we also have to respect our religion and preserve religious values, celebrate religious festivals.'

Traditions as 'origin/roots' were mentioned by a number of respondents who thought that traditions were the origins of their identity. One female (aged 15) explained: 'it is important to know your tradition and your culture. No matter where we live these are our origins/roots. And we have to respect and preserve these origins/roots wherever we are. It should not make any difference in what country you are living.' A seventeen-year-old female went on saying, 'I have got to know whole my family, where they come from, what they believe in. If I don't learn my cultural background I will lose my identity. Therefore we should never forget our culture and values.' These findings suggest that, parents and other family members appear to have managed to persuade their children of the importance and significance of traditional Turkish culture and values. Nauck's findings on the children of Turkish immigrants in Germany confirm this observation. His study on the intergenerational transmission of cultural values found that:

> [I]n spite of all intergenerational differences in attitudes and behaviour, the results reveal that intergenerative transmission is an essential and integral part of the socialisation of the 'second generation'. Despite all the differences between the generations in their assimilation behaviour and their behaviour to the receiving society, the dense interaction structure of the migrant families obviously results at the same time in a high level of co-ordination between generations in their basic value orientations and action preferences
>
> (Nauck 1994: 134; 1995: 82-83).[6]

Family life provides or imposes a social and cultural atmosphere for identity development. As Waters (1990: 19) puts it, the 'ethnic identification involves *both* choice and constraint. Children learn both the basic facts of their family history and the cultural content and practices associated with their ethnicity in their household.' A thirty-year-old single female interviewee who was brought to London when she was eight years old summed up the attitudes of the young generation when I asked her how she felt about Turkish traditions and values:

> I think that traditions and values are parts of my identity. They are significant for me, not only because I was born in Turkey but also I still live with my parents

who stick to these values and more importantly such traditions and values are the only part of Turkey we can have even on a symbolic level. I understand that there is a difference between Turkish and British identity, but I do not think that having one of them necessarily negates and rejects the other one. In my case for example, though I am fairly integrated into British society and absorbed being British, it is still important for me to have a Turkish identity.

However, as seen in Table 12, 13 per cent of the respondents differed from the majority and said that they would not totally support the preservation of traditions and values. The differences in attitudes surface more in relation to some cultural concerns that are regarded as constraining the choices of the young generation. Arranged marriage was the most often mentioned traditional practice that girls especially would like to see abandoned. One 17-year-old female expressed her partial disapproval of traditions as: 'I am Turkish and respect the traditions but I feel that traditions should not be so strict and our opinions should also be valued. Arranged marriage is one of the traditions that I do not want it to be imposed on me. I do not refuse all the traditions but some of them should accommodate changes at least.' Anwar's (1994: 27) findings on young Muslims' attitudes towards arranged marriages are similar. He points out that 47 per cent of his respondents disagreed with the custom of arranged marriage and 53 per cent thought that children's marriages should be arranged by themselves. Another female respondent (aged 16) expressed her disappointment with the unequal treatment of boys and girls. She saw the roots of overprotection of girls in the tradition and wished that girls would be recognised for being as responsible as the male members of the family and the community. She referred to the concept of chastity and honour of the family and said:

> When we (girls) want to meet our friends and spend time with them our mothers suddenly become our guardians and always limit the time and they control whom we are meeting. They do not tell us but we feel that they are checking on us. As you know, when a Turkish girl is seen with a male friend, let alone a boyfriend, everybody starts circulating a rumour about the girl. If a boy does the same thing, nobody takes notice of his behaviour. If that is the tradition you are asking about, it should be changed and not preserved at all.

Restrictive parental practices towards the girls is not only peculiar to the Turkish Muslim community in Britain. Ballard (1979: 117) and Joly (1995: 167) observed a similar phenomenon among South Asians and the Pakistani Muslim community. They note that some Pakistani Muslims are more lenient to boys than girls. Boys are allowed to go to cafés and discos and socialise with girls. Pakistani girls, however, are not allowed to follow the same pattern of behaviour and are more closely controlled. Similar findings on young people of Turkish and Pakistani origin suggest that both communities have corresponding cultural values. These similar cultural values seem to centre around chastity and the reputation of the girls and family honour.

Although the majority of the respondents were born and brought up in London, about a third were born in either Turkey or Cyprus, and joined or came with their families at an early age. The young people in the sample spent their childhood in Britain and were educated here. Therefore, it may be expected that the young generation might have developed a sense of attachment to the country where they were born and brought up. Families, on the other hand, constantly remind their children about where they come from and take them to Turkey and Cyprus. Young people are developing multiple allegiances and attachment to Turkey/Cyprus and England.

Table 13: Attitudes towards parent's country of origin and Britain. Where respondents feel happier?

	No.	%
Cyprus/Turkey	28	30
England	26	28
No difference	39	42
Total	92	100

When asked 'where do you feel happier, in England or in Turkey/Cyprus?', 30 per cent of the respondents replied that they feel happier in Turkey/Cyprus when they visit the country (Table 13). A sixteen-year-old male explained his source of happiness as 'there, it is easy to communicate with people. I can make friends easily than here. I feel that I am a part of the community in Turkey whereas here I am only an ordinary individual.' Another respondent (female aged 17) said that she felt happier when she went to Cyprus. When asked why, she said: 'because of the safe environment. I feel more safe and less protected in Cyprus where I am allowed to go out more freely. I cannot feel that much safe here and therefore my parents are more strict.' As this reply suggests, the young generation are given more freedom because of the nature of the society in the country of origin where exposure to threat is thought to be much less. Another reason for feeling happy in Turkey/Cyprus was expressed by a 17-year-old female who said: 'I like being with my own people who understand my background. In Cyprus, there is no racism and you are treated equally.' It seems that the experience of racism, discrimination and the lack of respect given to one's own culture alienate some young people from the society they live in and encourage them to develop a positive attitude to the country of origin.

In contrast to those who felt more comfortable in Turkey/Cyprus, 28 per cent of the respondents said that they were more at home in England. When asked why she felt more at home in England rather than Cyprus, a 15-year-old girl who visits Cyprus every year with her parents, said that England was her birthplace. She had spent all her life in England where she had made friends and received her education. Although she enjoyed visiting Cyprus for a short time, she did not feel as a strong an attachment to the country and its people as her parents did. She said: 'I see Cyprus as a holiday spot. I like being there for sometime and see my relatives. But I cannot imagine living there for a lifetime as I am used to a different kind of life in England. My parents' village is a very small one compared to London and not everything is available there.' A seventeen-year-old respondent expressed similar reasons for his preference for living in England rather than in Turkey. He said:

> Well, it is fun to go to Turkey and have a holiday. But when I stay there for a month or so I start missing our home in London and my friends here. Since I go to Turkey once a year and stay in a small village where my parents came from, I get really bored and want to come back soon. Moreover, I feel less restricted here. When I am in Turkey everybody tells me what to do, but here in London only my parents remind me of things to be done or refrained.

In addition to those who feel more at home in Turkey/Cyprus or England, there is a significant number of Turkish young people who seem to have developed a neutral attitude towards the country of their parents and their own birthplace: 42 per cent of the respondents said that living either in England or in Turkey/Cyprus would not make much difference. The explanation of a young girl, aged 18, clearly describes the development of a balanced attitude towards both countries:

> I think that I learned to be capable of living in both countries and both cultures. First of all, I was born in London and raised here. I feel that I am a member of this society. But, there is also another side of the coin. I remember that, since my

childhood Turkey was a central place of visit and was dominating the conversations at home. We were always told that our roots were in Turkey and I felt that may parents were right. As many of my friends, I came to the conclusion that we did not have to get rid of what our parents presented to us as national and cultural heritage. I can say now that, although I am not an active member of the society in Turkey, I still feel that I am member of the same culture.

Turkish parents exercise pressure on their children to develop commitment to their own country, society and its values. Twenty-eight per cent of the respondents do not seem to have been influenced by these pressures while 30 per cent seem to have developed the desired attitude towards their parent's country. The majority of the respondents, on the other hand (42%) seem to have developed a different strategy which accommodates both countries and both societies. In earlier research, Liebkind (1989: 186) also found a similar pattern among Turkish youth in Sweden regarding the country of origin. According to her findings, 28 per cent of Turkish respondents felt more at home in Sweden, 26 per cent felt more at home in the country of origin and 39 per cent felt equally at home both in Sweden and in Turkey.

Sexuality

Traditional family values are reproduced within the Turkish community. Parents try to control their children, and girls are particularly discouraged from going out with unrelated males as this is thought to damage the family's honour. This section will analyse the attitudes of the young generation towards relations with the opposite sex, sexuality and sexual behaviour. The analysis of the young people's attitudes towards these issues will enable us to understand continuity and change in their perception of Turkish culture and traditions. As Table 14 shows, despite parental insistence and cultural discouragement, young people are developing a more accommodating attitude towards social meetings with the opposite sex.

When asked 'do you approve of pre-marital male-female social meetings?', 13 per cent replied that they would not approve of such relations. It seems that cultural values, family pressure and religious beliefs have influenced this group. One male (aged 17) said: 'it is against our religion and as I can see from my friends, such relations lead to too many problems. I do not go out with other girls. And I do not want my sister to go out with boys.' A female, aged 17, on the other hand, mentioned social pressure rooted in the culture of the Turkish community. She said: 'I do not go out with boys because my family is strongly against it. If a boy goes out with girls and does whatever he likes, nobody talks about him. But when a girl goes out and is seen in the street, even with a classmate, everybody talks behind her and her family. I do not want to hurt my family with the gossip around. Therefore, I refrain from socialising with boys and go out with girls, and even this is limited.'

Table 14: Attitudes towards pre-marital male-female social meetings

	No.	%
Approve	50	54
Do not approve	12	13
Have no idea	31	33
Total	93	100

It seems that the circulation of gossip about the behaviour of girls has wide implications, and functions as a social control on the female generation. Research by de Vries (1995: 39) on Turkish girls in the Netherlands supports my argument that gossip becomes an effective means of social control. Young Turkish girls are in a situation similar to that of their counterparts in England. After interviewing twenty five Turkish girls, aged between 16 to 25, de Vries analysed the implications of gossip. She explains that 'most girls live surrounded, to a varying degree by compatriots who see it as their task to keep watch over the girls' behaviour: they must be chaste and remain Turkish', and if they become a subject of gossip, 'this will be directed, not only against her, but also against her parents' (*ibid.*: 39). As mentioned earlier, involvement of some members of the community in the circulation of gossip and the resulting damage to the parent's reputation produce social pressure which forces the girls to behave along the lines laid down by cultural attitudes towards male-female socialising.

A third of the respondents said that 'they have no idea' about male-female outings whereas more than half (54%) of the youngsters said that 'they approve pre-marital male-female social meetings'. The responses of the young generation indicate that a change is taking place in the attitudes of London-born and bred children in contrast to family pressure to conform to parental values. One female (aged 17), for example, challenged her parents' views on male-female outings and said: 'we are living in a different society.

It might have been really wrong in their own village, but here is not their village. What is wrong with seeing your male friends? My parents say it is wrong. Why? Because that is the culture. I do not believe that this is the culture. If it was the culture it should have been the same for the boys as well.' Another female (aged 18) also argued that parents must change their minds on certain issues such as male-female relations. She said: 'what harm you can get by seeing your friends? I always want to remain honest to my parents, but if they try to control everything, then I am forced to do things in secret. I think our parents should be more open minded and have more toleration as they have for my brothers.' This was also mentioned by several other female respondents. Some of them implied that their parents were using 'double-standards' in the treatment of boys and girls. Many females explicitly accused their parents of not being fair to them and of being too restrictive on their social life. As shown in Table 14, young people are developing a more approving view towards male-female social meetings which are not accepted by their community. Table 8, on the other hand, shows that parents do not approve of girls' relations with boys, whereas boys are tolerated if they have a girl-friend. The findings in Table 15 not only confirm this, but also indicate that young Turkish girls are trying to conform to the attitudes of their parents.

When asked, 'do you have a boy/girl friend?', an expected pattern of reply emerged. There is a significant difference between the genders in relation to boy/girl friendships. Sixty nine per cent of the male respondents said that they had a girlfriend whereas only 27 per cent of the females admitted having a boyfriend. In contrast to boys, 73 per cent of the girls replied that they 'have no boyfriend', whereas 31 per cent of the boys said that they 'have no girlfriend'. These findings support my earlier argument that parents are more lenient towards their sons and the community has less social control over the behaviour of its male members.

Table 15: Having a girl/boy friend

	Male	%	Female	%
Has a girl/boy friend	29	69	14	27
Does not have a girl/boy friend	13	31	37	73
Total	42	100	51	100

The attitudes towards pre-marital sexual relations also indicate that there is continuity and change among the young generation. Pre-marital sexual relationships are strongly rejected by the traditional Turkish culture and religious values. Some of the young people are still conforming to cultural and religious values and some of them are developing new attitudes which are in conflict with parental culture.

Table 16: Attitudes towards pre-marital sexual relationship

	Male	%	Female	%
Approve	23	55	17	33
Do not approve	12	28	27	53
No reply	7	17	6	14
Total	42	100	51	100

When asked whether they approved of 'pre-marital sexual relationships?', 14 per cent of the respondents did not reply to the question on the grounds that this was a personal matter. When the replies were analysed, a contrasting pattern of attitudes emerged between the males and the females. Fifty five per cent of the male respondents said that they would approve of pre-marital sexual relations whereas 33 per cent of the female respondents expressed the same attitude. In contrast to males, 53 per cent of the females said that 'they would not approve of pre-marital sexual relations'. The contrast between males and females can be attributed to the values of the Turkish community and to the attitudes of parents and the community who set different social roles for boys and girls.

It may be argued that a high approval rate of culturally and religiously prohibited practice indicates a meaningful change in the attitudes of the young generation towards sexuality. Forty three per cent of the total sample expressed their approval of pre-marital sexual relations. Since respondents were reluctant to talk about the subject, I can only make suggestions, based on my observations, as to why a high number of the respondents approved of such relations despite the strict Islamic prohibition. It may be argued that the first generation was not very successful in transmitting religious values to their children. It may also be suggested that the young people are adopting some of the values of the larger society where such relations are regarded as natural and practised by their peers. Nevertheless, while cultural changes are taking place which influence the identity development of the young generation, as much as 43 per cent of the respondents seem to display a continuity in their attitudes and behaviour. The tension between chance and continuity will remain as long as the young generation is exposed to conflicting value systems and multiple group belonging. However, whether one of - or which of - these forces will overcome the other remains as an open question

In addition to sexual relations, young people were also asked for their views on birth control. They were asked if they approved of birth control. Eleven per cent of the respondents gave negative answers (Table 17), and said that they would not 'normally' approve of birth control. About a quarter said that they would approve of birth control 'under some circumstances'.

More than half (54%), on the other hand, said that they would approve of birth control. During the interviews, only a few respondents were willing to talk about the reasons behind their approval or disapproval. Those who approved of birth control gave almost same reasons emphasising 'choice' and 'control' over their own lives. One seventeen-year-old female who volunteered to talk about this said: 'I think that this a personal issue which must be decided by the individual concerned. I do not think that we can look after too many children. Personally, I approve of birth control which means I decide and control my own life.' The reply was a typical one which suggests that young people would like to be less influenced by external agents when they are making their own decisions.

Table 17: Attitudes towards birth control

	No.	%
Normally yes	50	54
Normally no	10	11
Under some circumstances	25	27
No reply	8	8
Total	93	100

Conclusion

The above analysis shows that change and continuity are the underlying experiences of the Turkish young generation in London. Although they still respect parental values and Turkish traditions, there is a tendency among the young generation to change constraining customs. This means that they are developing a new identity in constant negotiation with parental values. The negotiation and redefinition of identity as a dynamic process is influenced by the socialisation of Turkish youth in a different cultural context. It seems that the Turkish youth are adopting some of the socio-cultural values of the larger society. They are, for example, demanding more freedom and responsibility. Girls, in particular, are complaining about parental control over their social behaviour. Turkish youth are also developing different attitudes towards sexuality in conflict with the values of their community. Generational differences are the natural outcomes of these sociocultural changes and negotiations which sometimes give rise to tension between parents and the younger generation. Language, culture, sexuality, control and freedom on the one hand and the multiple identity allegiance on the other, seem to be the sources of tension and conflict.

Although there is no wholesale rejection of traditional values, it appears that the young generation are developing different attitudes towards parental values. The analysis of the data shows that although most of the Turkish young people agree with the preservation of parental culture, they seem to attribute different meanings to some of the elements of traditional values. There is a tendency among young Turks to see marriage, social relations and sexuality in a somewhat different way than their parents. They have a desire, on the one hand, to preserve parental values at home, and on the other, to adopt some elements of the host culture outside. This means that there is an emergent identity construction taking place among the young generation. This emergent identity is not exclusively shaped by 'Turkey/Cypriot inspired perceptions', but rather is increasingly based on 'local/British inspired perceptions'. This argument might be taken a step further to suggest that British-Turkish identities are emerging among young Turks in London.

Notes

1. Kellner takes the view that one of the persistent and underlying properties of identity is its social character. Comparing identity in pre-modern and modern societies, he suggests that identity remained as social. In Kellner's (1992: 141) words 'in modernity, identity becomes more mobile, multiple, personal, self-reflexive, and subject to change. Yet in modernity [identity] is also social and other related.'

2. See Nauck (1988, 1995) for the changes that took place in parent-child relationships and socialisation practices in Turkish migrant families. For the educational problems of Turkish children, see Malhotra (1985) and Lindo (1995). For an analysis of identity, religion and ethnicity, see Abadan-Unat, (1985), Mandel (1989), Lange (1989), de Vries (1995) and Sunier (1995). On the employment chances of the Turkish young generation, see Faist (1995).
3. Sonyel (1988) carried out a survey on educational problems of Turkish children in schools.
4. Educational problems of Muslim children are dealt with by Parker-Jenkins (1992, 1995). Kelly's (1989) study compares ethnic identification among Pakistanis and Greek Cypriots.
5. See also Ladbury (1977: 140.)
6. For a discussion of variety in the orientations of ethnic youth, *see* Phinney, (1992); Phinney et al. (1992).

References

Abadan-Unat, N. (1985) 'Identity Crisis of Turkish Migrants, First and Second Generation', in: I. Basgoz and N. Furniss (eds.), *Turkish Workers in Europe*, Bloomington: Indiana University Press: 3-22.
Anwar, M. (1976) *Between Two Cultures*, London: Community Relations Commission.
Anwar, M. (1985) *Pakistanis in Britain: a Sociological Study*, London: New Century.
Anwar, M. (1994) *Young Muslims in Britain*, Leicester: The Islamic Foundation.
Ballard, C. (1979) 'Second-generation South Asians', in: V.S. Khan (ed.), *Minority Families in Britain, Support and Stress*, London: Macmillan: 109-130.
de Vries, M. (1995) 'The Changing Role of Gossip: Towards a New Identity, Turkish Girls in the Netherlands', in: G. Baumann and T. Sunier (eds.), *Post-Migration Ethnicity: De-essentializing Cohesion, Commitments, Comparison*, Amsterdam: Het Spinus: 36-56.
Faist, T. (1995) *Social Citizenship for Whom? Young Turks in Germany and Mexican Americans in the United States*, Aldershot: Avebury.
Joly, D. (1995) *Britannia's Crescent: Making a Place for Muslims in British Society*, Aldershot: Avebury.
Kellner, D. (1992) 'Popular Culture and the Construction of Postmodern Identities', in: S. Lash and J. Friedman (eds.), *Modernity and Identity*, Oxford: Blackwell: 141-177.
Kelly, A.J.D. (1989) 'Ethnic Identification, Association and Redefinition: Muslim Pakistanis and Greek Cypriots', in: K. Liebkind (ed.), *New Identities in Europe*, Aldershot: European Science Foundation/Gower: 77-115.

Ladbury, S. (1977) 'The Turkish Cypriots: Ethnic Relations in London and Cyprus', in: J.L. Watson (ed.), *Between Two Cultures: Migrants and Minorities in Britain*, Oxford: Blackwell: 301-331.
Liebkind, K. (1989) 'Identifications, Perceived Cultural Distance and Stereotypes in Yugoslav and Turkish Youth in Stockholm', in K. Liebkind (ed.), *New Identities in Europe*, Aldershot: European Science Foundation/Gower: 169-218.
Lindo, F. (1995) 'Ethnic Myth or Ethnic Might? On the divergence in educational attainment between Portuguese and Turkish Youth in the Netherlands', in: G. Baumann and T. Sunier (eds.), *Post-Migration Ethnicity: De-essentializing Cohesion, Commitments, Comparison*, Amsterdam: Het Spinus: 144-164.
Malhotra, M.K. (1985) 'The Educational Problems of Foreign Children of Different Nationalities in West Germany', *Ethnic and Racial Studies*, 8(2): 291-309.
Mandel, R. (1989) 'Ethnicity and Identity Among Migrant Guestworkers in West Berlin', in: N. Gonzales and C. McCommon (eds.), *Conflict, Migration and the Expression of Ethnicity*, Boulder, CA: Westview Press: 60-74.
Markstrom-Adams, C. (1992) 'A Consideration of Intervening Factors in Adolescent Identity Formation', in: G.R. Adams, T.P. Gullotta and R. Montemayor (eds.), *Adolescent Identity Formation*, Newbury Park, CA: Sage Publications: 173-192.
Nauck, B. (1988) 'Migration and Change in Parent-Child Relationships: The Case of Turkish Migrants in Germany', *International Migration*, 24(1): 33-51.
Nauck, B. (1994) 'Changes in Turkish migrant families in Germany' in: B. Lewis and D. Schnapper (eds), *Muslims in Europe*, London: Pinter: 130-147.
Nauck, B. (1995) 'Educational Climate and Intergenerative Transmission in Turkish families: A Comparison of Migrants in Germany and Non-migrants', in: P. Noack, M. Hofer and J. Younnis (eds.), *Psychological Responses to Social Change*, Berlin: Walter de Gruyter: 67-86.
Parker-Jenkins, M. (1992) *Educating Muslim Children*, Nottingham: School of Education, University of Nottingham.
Parker-Jenkins, M. (1995) *Children of Islam*, Stoke-on-Trent: Trentham Books.
Patterson, S.J., I. Sochting and J.E. Marcia (1992) 'The Inner Space and Beyond: Women and Identity', in: G.R. Adams, T.P. Gullotta and R. Montemayor (eds.), *Adolescent Identity Formation*, Newbury Park, CA: Sage Publications: 9-24.
Phinney, J.S. (1992) 'The Multigroup Ethnic Identity Measure, A New Scale for Use With Diverse Groups' *Journal of Adolescent Research*, 7(2): 156-175.
Phinney, J.S. (1993a) 'Multiple Group Identities', in: J. Kroger (ed.), *Discussions on Ego Identity*, Hillside, NJ: Lawrence Erlbaum Associates: 47-74.
Phinney, S.J. (1993b) 'A Three-Stage Model of Ethnic Identity Development in Adolescence', in: M.E. Bernal and G. Knight (eds), *Ethnic Identity, Formation and Transmission among Hispanics and Other Minorities*, New York: State University of New York: 61-79.
Phinney, J.S. and D.A. Rosenthal (1992) 'Ethnic Identity in Adolescence: Process, Context, and Outcome', in: G.R. Adams, T.P. Gullotta and R. Montemayor (eds), *Adolescent Identity Formation*, Newbury Park, CA: Sage Publications, pp. 145-172.

Sonyel, S.R. (1988) *The Silent Minority: Turkish Muslim Children in British Schools*, Cambridge: The Islamic Academy.
Sunier, T. (1995) 'Disconnecting Religion and Ethnicity: Young Turk Muslims in the Netherlands', in: G. Baumann and T. Sunier (eds), *Post-Migration Ethnicity: De-essentializing Cohesion, Commitments, Comparison*, Amsterdam: Het Spinus: 58-77.
Van der Lans, J and M. Rooijackers (1996) 'Ethnic Identity and Cultural Orientation of Second Generation Turkish Muslim Migrants', in: W.A.R. Shadid and P.S. van Koningsveld (eds), *Political Participation and Identities of Muslims in non-Muslim States*, Kampen: Kok Pharos: 174-189.
Waters, M. (1990) *Ethnic Options, Choosing Identities in America*, Berkeley: University of California Press.
Weinreich, P. (1986) 'Identity Development in Migrant Offspring: Theory and Practice', in: I. H. Ekstrand (ed.), *Ethnic Minorities and Immigrants in a Cross-cultural Perspective*, Lisse: Swet & Zeitlenger: 230-239.

8 Gender and Generation: Young Muslims in Copenhagen

Yvonne Mørck

[I]dentity only becomes an issue when it is in crisis, when something assumed to be fixed, coherent and stable is displaced by the experience of doubt and uncertainty

(Mercer 1990:43).

The subject of this paper is the perceptions of gender among young immigrants of Muslim background, although many of the issues touched upon are also relevant for young people from non-Muslim homes (see Bhachu 1991; Drury 1991). Two of my key questions are whether the position of 'second-generation immigrant' implies gender-specific advantages, problems, and consequences and how do the children of immigrants transform the gender culture they inherit from their parents? The cultures generally represented by first-generation migrants are not homogeneous entities but differ in many respects according to ethnicity, class, gender, age and religion. Nonetheless, people from Muslim backgrounds have many things in common, although the use and interpretation of Islam in different Muslim countries vary. Fusion with local cultures creates different representations of Islam. Furthermore, so-called 'second-generation immigrants' are not migrants in the strict term because most are born in Denmark. But due to lack of a better concept I use the terms 'second-generation (im)migrant' or 'young (im)migrant'.

Denmark has a population of about 5.5 million. In 1992 it was estimated that 3.3 percent of the population (roughly 160,000) held foreign citizenship (Danmarks Statistik 1992:7). Forty-two percent - or about 67,000 - are formerly guestworkers, now renamed immigrants, mainly from Turkey, Yugoslavia, Pakistan and Morocco (Bruun and Hammer 1991:5). Among immigrants and refugees at least 60,000 are Muslims.[1] Compared with many other European countries, Denmark has few immigrants and no large minority communities. On the other hand, Denmark, like many other West European countries, has ethnic-minority 'enclaves' of different sizes. Denmark can no longer be defined as a religiously homogeneous country.

It is difficult to study complex identities in so-called complex societies. In postmodern times there are no fixed identities, no small enclosed communities, no whole or complete cultures, nor are there fixed methods for studying them. Little research has been done on non-localised culture groups (Knudsen 1991), but refugees and migrants problematize both the concepts of identity and culture. Fog Olwig (1992: 92) notes that immigrant relations are primarily 'non-localised', i.e. they combine social ties with their homeland and create new ones with people in different migrant destinations. To understand these transnational social networks, I advocate the construction approach which implies that both identity (including gender identity) and culture are continuously constructed in various contexts in relation to other individuals. It is the cultural processes which are the interesting objects of study. The point of intersection between the Western-dominated processes of global homogeneity and locally defined processes of heterogeneity is an interesting place in which to study the construction of culture (Fog Olwig 1992; see also Mørck 1994).

Stuart Hall shares this understanding of identity as 'subject to the play of history, politics, representation and difference' (Hall 1992: 309). Because they are never likely to be 'unitary or pure', he advocates the use of the concept of 'translation':

> [t]his describes those identity formations which cut across and intersect natural frontiers, and which are composed of people who have been dispersed forever from their homelands. Such people retain strong links with their places of origin and their traditions, but they are without the illusion of a return to the past. They are obliged to come to terms with the new cultures they inhabit, without simply assimilating them and losing their identities completely. They bear upon them the traces of the particular cultures, traditions, languages and histories by which they were shaped. The difference is that they are not and will never be *unified* in the old sense, because they are irrevocably the product of several interlocking histories and cultures, belong at one and the same time to several 'homes'.
>
> (*ibid.*: 310)

He defines such immigrant contexts as 'cultures of hybridity', a new form of identity found in late modernity. People belonging to such cultures of hybridity, Hall says, have had to renounce the dream or ambition of rediscovering any kind of 'lost' cultural purity, or ethnic absolutism. They are irrevocably translated ... [Migrants] are the products of the new *diasporas* created by the post-colonial migrations. They must learn to inhabit at least two identities, to speak two cultural languages, to translate and negotiate between them.

(*ibid.:* 310)

So the migrant does not have to 'choose' between either returning to his or her roots or disappearing due to assimilation, as the process is often described in immigrant research. Culture, identity and roots are relational constructions which are in a state of constant flux and change:

The roots don't stay in one place. They change shape. They change colour. And they grow. There is *no such thing as a pure point of origin* ... but *that doesn't mean there isn't history.*

(Hebdige in Malkki 1992: 37 emphasis added)

Reflections on gender seldom arise among writers on the cultures of hybridity or among researchers interested in identity generally. Nevertheless, each society has more than one definition of human nature, which becomes obvious when we talk about gender.[2] Feminist research has shown that identity and gender issues cannot be separated. Identity is always gendered because all individuals are socialized into a culture-specific gender as part of the process whereby human identity is constructed.[3]

Complex identities demand complex methods. It is therefore difficult to use the field methods which are developed to study small social units such as villages in a modern context such as Denmark. It is difficult to do traditional fieldwork with participant observation with young immigrants because, like everyone else, they are found in many different places throughout the metropolis.

Nevertheless, I have conducted fieldwork among young immigrants in Copenhagen which included interviews and participant observation in different milieux. I interviewed Pakistani and Turkish youths and I did participant observation in three different cross-ethnic institutions. These were a youth organization for migrants and refugees, a film project and an organization for women. The Council of Europe Minority Youth Committee (CEMYC) is a national organization founded in 1989. Several of the female members of CEMYC were also involved in an organization for ethnic minority women, SOLDUE (Sun Dove). It had been dominated by first-generation and refugee women, but young women were having a growing influence. The film project was chosen for two reasons, both as a 'cultural meeting' between the participants and for the subject of the film itself. I also interviewed young people in high school. There were close connections between the different spheres of participant observation, so I had contact with the same group of people in different contexts. The majority of the interviewees were women, while most of those contacted in participant observation were men. In my view these young immigrants constitute an example of a hybrid culture in Denmark.

Preliminary results

One great difference between the gender ideology that dominates the homes of the young immigrants compared with those of the rest of Danish society is that among the former, an ideology of difference dominates whereas in the latter an ideology of sameness rules. The difference in gender ideology is significant in the encounters between immigrants and Danes, not least for the second generation. The daily contact with Danes, depending on the local contexts (e.g. Bhachu 1991),[4] gives the young immigrants experiences which their parents have not had. As a Turkish girl Fatima says:

> I have one foot in my own culture and the other one in the Danish culture ... I *am* different from my parents ... but I also feel that deep down there are many things which mean that I can't feel as a Dane ... for instance so much information is implicit when Danish girl friends talk together that I can't understand the conversation: discussions about parties and boys.

My research shows that young immigrants are caught between a wish for greater personal freedom and an emotional tie to the parents and to the ethnic group itself. It might be called a loyalty conflict between several identities which often force the young people into context specific identities.

Different power struggles take place: between generations, between the sexes, between the minority and the majority societies, among the minority communities and the young and between the minority communities and the different immigrant families. Although the first generation of immigrants is not a homogeneous entity, the parents seem to share a major worry, namely of 'losing their children'. Many of the girls I talked to said: 'I don't want to let my parents down. They trust me.' It is not only the parents' point of view that matters. The different local Turkish or Pakistani minority communities have great influence on the constructing of what is to be considered normative.

While in high school, the degree of personal freedom young people have depends a lot on the attitude of the parents: some attend parties in school and other social activities and enjoy it; others are never permitted to participate and others again take part but do not like it, because they are not allowed to participate on the same conditions as the Danes. They are not allowed to drink alcohol or to have sweethearts. How do the young talk about these issues? A Pakistani girl said: 'it is my mother who takes care of the home ... and she is the one who controls us ... and it is her fault if something goes wrong.' Freedom to be in the public sphere, the dress code, behaviour, relations to the other sex and to Danes are to a great extent controlled by the first generation both at a parental level and through the minority cultures. The young migrants therefore have an ambiguous relationship with both the parents and the local ethnic groups. Gossip plays a great part in the control system. As a young Turkish man commented on the role of gossip: 'they are faster than CNN!' The control system operates through gossip across borders such as between the country of origin and the different diaspora communities, which implies that both normativity and change have a global character. Perhaps the fear of 'losing their children' is especially great among people from Muslim background because they find themselves in a Christian culture which represents different values than their countries of origin (see Mandel 1989)?

The second generation has grown up in Denmark and often they have only experienced their parents' country of origin during a few visits which were akin to a tourist holiday. My informants often stress that they do not think the first-generation can (or will) change, for example their perceptions of gender, whereas they themselves do not know anything other than having two sets of values -- after all it is their first childhood (Knudsen 1991; see also Drury 1991). The young immigrants worry that they will 'let their parents down'. Conflicts between generations are of course not unknown to Danes but presumably the issue is felt more strongly in the context of a diaspora. The second-generation immigrants therefore have an ambiguous relationship with their parents and the local ethnic groups because they can be of both great support and at the same time exercise great social control.

The concept of honour is used in the negotiations concerning generation and gender, which implies that the idea of honour is still very important in Muslim diaspora communities. Atima - a Pakistani girl says: 'I don't want [my behaviour] to affect the honour of my parents ... [I don't want them] to regret ... that they brought me to Denmark.'

As far as I can see both sexes have problems concerning the parents' lack of understanding of their wish to choose their own partners or to postpone or avoid marriage. Put in another way, it is difficult for the young to refuse more or less arranged marriages. Research in Britain also concludes that many 'second-generation immigrants' 'reluctantly agree to arranged marriage because they [do] not wish to hurt their parents by ruining the family *izzat* (honour)' (Drury 1991: 396).[5] It is common for the second-generation in Denmark to live with their parents until they get married. I only know of a few who have broken the rule by living with siblings, at a college or in a flat of their own. Several of these are women and one argument could be that women both have more to lose and more to win than men by breaking this norm.

Many of my informants agree that they are exposed to more severe rules of behaviour in Denmark than they would have been if they lived in the big cities in their countries of origin. After visits to Turkey or Pakistan they are often surprised how 'modern' the city youth are and how independently they behave. One of the reasons given by my informants for this difference of rules is that the parents react more strongly in Denmark because they are afraid of 'losing their children'. If they lived in Turkey or Pakistan they would be in 'safe' surroundings, whereas in Denmark they live in an 'hostile' environment in which the youngsters can 'go astray'. But the rules of behaviour differ according to gender, and they are harder on women than on men. At the same time the first generation of immigrants are often out of touch with the transformations in the gender culture in their home country. Sometimes they discover the changes in curious ways: for instance it is now possible to watch Turkish television in Denmark. It brings fashionable female speakers dressed in very short miniskirts right into the living room. This leads to discussions between mothers and daughters over such things as whether it is proper for women to show their legs.

Young men have more personal freedom than young women. They are out in public more, going to discos, movies and sporting events or just hanging around in the streets and shopping malls. Danish girlfriends are not accepted by the parents but young men seem to act according to a well-known motto: 'what they don't see, can't hurt them'. They seem to think that if their parents do not know that their sons are dating Danish women, they are not hurt. Male youths often get their first experience with the opposite sex with Danish women even though they know that they eventually will marry one of their 'own kind', which generally means someone from their country of origin.

Many young people want to marry another immigrant. But the consequence of such a marriage, as one male informant explained, would be that two other people from the country of origin lose the opportunity to come to Denmark. Most families prefer to create marriage alliances in the home countries with other parts of the family or with families they know well - families with a good reputation. As Fatima says, 'perhaps it is to do some relative a favour so he can get his son to Denmark, because it is also a kind of business; it has been that for many years.' Several of the youngsters pointed out that there is money and prestige involved in the choice of marriage partners. Suna, a Turkish girl says:

> It is a major problem for the young immigrants ... because we somehow are pushed to marry someone from [the country of origin] ... we could easily choose one from up here because there are lots of young men up here.

Many of my informants tell stories about how the family in the country of origin call on the telephone, asking how the children are doing, if they will visit Turkey or Pakistan soon and if they do, family members often drop in to 'check out' the young immigrants for potential marriage partners for their own children. Suna concludes:

> In a way both boys and girls who grow up abroad are misused by those in Turkey because they have found out that it is easiest to get a residence permit in Denmark. After two years of marriage they kick out the spouse and marry one they known from before.

And she concludes that the family in Turkey 'have turned marriage into a game.'

Being the oldest of the children in a family is a difficult position because they have to construct new boundaries. The oldest have had to create a framework of how to be young in a Turkish-Danish or Pakistani-Danish context. The first child who wants to go to high school might have to face a struggle with the parents, while for the younger children a longer school education is accepted. At the same time young women, and perhaps also men, use the desire for an education as a reason to postpone marriage. The same goes for behaviour in high school. Once new boundaries are created by the oldest child, the younger have an easier time. Some parents are nonetheless, very interested in giving the children an education and almost force them into high school, as several of the interviewees said.

In the Western world, youth or the 'teenage years' has a different meaning than it does in Turkey or Pakistan. In the countries of origin it is not common to use the category of 'youth', because someone is either a child or married adult. New forms of praxis concerning both youth and gender are developed among the young immigrants due to, among other things, influences from Danish or Western youth culture. This does not mean that all changes come from the outside. Social change also happened in the countries of origin. My informants take part in a social mobility which implies transformations in norms, gender behaviour and gender relations. 'If the second-generation immigrants are not going to be second-generation cleaning assistants, then they need education. This our parents know,' as a female informant pointed out. Perhaps here is a paradox: the parents want the children to get educated but not 'Westernized' because they consider that equivalent to 'losing' them. But is it possible to have the one process without the other?

The first generation has paid a high price for economic improvements because they *have* lost their children to the extent that the second generation has not developed in the image of their parents; they have not always turned out as the parents expected (Ganguly 1992).[6] Modern city life offers some possibilities in which young people want to take part (Wilson 1991). Thus they wish to choose their partners, to have greater personal autonomy, less social control, a life which is less directly dominated by religion etc.. These issues constitute a 'negotiation zone' where the young in different ways try to present their wishes. Sometimes they do so by direct confrontations and other times by more indirect means. Some of the informants said that they do not want to 'beg' their parents while others have a more context dependent strategy. Depending on how strongly the young person wants something, such as to study in high school, she or he argues with their parents and sometimes they defy them.[7] For instance one Turkish girl went to Paris on a schooltrip without her parents' consent. She thought that this trip was so important for her that she chose to have a direct confrontation with them. No matter their strategies, young immigrants are in a process of reconstructing their inherited gender culture.

Young people operate as cultural brokers, for example between the first generation and the wider Danish society. Brothers can be brokers between parents and sisters by supporting the sisters in greater personal freedom and access to education and/or work. Older brothers and sisters can work as brokers for younger siblings, and some families function as brokers by letting their daughters do non-traditional things like postpone marriage or travel to other towns in order to get an education, which is the case with several of my informants. Some young people did not want to be placed in such an adult role, because they had to deal with subjects they were not supposed to know about, e.g. sexuality or economic issues.

For boys and young men there is a further problem with this brokering role (Bøggild Mortensen 1989). In a Muslim peasant culture, there is no direct dialogue between father and son. Conflicts are rare, or they are seldom expressed openly (Drury 1991). In Denmark, the father loses his traditional role, yet he cannot help his son acquire Danish norms of family relations. Problems of this nature are especially acute when parents get divorced.

Young people also have to be brokers *among* themselves, because their position as second-generation immigrants gives access to several perspectives, identities and cultural languages. They must be able to shift between different and often mutually contradictory cultural norms. Sometimes they break a Danish cultural norm by wearing a headscarf or by entering into an arranged marriage. Other times they break a cultural norm which belongs to the country of origin by for example, having a sweetheart or drinking alcohol. To break their parents' rules can create a 'totally bad conscience' as one of my female informants put it.

Conclusion

Most research on immigrant youth in Denmark focuses on problems but I want to stress that there are more than just problems and hardship. Many of the subjects of my study are very bright and have strong personalities. In many respects they have managed to combine several cultural norms. The Danish anthropologist Anne Knudsen has suggested the concept 'constructive schizophrenia' for this kind of talent (Knudsen 1991: 5). It could be argued that some second-generation immigrants only become 'schizophrenic' and not 'constructive' but I think it is also important to stress positive processes. There are many ways of being a 'second-generation' or 'young Muslim'. My research finds that some second-generation immigrants do come together across ethnic and gender boundaries. While making daily choices, the young create a 'Danish' version of a culture of hybridity. In a variety of contexts or cultural niches new gender specific identities, values and possibilities are negotiated, explored and developed. It is important for young people to develop strategies which can maintain a relationship between continuity and change, or what Gilroy calls a 'syncretic conscience' (Gilroy 1987). Gender is a significant part of this process, as Ålund's work in Sweden shows (Ålund 1991). In Denmark this process of hybridity happens on a smaller scale than many other places in the world, but it happens nevertheless.

Notes

1 The exact number of Muslims in Denmark is unknown, partly because of lack of registration and partly because immigrants keep their country of origin's citizenship: for instance one third of the Pakistanis keep their Pakistani citizenship. The remaining majority are therefore registered as Danish citizens but presumably still consider themselves as Muslims.
2 That each society has more than one definition of the human nature is seldom incorporated into the mainstream academic work. See for instance books on the concepts of person and self: Heelas and Lock 1991; Carrithers et al. 1985; Dumont 1986.
3 Each society has at least two definitions of human nature: a male and a female. In rites de passages, in work, economic, political, religious and family dimensions you find differences according to gender. Or as Jonathan Rutherford says: '[Identity] is constituted out of different elements of experience and subjective position, but in their articulation they become something more than just the sum of their original elements. For example our class subjectivities do not simply co-exist alongside our gender. Rather our class is gendered and our gender is classed' (Rutherford 1990: 19).
4 In an article about second-generation Punjabi Sikh women in Great Britain, Bhachu (1991) argues that their 'cultural locations are constantly renegotiated and filtered through the *same* economic, political and media forces that affect white "indigenous" women,' (*ibid.* 401). At the same time though 'their patterns of consumption and cultural styles grow out of the *specificities* of their regional and class locations and from *particular* niches within the large metropolis ... This is not because there is no common "ethnic" cultural base, but because younger Asian women emerge out of the *particular* localities in which they have been raised, and from *particular* class cultures, to which they have been socialised,' (*ibid.* 408-409, emphasis added).
5 Drury (1991) describes Sikh girls and their maintenance of their ethnic culture in Nottingham, England. Her study included 102 second-generation females of Sikh origin. On the issue of arranged marriage among Sikhs in Britain, her research confirms previous studies, namely that it still prevails: 92% of her respondents expected to have an arranged marriage. She concludes: 'even those who secretly

went out with boyfriends (22%) would nevertheless accept an arranged marriage for themselves ... a majority expressed strong feelings about their relative lack of freedom vis-à-vis Sikh males ... 58% of my respondents complained bitterly about not being allowed to go out with boyfriends openly ... and said that although they preferred to have a "love marriage" they would reluctantly agree to an arranged marriage because they did not wish to hurt their parents by ruining the family *izzat* (honour) ... Thus, a majority of my respondent (66%) no longer supported the traditional marriage, although most of them expected to be married in this way' (*ibid.* 396). Her main conclusions also seem to fit my findings.

6 Ganguly (1992) describes a group of male middle-class professional Indians who emigrated to the United States in the late sixties and early seventies. Ganguly studies the gender differences between the first generation with respect to their view on their life in India in the past and their present life in the US. Most of the men play down their experiences of marginality and emphasize the fact of their material 'freedom' in the present, whereas the women (their wives) romanticize the past. The research illustrates the fear among first-generation immigrants of 'losing their children'. As a male informant says to Ganguly: 'even if I don't get nearly the same kind of respect or attention [as in India], I've got what I need. And if the children don't go astray - become hippies, or start dating - then I'll be satisfied' (*ibid.* 36). As Ganguly concludes: 'for, if his children *were* to "go astray", it would almost be a betrayal not only of his decision, but also of his identity -- as male, father and Indian' (*ibid.* 36). Furthermore, 'the anxiety about and concern with power and masculinity signal ways in which colonial discourses continue to interpolate postcolonial subjects' (*ibid.* 37) and 'the devaluation of the past indicates and itself produces the present, hybrid identity of immigrant men' (*ibid.* 38). I have not analysed this aspect but I expect differences between the hybrid identity of first- and second- generation immigrants, as well as by gender.

7 One of Drury's (1991) main conclusions is that there was very little evidence of overt intergenerational conflict among her Sikh respondents: 'indeed, very few members of the second generation openly went against their parents' wishes and, even, when there were acts of "rebellion", these mostly took place secretly, thus avoiding confrontation' (*ibid.* 398).

References

Ålund, A. (1991) 'Ungdom, multietnisk kultur och nya gemenskaper', *Kvinnovetenskaplig Tidskrift* 3: 18-30.

Bhachu, P. (1991) 'Culture, Ethnicity and Class Among Punjabi Sikh Women in 1990s Britain', *New Community* 17(3): 401-412.

Bruun, I. and Hammer, O. (1991) *Statistik om indvandrere og flygtninge 1991*. MS Nr.2.

Bøggild Mortensen, L. (1989) *'At være eller ikke være' Tyrkisk ungdom i København og Ankara*. København: Akademisk Forlag.

Carrithers, M., Collins, S. and Lukes, S. (eds.) (1985) *The Category of the Person*, Cambridge: Cambridge University Press.

Danmarks Statestik (1992) *Dokumentation on Indvandrere: Unge indvandrere og kriminalitet*. MS Nr.3.

Drury, B. (1991) 'Sikh Girls and the Maintenance of an Ethnic Culture', *New Community* 17(3): 387-400.

Dumont, L. (1986) *Essays on Individualism*, Chicago: University of Chicago Press.

Fog Olwig, K. (1992) 'Kulturel komplexitet', *Jordens Folk* 3: 89-94.

Ganguly, K. (1992) 'Migrant Identities: Personal Memory and the Construction of Selfhood,' *Cultural Studies* 6: 27-50.

Gilroy, P. (1987) *There Ain't No Black in the Union Jack*. London: Hutchinson

Hall, S. (1992) 'The Question of Cultural Identity', in S.Hall, D.Held and T.McGrew (eds) *Modernity and Its Futures*, Cambridge: Polity Press: 273-325.

Heelas, P.L.F. and Lock, A.J. (eds) (1991) *The Indigeneous Psychologies: The Anthropology of Self*, Academic Press.

Knudsen, A. (1991) 'Interpreting Identity', paper presented at UNESCO European Expert Meeting: Overlapping Cultures and Plural Identities, Vienna.

Malkki, L. (1992) 'National Geographic: The Rooting of Peoples and the Territorialization of National Identity Among Scholars and Refugees', *Cultural Anthropology* 7(1).

Mandel, R. (1986) 'Turkish Headscarves and the "Foreigner Problem": Constructing Difference Through Emblems of Identity', *New German Critique* 46: 27-46.

Mercer, K. (1990) 'Welcome to the Jungle: Identity and Diversity in Postmodern Politics', in: J.Rutherford (ed.) *Identity, Community, Culture, Difference*. London: Lawrence and Wishart: 43-71.

Mørck, Y. (1994) 'Identity, Gender and the Culture of Hybridity: Muslim Youth in Copenhagen', unpublished paper presented at the 4th Nordic Youth Research Symposium, Stockholm.

Rutherford, J. (1990) 'A Place Called Home: Identity and the Cultural Politics of Difference', in J.Rutherford (ed.) *Identity, Community, Culture, Difference*. London: Lawrence and Wishart.

Wilson, E. (1991) *The Sphinx in the City: Urban Life, the Control of Disorder, and Women*. Virago Press. London.

9 Good Girls, Bad Girls: Moroccan and Turkish Runaway Girls in the Netherlands

Lenie Brouwer

A nineteen-year-old Moroccan girl - I will call her Faithy - told me of her problems with her parents. She has lived with her family in the Netherlands for thirteen years. Faithy was more restricted in her movements than her Moroccan girlfriends: 'I was not allowed to go out with my girlfriends and had to return home immediately after school. I had to return home immediately. By changing my school schedule, saying that school was finished at half past four instead of three o'clock, I had more free time.'

She secretly took a boyfriend which caused many in the Moroccan community to gossip about her. When her parents found out they confined her to the family home. They planned, moreover, to marry Faithy to her cousin. 'I had to stay at home the whole day, it felt like a prison.' Finally, she managed to run away one day when her parents were out. When I spoke to Faithy one year after these events, she had returned to her parental home on several occasions - but never stayed for very long. The events of the past had caused her parents to not want to see her anymore. Faithy regrets this situation. 'I would like to become a policeman,' she says, 'to prove to my parents that I didn't run away to play a whore. I want to show them that I have learned a good profession.'

Turkish and Moroccan male migrants first arrived in the Netherlands during the 1960s hoping to earn quick money to invest in their country of origin. Yet by the 1970s their attitude had changed. Instead of returning to their native country, they began to bring their wives and children to the Netherlands. Their daughters were brought up according to Moroccan or Turkish tradition, although they were also strongly influenced by what they learnt at Dutch schools and through contact with members of their peer group. Turkish and Moroccan adolescent girls have to cope with various cultural frames of reference. Most will probably live quite happily with this situation, but some do not.

The past ten years has seen an increase in the number of Moroccan and Turkish adolescent girls in the Netherlands who run away from home.[1] By leaving home, they run the risk of severing ties of kinship and becoming isolating from their family and community without any certainty of being accepted by Dutch society. Moroccan and Turkish runaways have a bad reputation within their own communities. They are considered whores who will come to a bad end, unlike the image of good Muslim girls who have listened to their parents. But what do parents mean by 'good' girls and 'bad' girls? And what is their daughters' perspective on 'good' and 'bad' behaviour?

I approach these questions in the light of the research conducted among Moroccan and Turkish runaway girls in the Netherlands. I analyze the process of running away from home using perspectives on ethnicity developed by Fredrik Barth (1969) and Anthony Cohen (1989) to consider the relations between Muslim parents and their daughters in the Dutch context. What is the girls' relationship to their families, their own communities, and to Dutch society? What are the reasons for running away and what different strategies do runaway girls apply in their negotiations with their parents? Are runaway girls always cut off from their family and community and how do they define their new situation?

Turkish and Moroccan girls in the Netherlands: a sample

Between 1987 and 1989 I conducted qualitative research among forty-five runaway girls: twenty-eight of Moroccan, and seventeen of Turkish, descent.[2] In order to establish contact with my informants I spent long hours at a hostel for Muslim women and girls, and at another for Muslim girls only.[3] Meeting them regularly, I built confidential relationships with and maintained contact when they moved to a different hostel or to another setting. In addition, I interviewed a number of girls who had not sought refuge in Muslim hostels or who had run away from home some years previously.

Twenty Dutch, Moroccan and Turkish social workers were also included among my informants in addition to two mothers (one Moroccan and one

Turkish). To get an impression of the parents' views I conducted interviews with the runaway girls, with social workers and consulted dossier material. Most of the runaway girls I interviewed were aged between fifteen and seventeen when they left home. The youngest was thirteen and the oldest, twenty-three. Almost a third of the Moroccan and Turkish girls I interviewed had run away from home on more than one occasion. More than sixty percent of the Turkish girls and half the Moroccan girls were either born in the Netherlands or had come here before the age of six. Generally speaking, the Turkish girls had lived longer in the Netherlands than had the Moroccans. A small number of the latter had arrived after their thirteenth birthday and had lived with their families for about two years before leaving home.

The scope of this paper does not allow me to describe in detail the differences between Moroccan and Turkish girls; however, I feel it is necessary to make some comments of a more general nature. While in absolute figures there are more Turkish than Moroccan adolescent girls in the Netherlands,[4] more Moroccan girls run away from home. Differences are also to be found in literacy levels and knowledge of the Dutch language between Moroccan and Turkish parents. Most Moroccan mothers - especially those belonging to the Berber-speaking group - and approximately half the mothers of Turkish origin were both illiterate in their own language and barely able to express themselves in Dutch. The majority of Turkish fathers were literate and spoke Dutch rather fluently, at least when compared to Moroccan fathers. On the question of family stability, divorce is more common among Moroccan parents of runaway girls than among the Turkish. This pattern can be also found in their respective home countries (Mernissi 1978: 318).

The socio-economic position of Turkish and Moroccan migrants varies little from that of other migrants in Western societies. Their situation is characterized by high levels of both unemployment and industrial disadvantage. In the labour market as in daily life, they are faced with various kinds of prejudice and discrimination. Their response to this negative categorization is to place greater emphasis on their ethnicity (Jenkins 1986: 178). The younger generation of these migrant groups are not likely to have the opportunities their parents would wish them to have. In many ways, one could say that life in the Netherlands has not been a success for most Moroccan and Turkish migrants (Penninx 1989).

Ethnic boundaries

Turkish and Moroccan migrants in the Netherlands[5] can be considered as ethnic groups. Barth has defined one aspect of such groups as 'categories of ascription and identification by the actors themselves' (1969: 10). Although social interaction does take place between these migrants and the Dutch population, cultural differences still persist - but only those which migrants themselves regard as socially relevant. These differences may be marked by such 'overt signals' as dress and language or by 'basic value orientations' on, for example, sexual relationships (Barth 1969: 14). The continuity of the ethnic group is dependent upon maintaining these boundaries.

Eriksen (1993: 41) has likened social boundaries to invisible lines running between groups. The cultural content highlighting the boundary may change but the dichotomization between group members and outsiders remains. According to Barth, it is this ethnic boundary that defines the group. Where migration is involved, maintenance of the boundaries becomes an imperative as the group may perceive itself to be under pressure.

Anthony Cohen (1989) takes the view that ethnic boundaries are largely symbolic. By stressing certain symbols Moroccan and Turkish migrants are able to differentiate themselves from the dominant Dutch group. Moroccan and Turkish parents feel, for example, that their Islamic faith offers them a moral frame of reference, and this they consider to be one of the biggest differences between themselves and the Dutch. In fact, Muslim values pertaining to sexuality, honour, virginity, respect, obedience and marriage are violated by dominant Dutch norms.

As Floya Anthias (1992: 26) observes, 'the relations around sexuality and gender are central in defining the boundaries of the ethnic group'. Female virginity, which is often associated with female purity, must be considered as one key aspect of sexuality. The purity of the group is dependent upon the purity of its women, whose task it is to ensure group continuity (Hastrup 1978). Kirsten Hastrup has emphasized how a particular sexual state of women, for example a girl's chastity, can act as a means of establishing distinct social categories. With Turkish and Moroccan migrants a girl's virginity is not her own business, but becomes the concern of her whole family.

In order to preserve the boundaries of the ethnic group in the Dutch context, a high level of social control over the girls' conduct is felt necessary. Moroccan and Turkish parents fear losing their daughters to Western society or that their daughters might become alienated from their own cultural background. In the Dutch context, Moroccan and Turkish girls serve as ethnic markers of their communities. This symbolic aspect of the ethnic boundary is crucial in understanding the relations between parents and daughters.

'Good' girls

The majority of the runaway girls I interviewed described a number of strict rules, common to both Turkish and Moroccan migrant communities, to which a 'good' girl has to acquiesce. Obedience of, and respect for, one's parents are two values strongly emphasized during their socialization. Generally speaking, generational stratification dictates that individuals have to yield to anyone older than themselves. Daughters may certainly not disobey their father in public (Kagitcibasi 1989; Davis and Davis 1989). A girl has little say in family affairs; the father is the authority figure and is presumed to know what is best for his daughter. Matters of honour and shame are crucial to both the family and the individual since breaking these codes will bring dishonour not only to the offending person but to the whole family unit.

Men take on the responsibility of maintaining the honour of the family, and try to discourage 'bad' behaviour by their daughters which could bring shame upon the whole family. In their perception a 'good' girl behaves properly and is, for example, forbidden to meet or talk with boys in public lest she gain a bad reputation and bring shame on the family. Contacts between men and women take place within the confines of marriage and family life. As virginity is a prerequisite of marriage, fathers and brothers feel it their responsibility to strictly supervise the sexuality of young female family members.

Virginity can be seen as a boundary-expressing symbol. Following Cohen's (1989: 18) definition of symbols 'as things standing for other things', these symbols have not only visual expression but also stand for ideas. They are 'mental constructs' - although Cohen's analysis emphasizes that sharing symbols does not imply shared meanings. Meanings are not fixed and uniform. As a symbol it is held in common by the members of a group but its meaning varies with each member's unique interpretation of it.

Culture, manifest in symbols, is not so constricting that it demands that all group members make the same sense out of the world around them. Neither is it the case that individuals give random interpretations to their world. Interpretations tend to be drawn from within the framework of a given society and are influenced by such factors as language, beliefs and ideology. They are responsive to the circumstances of social interaction, both among the individuals who constitute a society and between the society as a whole and those falling beyond its boundaries. The vehicles of such interpretations are symbols. By their very nature, symbols permit interpretations and provide scope for interpretive manoeuvre by those who use them.

Symbols are effective because they are so imprecise. They are the ideal medium through which people can speak a common language, behave in seemingly similar ways, participate in the same rituals, pray to the same gods, wear similar clothes and so forth. They constantly transform the reality of difference into the appearance of similarity with such efficacy that people can still invest the community with ideological integrity. This unites people in their opposition, both to each other and to those outside. It gives reality to the community's boundaries.

Virginity is an important virtue within Islam. Islamic norms clearly stipulate what the decent behaviour of girls includes. It provides 'some unifying concepts on female sexuality, linking female sexual virginity to male honour and the segregation of the sexes' (Kandiyoti 1987: 326). Any misbehaviour on the part of girls or women can bring shame and dishonour to the male members of a whole family or community. Although control over sexuality may continue to prevail, the actual nature of acceptable sexual conduct is constantly being challenged and re-negotiated.

In the Dutch context, Muslim parents consider virginity as a boundary marker delineating them from their social surroundings. In this respect, it symbolizes their differentiation from the Dutch majority. The decent behaviour of girls is closely linked to the honour of the family. In the socialization of girls, it is stressed that they must remain a virgin until marriage, by which is meant keeping the hymen intact. The girls say 'as long as we live at home, we have to agree with it.' Some of them also associate virginity with self-respect; this finding has been confirmed in other studies of Turkish girls in the Netherlands (De Vries 1987).

In order to preserve their daughters' virginity, parents feel it necessary to control their movements. This can include not allowing them to attend school after the minimum leaving age of sixteen, or objecting to them meeting or talking with their friends. How strict the parents' interpretation of virginity is, is dependent upon such factors as whether the family has a rural or urban background, their educational level, socio-economic status or degree of religiousness. The girls I interviewed share the symbol of virginity with their parents although they do not accord the same meanings to it, nor do they agree with the consequences it has on their freedom of movement. This is an important source of conflict between the girls and their parents.

Reasons for running away

The girls mentioned a wide range of subjects which had led to conflict, especially with their fathers. There was no one single reason for running away from home; their decision was rather the result of numerous quarrels that had escalated over the course of years. Two-thirds of all conflicts involved punishment, and some of the girls also referred to maltreatment and sexual abuse (see Brouwer 1992). Half of the runaway girls I interviewed came from so-called problem families. These girls referred to conflicts between their parents and the beatings their mothers were forced to endure. Other factors mentioned by the girls were financial problems, parental drinking, marital problems or the presence of a step-parent. One-third said that although they had not been beaten they had, however, been subjected to intimidation or humiliation.

The girls usually described three major areas of conflict. These concerned their education, their association with boys and with their marriage prospects. More than half the runaways told me they had had problems with schooling. In families where girls' education is not considered important, girls of school age were often kept at home, or were not allowed to attend school after the minimum leaving age of sixteen. They expressed opinions such as, 'girls are not important', 'education is not necessary' and 'at school I can meet boys and that is forbidden.'

In the few families where importance is placed upon girls' education, they often had little say in their choice of curriculum or school. Their fathers made these decisions, and the daughters were expected to simply obey. Recognition of the importance of female education is often related to the parents' own level of educational achievement. To some extent most Moroccan and Turkish parents' negative attitude toward their daughters' education is related to their rural background and low educational level. This was particular true of the mothers. However, this is only one part of the explanation. Parents who regard Dutch culture as a threat were also worried about the vulnerable position of girls in the Dutch context. Some Moroccan and Turkish girls I spoke with made statements such as: 'I know that getting my diploma was the only way to get out of this situation and be free of the influence of my family'.

The other problems mentioned by the girls, for example the prohibition on contacts with boys or the tradition of arranged marriages, arise from the meaning parents attach to virginity. About half the Moroccan and Turkish runaways said they had had quarrels about contact or supposed contact with boys. From their parents' perspective, contact between men and women should been confined to marriage. Virginity is considered a prerequisite of a good marriage. Girls generally agree with the symbol of virginity, but not with the meaning their parents attach to it. The Moroccan and Turkish girls I interviewed do meet boys, and a third of them secretly had a boyfriend although they did not have sexual intercourse with him.

Almost half of the girls ran away from home to avoid a marriage arranged by their parents without the girls' consent. Muslim marriages are considered the responsibility of the family and not the individuals involved. Intra-ethnic marriage must be seen in the context of maintenance of the ethnic boundary. Girls agree with the principle of parental involvement in marriage but say they also wish to be consulted on the choice of partner. In addition, in these families it is said that Islamic law requires that they consent to any proposed wedding.

In the case of the runaway girls, the father-daughter relationship was too disturbed to provide a solid basis for communication and confidence. If parents were afraid of losing control over their daughters, then they tried to force them into an arranged marriage. The girls themselves did not want to get married but wished instead to finish school first, or to postpone the wedding to a later date. In some cases, they did not agree with their parents' choice of suitor. In others, they already had another boyfriend. Often they were afraid of being shipped back to relatives still living in Turkey or Morocco.

Power relationships

To fully understand the relationship between parents and daughters, we have to analyze them within the context of existing power relations. Moroccan and Turkish families are characterized by hierarchical power structures in which the father holds formal authority, and daughters show deference to that authority. Fathers also try to control the meanings of symbols by imposing their interpretation upon their daughters (Tennekes 1990: 67). The fathers reinforce these interpretations by claiming them to be sanctioned by religion, the family and the father's network of friends.

Following Cohen (1989: 17), I consider social interaction within families as 'the transaction of meanings'. Again, these meanings are not fixed. Muslim girls are socialized by their parents within the home, yet at school they are confronted with other values. Their parents have passed on to them certain meanings which the girls no longer take for granted. The fact that the girls have a better command of the Dutch language and a higher level of education than their parents has only served to strengthen their social position within the family. Access to Dutch society gives the daughters an important power resource to challenge the formal authority of the father.

In the social interaction between parents and daughters, the meanings of important ethnic symbols - virginity or how a good Muslim girl is supposed to behave for example - are contested. The girls I spoke with attempted to obtain a broader interpretation of the meaning of important symbols than their parents wish to attach to them, but it is not their intention to challenge their cultural frames of reference. They are left with a number of options: (a) they can try to negotiate with their parents; (b) they can choose the strategy of secret behaviour; (c) they can attempt to gain the support of others; or (d) they can run away from home.

In regard to the first option, some girls did try to negotiate with both parents, or the mother only, on the meanings they attach to education. A common response of girls of school age to being kept at home was: 'I did not accept it; I wanted to go to school, otherwise I would have gone crazy!'

Some succeeded. These girls had the support of Dutch laws on compulsory education to which their parents were forced to adhere. Matters become more complicated after they had passed school leaving age. Since Muslim mothers can be important intermediaries between father and daughter, some girls made attempts to speak to their mothers about some of their future aspirations. One Moroccan mother I interviewed told me of her husband's increasing religiousness as his daughters approached puberty. His various demands included that they wear a headscarf outside the family home. This mother advised an 'out of sight, out of mind' philosophy by telling her daughters to obey their father only as long as he could see them. On subjects such as school attendance and the timing of marriage, the girls were able to negotiate with their parents for a more broad interpretation.

Whilst these two subjects were open to negotiation, the subject of having liaisons with boys - however innocent such relationships may be - was, in the girls' view, a matter not open to discussion. According to their parents, a good Muslim girl is not allowed to meet boys in public for fear of public rebuke or censure. The girls are in agreement with their parents' symbolism of virginity as meaning keeping the hymen intact. They were not, however, in agreement with any interpretation the consequences of which are that they should not meet boys at all. In dealing with this conflict most girls choose for the second option, the strategy of secret behaviour. In order to give meaning to their interpretation of virginity, they led a double life doing what they wished but doing it secretly. One possible strategy to achieve this aim was to change their school schedule. School is one important setting where they are able to freely associate with (male) members of their peer group. As long as this strategy is not discovered no problems would result.

Since social control in their communities is very strong, such secret activities are full of risk. Often they served to feed the suspicions of fathers who already have little trust in their daughters. They often result in the girl being placed under an even stricter regime. If their secret behaviour was discovered then they would be in deep trouble with their parents. This happened to Faithy, the girl I quoted in my introduction. Most conflicts of this kind lead to heated quarrels and often end in beatings. Unable to withstand this situation, and fearful of more beatings, some girls decide rather to run away from home. This was particularly true of girls who had never thought of running away before. The severity of the crisis forces them to take this drastic step.

In Morocco or Turkey, such girls have more opportunity to resort to the third option: to seek the help of others to intervene in quarrels. Bonds of kinship, and other social networks, play an important role here. However, the few girls who did have relatives resident in the Netherlands said they would not ask them for help as they expected a negative response. As one Moroccan girl told me: 'If I tell them my father beats me, they will beat me even more.'

The father of a seventeen-year-old Turkish schoolgirl was criticized by his friends for not making his daughters wear a headscarf to school. The criticism was based upon their interpretation of such behaviour as 'Dutch', this notwithstanding the fact that in their home countries the same behaviour would simply be considered 'modern'.

While it was often impossible to ask for help from relatives, several Moroccan and Turkish girls I interviewed did seek assistance from their teachers or social workers. The girls spoke to these professionals without informing their parents. They knew that discussing internal family matters with outsiders would meet with their disapproval. Moroccan and Turkish parents view Dutch social workers rather suspiciously, believing they encourage their children to run away from home. The girls informed me, however, that explaining their problems to social workers gave them the courage to speak up for themselves. Whereas before they simply suffered in silence, now these girls asked for information on facilities for runaway youngsters and began to make preparations for leaving the family home.

The fourth and final option left open to these girls was to run away from home. Daughters who did this witnessed a dramatic change in their power relations with their parents; it strengthened their negotiating position considerably. In several cases social workers acted as go-betweens able to negotiate an amicable agreement between parents and daughter. Almost one-third of the girls I interviewed later returned to the family home. Some girls also realized their demands of, for example, having an unwanted marriage canceled or receiving permission to attend school. One wonders, however, how long this new situation will persist. The picture here becomes particularly clear where girls who have run away from home several times are concerned.

After running away: 'bad girls' and ambivalent feelings

By running away from home Moroccan and Turkish girls gain a bad reputation. Within their own community they are seen as whores. What was the reaction of the runaway girls to this stigmatization? What meanings do they now attach to the symbol of virginity, embodied as it is in the concept of the 'good' girl? And how do they cope with being stigmatized a 'bad' girl because of running away from home?

Various social workers with whom I spoke had observed a strong tendency towards ambivalence in the girls. On the one hand, they desired to prove to their parents that, despite the stigma, they are still 'good' girls and had not run away from home just to meet boys. On the other hand, they develop a strong negative self-image. They think of themselves as 'bad', or fear that their community views them as such. 'It doesn't matter how I behave' is a commonly heard viewpoint.

Most girls who had only recently run away from home stated that virginity - in their interpretation, where the hymen is still intact - is still of great importance to them. As one Turkish girl explained 'this is drilled into our heads.' However, the further implication of virginity - that of not meeting boys - remains a matter of disagreement. Some of the runaway girls had already concluded that 'if people just see me as a whore then I will behave like it. I will enjoy life.' They react to stigmatization by doing everything their parents have forbidden. They cut their long hair, wear make-up and tight clothes, start smoking and visit Moroccan or Turkish coffee shops[6] where they are able to meet boys.

If it appears unlikely they will ever return home then, over time, their perspective on virginity gradually changes. Slowly they begin to question its importance. A seventeen-year-old Turkish girl who had been living in a Dutch hostel for several months and recently found a boyfriend told me: 'I know for sure that I will not return home. So why should I stay a virgin? It is not important to me anymore'.

Their doubts on the importance of virginity become particularly strong if they fall in love with a boy. This tendency can be seen in the case of one Turkish runaway I interviewed several times during the course of a year in which she only saw her parents now and again. At our first meeting she emphasized the cultural connotation of virginity for Muslim girls. She also interpreted it as a form of 'self respect'. A year later she had fallen in love with a Turkish boy whom she wished to marry. He had already been married once before and urged her not to value her virginity. Under his influence her interpretation of virginity had now altered. 'Virginity is not important to me,' she said, 'I don't care anymore. I am sure my boyfriend will choose me and will marry me.'

Another Turkish respondent told me of her boyfriend with whom she had lived for several years. At the time of our interview this relationship had been finished for some time:

> Just after I had run away from home, I was very prudish. I would never sleep with a boy before marriage. When I met my boyfriend I changed. I was head over heels in love. I was very romantic at the time. After six months I wanted to go to bed with him. Now I am sorry that I did it although I have had a good time. When I lost my virginity I did not dare to tell my sister with whom I ran away from home. We often check up on each other.

Some girls confessed to me that later they had had some difficulty with the way in which they had lost their virginity. A seventeen-year-old Moroccan girl who had not spoken to her parents in the four months since running away described why she burned her arm with a cigarette:

> I was angry with myself. I just had to cry. My boyfriend said I could decide by myself but in fact he ... how shall I put it ... he said, it's up to you. But I thought

to myself that if I refuse to sleep with him, then I will lose him. I really loved him
... I did not want to lose him.

Some runaways become very critical of the importance their community places on virginity. One Turkish girl explained:

> From the moment I first left home I started to think more about virginity. I realized that I was changing very fast. At first I thought it would be impossible for me to lose my virginity because I would no longer be accepted by the Turkish community. Then I thought: I don't care anymore. I do not like this tradition. My sisters told me to be patient and were afraid I would have regrets later. Careful what you do, one warned me. My other sister was shocked but she was against my Dutch boyfriend anyway. She said that I had ruined my life and that I was no sister of hers.

Whilst in their own ethnic communities these runaway girls are considered whores, among the girls themselves a finer distinction is drawn between the concept of 'good' and 'bad'. Some girls try to differentiate themselves from others they perceive as being really 'bad'. Although they too have lost their virginity they still feel themselves different to the 'others'. One sixteen-year-old Moroccan explained:

> I'm not the kind of girl who goes from one boy to another. I will not deny that I have visited coffee shops but I know what I am doing. I know a lot of girls who are caught up with everything. If a boy tells them they are beautiful, they allow him to abuse them. I know they went to bed with boys for money. That will not happen to me.

They call these other runaway girls 'boy-crazy'. 'A boy only has to look at them,' it is suggested, 'and they fall in love.' They also strenuously criticize girls who have relationships with married men.

> I'm angry with my girlfriend. She lets her boyfriend abuse her even though she knows he will not marry her. At home he has an obedient wife and my girlfriend is only a whore in his eyes. I'm sure that after a while he will say: piss off whore, I'm fed up with you.

The differentiation between these runaway girls and those they suppose to be 'bad' is not simply a question of whether they are virgins or not. The distinction turns on the way the 'bad' girls associate with boys. The 'good' girls view their loss of virginity as a response to falling in love with the prospect, if they so chose, of marriage. The others, again, are simply 'boy-crazy'.

Many of my respondents did not limit their criticism only to the behaviour of other runaway girls. They also pass judgement on Moroccan and Turkish boys. As one Moroccan girl put it: 'girls who run away from home are whores to them. No doubt about it.' This view was confirmed by a Turkish girl who says that: 'All Turkish boys are the same. At first they look rather modern. But later they all think in Turkish terms. After you are married, you are not allowed to do anything.' Another Turkish girl who had lived together with her boyfriend told me: 'When we had a fight, he always argued that I was bad because I had run away. He told me that he was superior. I could not stand it and I asked him whether that meant he had three noses or three ears!'

It is interesting to compare the opinions of some Moroccan or Turkish boys on this subject. Several studies have been published recently on Moroccan and Turkish boys in the Netherlands (see Buijs 1993; Feddema 1992). Their findings concur with the views expressed by many of the runaway girls I interviewed. Most boys reported that they had had various girlfriends of Moroccan, Turkish or Dutch descent. They admitted to often having secret sexual liaisons even though they were aware of how complicated this could be for Moroccan and Turkish girls. These actions have to be juxtaposed with the view that when it came to marriage they preferred their prospective wife to be a virgin. As a Turkish boy put it: 'I don't want to have a second-hand wife' (Feddema 1992: 58).

Relation with their parents

By the time I had concluded my research half of the girls I had interviewed were no longer on speaking terms with their parents. The remaining fifty percent did have contact - at least with their mothers - from time to time. Of course, the level of contact can change in either direction over the course of time.

When living with her parents, a girl must behave like the 'good' and decent daughter. Runaway girls, on the contrary, seek other meanings for the concept of the 'good' girl. For those who have lost their virginity another acceptable construction has to be found to compensate for the low status that running away brings. Educational achievement is an important source of status mentioned by a number of girls. 'I want to study, because it gives you power.'

The girls who see their parents only now and again do not wish to return to the parental home. As one Moroccan girl explain after a weekend visit to her parents: 'It's impossible! I have changed too much. I have to adjust myself to their situation. I don't smoke, I don't use make-up and I don't feel comfortable! I can't just talk about marriage and children!'

They do not, however, want to lose contact with their family all together. They claim they need family contact for their own personal well-being. Most girls who do lose touch with their family find it very difficult to adjust to the situation. As one Turkish girl who has not seen her parents for five years told me: 'I have still problems with it, but they wanted to kidnap me.'

Turkish and Moroccan parents feel that a girl should live with her family. Girls who live independently, or together outside of matrimony with a boyfriend, are stigmatized by their ethnic group. Although the girls claim not to like living on their own, they are also confronted with the difficulty of participating as an individual in the life of their own community. The ambiguous relationship they have with their own community causes them to avoid regular contact with their fellow countrymen. This is, however, not always possible. At school, or in the workplace, they are generally confronted with members of their own community. The girls try to avoid intimate questions on their background particularly those concerning where, and with whom, they live. This is not always easy as casual conversations between migrants invariably begin with questions on this subject. As one Turkish girl put it: 'It is only acceptable to live apart from your parents if you were unable to find a job in your own neighbourhood. But I don't tell the parents of the Turkish children I work with that I live unmarried with my boyfriend. If I did then my status would go down.'

Girls who lose contact with their family fear their parents discovering their present address. This is sometimes a reason for them to move to another city and take an assumed name.

Relationship with Dutch society: 'But you are different'

Although these runaway girls have a bad name in their own community, this stigma does not extent to their contacts with Dutch people. Most of these girls have a modern outlook on life which does not fit easily with the stereotypical image of traditional Turkish or Moroccan womanhood. In their contacts with Dutch society much emphasis is placed upon their ethnic background. What is their response to this reaction? One Turkish girl told me:

> Most people think I'm Italian as I do not really look Turkish. When I tell them my real descent, people are surprised because I don't wear different clothes and a headshawl.

The Dutch often ask the runaway girls how long they have lived in the Netherlands or compliment on their Dutch. This they do even with girls who have lived their whole life in the Netherlands.

> A Dutch woman told me that I was so different. When I asked her how many Moroccans she had ever spoken to, it appeared that I was the first one. How can she know that I'm different. She has no right to say this. I'm not different. I'm Moroccan, and there are thousands of Moroccans like me. What really annoys me is that Dutch people do not let me have a private life. People think Moroccans are all the same. For example, they ask me questions about my virginity. I think this is none of their business.

Girls are also confronted with negative remarks made by the Dutch about their own ethnic group.

> They expect that Turkish girls may not choose their own husbands. Why do they always think so negatively about Turkish people? They stated that these remarks were not meant for me, they did not consider me Turkish. They regard me as Dutch because I speak the language so well. But I am not Dutch.

As Richard Jenkins (1986: 178) has pointed out, ethnicity is often stressed as a response to such stereotyping. This would appear to be the case with the runaway girls I interviewed. In their daily association with the Dutch they emphasize their ethnicity above all else while affirming a desire to be accepted as individuals. They perceive themselves as open-minded towards the Dutch, yet feel neither comfortable nor accepted in their contacts with everyday Dutch society. Although their relationship with their own ethnic community is ambiguous, they appear to be more Turkish or Moroccan than they had originally thought.

In their interaction with Dutch people the girls are made aware of their own cultural values which they had previously taken for granted. A few have a relationship with a Dutch boyfriend which further confronted them with different cultural norms, this time in the private sphere. They claim, for example, to attach a different meaning to such concepts as the family and hospitality, two areas of social life where ethnic boundaries are particularly demarcated, and where differences become especially clear. As one Turkish girl who lives with her Dutch boyfriend told me:

> What I have noticed is that for a lot of Dutch people the family is not very important. It's just nice. If one does not live at home anymore then they see each other only on birthday parties. There is not a very strong bond. Turkish people are very close. My sister plays in a theatre group and when she has a performance we all go to watch her. In my boyfriend's family most of them do not even know what the others do.

A Moroccan girl told me of her past experience of visiting Dutch friends around dinner time:

> They told me to sit down and wait until they had finished. Once, when I called to ask a Dutch girlfriend to come and play outside, her parents asked me to return after they had finished dinner. Moroccans would ask you to come in and have some dinner with them. We don't say straight away that it is not possible.

These sort of reactions by the Dutch cause runaway girls to become more aware of their ethnic descent rather than to feel accepted by the host community. They discover that everything is not as positive in the Dutch culture as it at first appears to be.

The runaways interpret Dutch family bonds as being weak and, for this reason, reject them. Although their relationship with their own family remains problematic, it is still of great importance to them. When faced with Dutch social norms on, for example, how guests are received, they feel these norms to be lacking a sense of hospitality essential to own their ethnic group. The net result of such realizations is to further enhance their appreciation of their own culture.

Synthesis

Who do runaway girls[7] mix with when they live on their own? If they do still have contact with their families, then they often feel uncomfortable in the parental home. Associating with Dutch people is also not easy, although a few do have Dutch friends. They seek the company of other Moroccan or Turkish youngsters with similar experiences. Unfortunately, this is not easy as their numbers are so few. Some still maintain friendships with other runaway girls whom they met during their stay in hostels. Others told me of the closeness of their relationship with their sisters. Runaway girls form their own tiny youth culture together with other youngsters from a whole range of cultural backgrounds.

A few of the Turkish runaway girls I spoke with maintained regular mutual contacts. Their often lukewarm reception in Dutch society, in combination with their marginal position within their own community, caused them to become more conscious of their own ethnic identity than they were when living at home with their families. Runaway girls still consider themselves as Moroccan or Turkish. Yet how can they give meaning to this identity? The response of one girl, already a runaway for seven years, offers us some insights into this question:

> For long time I denied my Turkish descent. I never told people I was Turkish because I did not feel really Turkish. When I first left home, I didn't meet a lot of Turkish people anymore. Now I want to change this situation. I am Turkish and I want to stay Turkish.

As we saw earlier, the implicit meanings attached to both the family and to hospitality would qualify them as ethnic markers. Only the demarcation they symbolically represent is minimal when compared to the cultural divide that attitudes on virginity create between the Moroccan or Turkish parents on one hand, and the Dutch on the other. Runaway girls no longer fit with their parents' conceptualization of what constitutes a 'good' Turkish or Moroccan girl. Their general views on gender relations do not differ significantly from their Dutch peers. As I explained earlier, they are also not recognized immediately as Moroccan and Turkish in their daily contacts with Dutch people.

They seek symbols able to give meaning to their ethnic identity. The girl I quoted above continues her story:

> I have started to listen more to Turkish music. It disgusted me before but now I appreciate it more and go to Turkish music events now and then. I used to dislike Turkish food very much. At home I was a bad eater. Now I prepare it myself. In a certain sense this belongs to you, it is still a part of what you are.

Her Turkish girlfriend told me how they were taking belly-dancing lessons together, desired to learn their language better, and were planning to holiday in Turkey. A similar attitude could found among the Moroccan girls: 'when I visit Moroccan parties I enjoy myself very much. I am glad to be Moroccan.'

Counterpoised to this desired return to their ethnic 'roots' is the influence that living in the Netherlands exerts upon their development of a cultural identity. Faithy and others told of their partial adoption of a number of Dutch cultural traits. Although they wished to be hospitable in the terms laid down by their own community, they found this too time-consuming within the Dutch context and so reinterpreted this practice giving it another meaning which is more in the mode of a Dutch attitude. As Faithy explained: 'sometimes I like to be alone, listen to music and do some reading. When a friend rings on the door, I often ask them to return another time.'

This behaviour is contradictory to the norms of Faithy's ethnic community. The net result is a synthesis of her parents' cultural identity with that of the dominant Dutch culture.

Concluding remarks

In this chapter I have reviewed the kinds of conflicts Moroccan and Turkish girls have with their parents which lead them to run away from home. The low social position of Moroccan and Turkish migrant families, and their sometimes unstable family situation, makes for a very complex situation in the Dutch context. Parents want to protect their daughters against 'bad' Western influences by exerting severe control over them and restricting their movements.

The girls are, however, not socialized only by their parents. Compulsory school attendance also has a considerable influence. Through education they come into contact with their peers. The fact that the daughters function more adequately in Dutch society than their parents strengthens their position in the family. Daughters share symbols like virginity with their parents but not their meanings and consequences. They try to negotiate with their parents on the meanings in order to obtain a broader interpretation. As a final desperate measure, when no common definition can be reached, the girls run away from home. One-third of the girls I interviewed had later returned home. By running away they had increased their negotiating position with respect to their parents, and some girls even managed to force through several of the changes they wanted. The other girls I spoke with stayed away from home.

Moroccan and Turkish runaway girls have a bad reputation in their communities; they are stigmatized as 'whores'. Runaway girls try to find other meanings for a 'bad' girl. Shortly after running away most girls say that virginity, especially in the meaning of the preservation of the hymen, is still significant for them. Soon, however, if they fall in love or do not return home, they start to question its importance. They try to distinguish themselves from the so-called 'bad' runaway girls, those who they consider to be 'boy-crazy'. Although the girls themselves are also no longer virgins, they were in love or had plans to marry.

The girls look for other acceptable means to compensate for the low status that being a runaway brings. To the parents and members of their ethnic community, a 'good' girl lives with her parents, is a virgin and behaves decently. The runaway girls, most of whom live on their own, try to give another meaning to this concept. In their view, being a 'good' girl is not necessarily related to virginity but more to educational achievement or the attainment of a good profession. Contacts with boys are not forbidden; a girl may have one serious boyfriend with whom she will eventually go to live. However, their parents, and their ethnic community in general, still define 'good' girls more by their decent behaviour and less by their school record. The runaway girls try, therefore, to avoid regular contact with their own ethnic group, something that is not always easy or possible.

Runaway girls have a bad name in their own community. Most of those I interviewed have a modern outlook and do not easily fit the stereotype image of the traditional Turkish or Moroccan woman. In their daily contacts with the Dutch, hence they do not feel comfortable and accepted in their contacts with host community. Although their relationship with their own ethnic community is an ambiguous one, contact with Dutch people generally causes them to feel more Turkish or Moroccan than ever before. They become more aware of their own cultural values, which they had earlier either rejected or taken for granted. Runaway girls are no longer part of their parents ethnic community, yet neither do they feel accepted by the Dutch. They have crossed the ethnic boundary delimited by their parents and respond by starting to form a youth culture together with friends of different cultural backgrounds in which both ethnic and Dutch symbols are employed.

Notes

1 It is estimated that every year 30,000 Dutch youngsters aged between twelve and eighteen (two percent) run away from home (Angenent 1993:20). Exact figures cannot be given because not all runaways are registered with police or social service institutions (*ibid.* p.19). The figures I give here are taken from a Youth

Social Welfare Institution (JAC) in Utrecht. In 1982 11 runaway girls of Moroccan and Turksih origin asked the JAC for assistance. By 1984 that figure had risen to 50 (*Vrij Nederland* 5/3/85).
2   Research has also been conducted with fifty-one Surinamese runaway girls (Brouwer, Lalmahomed and Josais 1992)
3   Between 1986 and 1989, 95 Muslim girls (two-thirds Moroccan and one-third Turkish) stayed at the first hostel. Sixty-eight Moroccan and 32 Turkish girls sought refuge at the girl-only hostel over a period of one and a half years (Brouwer, Lalmahomed and Josais 1992: 74-75).
4   In 1989, 7455 Turkish and 5850 Moroccan girls aged between fifteen and nineteen years were resident in the Netherlands (Brouwer, Lalmahomed and Josais 1992:13).
5   As of January 1989, the total number of foreigners resident in the Netherlands was 624,000 (4.2% of the total population). The largest group were Turkish (177,000) followed by the Moroccans (140,000) (see WRR 1989: 66-67).
6   Coffee shops are not desirable places for girls in the eyes of parents; they are places where men congregate and where hash is sometimes smoked.
7   This question I can only answer from the responses of my research sample of twenty runaway girls. One-third eventually returned home while the rest remained at a hostel.

References

Angenent, H. (1993) *Weglopers*, Nijkerk: Intro.
Anthias, F. (1992) *Ethnicity, Class, Gender and Migration: Greek-Cypriots in Britain*, Avebury: Aldershot.
Barth, F. (1969) 'Introduction', in: F. Barth (ed.) *Ethnic Groups and Boundaries: The Social Organisation of Culture Difference*, London: George Allen & Unwin: 9-38.
Brouwer, L. (1992) 'Binding Religion: Moroccan and Turkish Runaway Girls', in: W.A.R. Shadid and P.S. Van Koningsveld (eds.) *Islam in Dutch Society: Current developments and future prospects*, Kampen: Kok Pharos: 75-89.
Brouwer, L., H. Lalmahomed and H. Josias (1992) *Andere tijden, andere meiden. Een onderzoek naar Marokkaanse, Turkse, Hindostaanse en Creoolse wegloopsters*, Utrecht: Jan van Arkel.
Buijs, F. (1993) *Leven in een nieuw land. Marokkaanse jongemannen in Nederland*, Utrecht: Jan van Arkel.
Cohen, A.P. (1989) *The Symbolic Construction of Community*, London: Routledge (first published in 1985).
Davis, S. Schaefer and D.A. Davis (1988) *Adolescence in a Moroccan Town. Making Social Sense*, New Brunswick and London: Rutgers.

Feddema, R. (1992) *Op weg tussen hoop en vrees. De levensoriëntatie van jonge Turken en Marokkanen in Nederland*, Utrecht: Jan van Arkel.
Hastrup, K. (1978) 'The Semantics of Biology: Virginity', in: S. Ardener (ed.) *Defining Females: The Nature of Women in Society*, London: Croom Helm: 49-66.
Jenkins, R. (1986) 'Social Anthropological Models of Inter-ethnic Relations', in: J. Rex and D. Mason (eds.) *Theories of Race and Ethnic Relations*, Cambridge: Cambridge University Press: 170-187.
Kagitcibasi, C. (1989) 'Child Rearing in Turkey: Implications for Immigration and Intervention', in: L. van den Berg-Eldering and J. Kloprogge (eds.) *Different Cultures, Same School: Ethnic Minority Children in Europe*, Lisse: Swets en Zeitlinger BV.
Kandiyoti, D. (1987) 'Emancipated But Unliberated? Reflections on the Turkish Case', *Feminist Studies* 13 (2).
Mernissi, F. (1978) 'The Patriarch in the Moroccan Family: Myth or Reality?', in: J. Allman (ed.) *Women's Status and Fertility in the Muslim World*, New York: Praeger: 312-333.
Penninx, R. (1989) *Minderheidsvorming en emancipatie. Balans van kennisverwerving ten aanzien van immigranten en woonwagenbewoners*, Alphen aan den Rijn/Brussel: Samsom.
Tennekes, J. (1990) *De onbekende dimensie. Over cultuur, cultuurverschillen en macht*, Leuven/Apeldoorn: Garant.
Vries, M. de (1987) *Ogen in je rug. Turkse meisjes en jonge vrouwen in Nederland. Met een bijdrage van Willem van Schelven*, Alphen aan den Rijn/Brussel: Samsom.
Wetenschappelijk Raad voor het Regeringsbeleid (WRR) (1989) *Allochtonenbeleid*, Den Haag: SDU.

10 Growing Up as a Muslim in Germany: Religious Socialization Among Turkish Migrant Families

Lale Yalçin-Heckmann

Research on labour migrants in Europe forms the main body of work in migration studies and in the sociology and anthropology of migrant groups. In each European country sociologists, social geographers, historians and anthropologists approach various aspects of migration and, depending on their own academic focus and scientific interest, emphasize one or several aspects of the migration phenomenon over the others. For instance, sociological approaches to migrant populations in Germany have tended to focus on social integration and identity questions, whereas anthropological studies emphasize more cultural distinctiveness and change within the migrant community. The social scientific debate on the nature and status of labour migrants' presence in Germany is based mainly on studies of Turks. However, depending on the purpose and context of the study, sometimes the object of analysis is defined as Turks and other times as Muslims.[1] This is not only an inevitable outcome of the multiple and complex social markers containing this particular migrant population, but it also reflects at least two more dimensions of representation, which are at times problematic and controversial.

To begin with, sociological studies of Turkish migrants, especially those working with 'integrationist' or 'assimilationist' assumptions, tend to group together all the norms, values and attitudes of migrants. This is especially the case for first-generation migrants, who are thought to have brought their 'cultural-baggage' with them from the country of origin, under the label 'tradition' or more specifically, as Islamic cultural heritage. Various symbols and forms of behaviour (such as the issue of women wearing or not wearing the headscarf or parents allowing or not allowing their daughters to mix with boys or go swimming) are classified as reflecting strong or moderate Islamic views. Moreover, religiosity is measured by the frequency of attending the mosque, being able to read the Koran or the performance of the prescribed daily prayers. Hence, one outcome of this approach of assessing religiosity and the nature of Islam among Turkish migrants is the prominence given to the exoteric and visible aspects of Islam as criteria for measuring and quantifying religiosity.

A second dimension in such studies is that they mirror the dominant representation of Islam in the wider European context and discourse: migrants are perceived by the majority non-Muslim society as Muslims in certain contexts and instances. For example, Muslims are identified primarily as such when they are visible in the public (with headscarves, beards, mosques, halal butchers etc.). They are perceived as Muslims more at certain moments of political and historical developments than others, i.e. more so during the Gulf War but less so during the xenophobic attacks on foreigners in Germany after the reunification. How Muslim migrants themselves manage these various contextualizations of definition and perception and how they manage the varied emphases put on their Muslim identity and its markers are themes which are not sufficiently discussed in sociological studies on Muslim migrants in Germany.

This chapter aims to reveal such omissions and emphasize the role of religion in the everyday life of Turkish migrants, the processes of religious socialization and religious practice within the migrant family. It explores such questions as the centrality of religion in migrants' daily lives, religion as a source of identity and identification, interpretations of religious attitudes and practice depending on various socio-economic factors, as well as migration-related and symbolic particularities.

The above-mentioned sociological approach of placing religion in a central position in migrants' lives arises partly from the difficulty of assessing the relative impact of other social, economic and political processes in migration. According to Turner (1991), the role of religion in modern and pre-modern societies still needs further analysis and theoretical debate. As for the migrants, 'the persistent sociological assumption that in pre-modern societies the lives of people were thoroughly embraced by a common culture which gave immediate significance to human existence' (Turner 1991: 238) has been taken as literally applicable to migrants, and understood as meaning that common culture, religious culture and immigrant culture are one and the same. Inquiries into the religious experience of lay people have also borrowed concepts such as 'folk Islam', 'traditional Islam' or 'official Islam' from the studies on Islam in traditionally Muslim countries, without sufficient critical assessment of the possible modifications these multiple traditions have gone through during the 30 years of migration. Without paying due attention to the complexity of migration experience, which contains various processes of adaptation, accommodation, individual and/or collective organisation and change, it is not possible to attain an accurate and differentiated picture of 'migrant Islam'.[2] A fruitful approach to the convergence of Islam and migration should combine the concerns with the subjectivity of the social actor and the subjective religious experience together with the effects of religious practices and institutions.

The study presented here takes up specific aspects of Islam among Turkish migrants in Germany, although it also holds wider implications for the role and status of Islam in Europe in general. Entitled 'Religious socialization among the Turkish migrant families in Germany',[3] the research deals with various aspects of religious socialization of Turkish children and youth in Germany. It involved 82 qualitative interviews with members of 30 households. Seventeen of the interviews were with children aged 8-9, 17 aged 14-15 and the rest with parents. Turkish teachers who teach Turkish children in different types of classes and schools were also questioned. Lastly, participant observation at school, in the classroom and in mosques provided important insights and background information. In the course of the research the following questions were asked:

- How and what kinds of religious concepts and ideas are transmitted within the families of Turkish migrants? How and what types of religious practice are children taught within the family?

- How do children and teenagers perceive the transmission of this knowledge and belief system, and how do they interact with it?

- What sorts of dynamics shape the transmission and socialization of religious values and concepts?

- To what degree do parents or other persons within or outside the family act as models for behaviour?

- Are there similarities and/or differences between the parents' and children's attitudes towards Islamic institutions, mosques and towards teaching religion at local schools or at the mosque?

- How do families as a group and as individuals practice religion, and how are differences within the family and between members explained and accommodated?

- What are the attitudes towards the non-Muslim social environment, and what differences are there between the parents' and the children's points of view on this?

These research questions have been explored for a particular sample of Turkish migrant families living in Nürnberg. As a result of the sampling technique,[4] the parents I interviewed varied considerably in terms of place of origin within Turkey and their level of education. The length of stay in Germany for 96 per cent of the parents, however, was at least 11 years; and 92 per cent of the parents had been living in Nürnberg for 10 years or more. This means that almost all (94%) of the children aged 8-9 were born in Germany, even if some of them had spent a few years in Turkey and were taken care of by relatives. As for the teenagers, 70 per cent of them were born in Germany; some had lived there all the time, whereas others had either migrated later in childhood or spent several years intermittently in Turkey. Some of the latter, a group composed of late-comers and temporarily absent children, had irregular and disrupted school histories and migratory biographies, having changed their place of residence more than once between Turkey and Germany.[5] In fact, separation within the family is the most typical characteristic of Turkish migrant families. Not only are teenagers and younger children separated from the parents due to migration and work conditions, but also husbands and wives are separated from one another due to migration policies and economic considerations. The wives especially had waited to join their husbands; within the sample, 24 out of 27 wives had experienced a type of separation from her other family members. The migrant women who started working after having children often sent them to their relatives in Turkey, hence being separated first from the husband while waiting to be taken to Germany, and then being separated from their own children, because of child minding difficulties. All of these disruptions within the family are bound to have an effect on socialization practices and attitudes.

In terms of occupation, the majority of parents were unqualified factory workers but there were a few self-employed and white collar employees. About one in five of the mothers and one in twenty of the fathers were illiterate, and there were very few parents who had finished a secondary school education in Turkey. The mean household size of the sample was 5.6;

Growing Up as a Muslim in Germany 171

55 per cent of the households had 3-5 members and 44 per cent had 6-8 members, which means a relatively high number of large households.

In order to discuss the particular characteristics of 'migrant Islam' among Turks in Germany, I shall first list some general trends of the attitudes of parents and children in relation to religious education at home and at school versus the mosque. As a way of illustrating the nature of information available from family visits and individual interviews with family members, and of contrasting them to general trends, I then present four case studies of families. The types of religious beliefs, meanings and practices within these families are discussed and compared.

A selection of findings and general trends

One of the most striking outcomes is the high proportion of parents who acknowledge the need for Koran courses, which are organised by various mosque organizations. There were only 4 or 5 parents (out of 49) who definitely rejected a need for them altogether. The approval of Koran courses is for many, nevertheless, a matter of principle. They almost all support the idea, but whether the parents really would consider or do send their children to such courses varied significantly. In fact nearly half (16 out of 34) of the children and teenagers had never visited a Koran course in the mosque. Many parents expressed their dissatisfaction with such courses because of the alleged involvement of the religious organizations with politics. Others gave the quality of imams as their reason for not wanting to send the children to them. Yet others expressed the objection that Koranic teaching was an extra burden for children in addition to their school work. Similar arguments have been made about Koran courses in Britain and France (Joly 1988; Leveau 1988).

In addition to acknowledging the usefulness of Koran courses, many parents stressed the value of possessing 'knowledge' about Islamic religion and culture. A significant number valued Islamic teaching for the sake of the 'knowledge' which is transmitted. For some this was needed for social skills and was important for the individual's identity within the ethnic community. Others stressed the value of such knowledge for transmitting basic moral values. For yet others such knowledge was a prerequisite for belief, and a life without the belief was unthinkable.

Knowledge on Islam was often described as 'technical' knowledge. Parents reported that their children 'know' about Islam, giving examples as to how many and which prayers they could recite by heart, if they know the pillars of Islam (*-slam'-n -artlar-*) and the pillars of belief (*iman-n-artlar-*) by heart. Having said this, it should be added that the interpretation of religious knowledge as a kind of 'technical' knowledge was considered to have a potential (sacred power) which could be channelled into different spheres. Apart from being the basis for practice and belief (a point which I elaborate below), parents referred to this knowledge as laying the fundaments for proper moral education, through which children were expected to develop balanced and responsible personalities. For instance, a father explained the use of teaching Islam (at home and at school) with the following argument: the knowledge on religious sins (*günah*) and prohibitions (*haram ve yasaklar*) would protect the child from evil deeds (literally from 'dirt' and 'dirty things', in Turkish *pislikler*). His wife, however, underlined another dimension, the unexpected and sometimes undesirable effects of this knowledge: her elder son, who had attended Koran courses, got so involved in religious matters (*kafay- kapt-rd-*, literally 'he lost his head'), that he wanted to change his own life style (by sleeping in the mosque, wearing ostensibly non-European style of clothes, not going to school on Friday and getting the school authority's permission to attend the Friday prayers in mosque instead), as well as his mother's lifestyle (the son demanded that the mother start covering her hair and dress herself according to the Islamic code). Here the mother's emphasis was on the uncontrollable effects of religious knowledge, without necessarily connecting it to political Islam or to the political activities and education by mosque organizations.

Although the transmission of religious knowledge in Koran courses or otherwise was conceived as a prerequisite for attaining belief, the relationship between belief and practice, that is practising the rituals and prescriptions, was seen and described as a complex phenomenon. Many parents (women more often than men) expressed the strength of the wish to practice religion as *the* determining factor. In other words, knowledge was to come first and belief afterwards. Many parents saw their duty towards their children as enabling the transmission of this knowledge, through teaching them at home, sending them to Koran courses or only in local schools. Nevertheless, belief could not be maintained or enriched without practice, and practice (especially but not only for children) is possible only if there is a strong wish and psychological disposition for it. This wish is explained as something coming from 'inside', from *'gönül'* (heart) and formulated as *'içten gelmek'* in Turkish (coming from the heart). Parents often used this expression to refer to the particular moment of beginning the practice, not only for themselves but also for the children. Hence a child wanted to fast in Ramadan, because it was his or her wish to do so (*içinden geldi*, 'it came from her heart'); or else a parent had all the knowledge and knew his/her duties towards Allah, but somehow had not started or carried on with the practice, because it had not come from 'inside' (*içinden gelmedi*). What is significant here is that this wish coming from 'inside' was not mentioned as an excuse for the lack of practice alone. It was used for explaining the existence *or* the lack of practice, by believers of varying kinds, including parents engaged in political and organised Islam, to those for whom religion was a secondary issue.

Children 8 to 9 years old mostly had a depth and strength of religious knowledge reflecting the attitudes and orientations of the parents. The religious concepts of sin (*günah*) or merit (*sevap*) reflected primarily the everyday knowledge of proper religious *and* social behaviour. For instance, in children's answers, the attributes listed as sin range from disobeying parents, eavesdropping, quarrelling with friends to stepping on bread on purpose, stealing, smoking hash or selling it. Therefore, 8-9 year-old children hardly differentiate the concept of sin from the concept of bad deeds valid also in non-religious contexts. This reflects the overlap of moral categories derived from religion and ethics. From the actor's point of view, however, the religious category of morals 'encompasses' the non-religious category, in the sense Baumann has used the term 'encompassement' between different religious traditions (Baumann 1995). From the emic perspective, therefore, the religious category of morals has a priority over the non-religious. As a result, it would be categorically difficult (if not impossible) to imagine morals without religion.

Nevertheless, to the question of 'whether all Muslims were good', children answered with a significant degree of variation. The answers partly reflected the points of view of the parents, which qualified some Muslims as being better than others; but, nevertheless, the answers suggest highly differentiating cognitive processes in general,[6] especially concerning the differences and diverging points of views within the ethnic community. For instance, 8-9 year-old girls had adjusted their perceptions of good/bad Muslims on the basis of the adults' expectations from them, such as adopting the Islamic dress code. Hence, for this age group the debate among the

Turkish migrants on the Islamic female dress and the headscarf is already accepted as a criterion for classifying Muslims, good or bad.

Another significant trend for this age group is the undifferentiated usage of national/ethnic and religious identity categories. For many children not only was the concept and term 'religion' *per se* foreign,[7] but being a Turk was necessarily understood as being also a Muslim, and hence being German, being also Christian. That some Germans were or had become Muslims was known, but this was seen as an aberration, articulated by a few children as if Germans had become Turks.

That Turkish and Muslim identities overlap and that this was seen as natural is also evident in attitudes towards teaching Islamic religion at local schools. The Bavarian school system allows for a choice between taking religion or ethics as part of the curriculum. However, many pupils and parents were not aware of this offer, and for almost all of them the fact that Turks go to the Islamic religion class was only natural. Moreover, in schools where Islamic religion is not offered within the curriculum, ethics is compulsory. Turkish pupils attend this course even if they are religious and believers. The noncommittal content of the course and the particular composition of the class with pupils from all types of denominational (from atheists to independent church membership) backgrounds is also a concern for the Turkish pupils and their parents.

Although almost all Turkish children go to Islamic religion courses at primary and secondary schools, only the children who visit additional Koran courses organised by religious associations had visited a mosque. Other children had either never seen a mosque from inside, or else they visited one during vacations in Turkey.

The type of schooling, that is Turkish-speaking national class or German class attendance, is directly correlated to (even if there is no causal relationship to) Koran course attendance. In other words, children who visit Turkish classes show a higher propensity to attend Koran courses than children in German classes. The attendance of Koran courses also seems to be closely correlated to the family type. Nevertheless, many of the children who are referred to here as attending Koran courses are actually attending the religion courses offered by the mosque organizations. These are religion courses of varying length, and many children have gone to them without being able or wishing to continue to the advanced religion courses, where reading the Koran begins. Less than a quarter of the children and teenagers had attended the courses offered by the mosque organisations for a period of more than one year, where they are likely to have started reading the Koran. Social contacts between Turkish and German pupils seem to show significant differences according to the type of schooling. Turkish pupils in German classes all had at least one good German friend, although this was an exception rather than the rule for the children in Turkish classes.

For 8-9 year-old pupils as well as the teenagers, religion was not a topic of discussion or conversation among peers and friends. This issue needs further exploration, but one interpretation may be that religious themes and symbols are particularly difficult to take up as a theme by children and youth from different religions.[8] A dialogue between youth of different religions in daily life and within face-to-face relationships, in the classroom as well as in the neighbourhood, does not happen automatically. In fact, teenagers say they try avoid religion as a theme of discussion within their peer group. Some teenagers mentioned having talked about Islam and Christianity particularly in the context of the Gulf War, at a time when many pupils in Nürnberg were involved in demonstrations against it. These discussions in classroom and among friends seem to have been an intellectual as well as emotional challenge for Turkish pupils.

The teenagers' attitude towards religion, religious belief and practice seems to be related to their overall status within the family and social group. Those teenagers, who seem to have inter-familial or cross-generational problems of being accepted by and autonomous from parents, are not so outspoken in their religious motivations and convictions. Those who seem to have established some status within the household however, are more open in their differences of opinion or acceptance of parental points of view on religious belief and practice.

Children and teenagers' views on attending Koran courses depend on the circumstances and context in which this takes place. Those who actually attended Koran courses mostly did so together with other siblings, friends and neighbours. Therefore, for some it was just another area of playful competition between siblings. In the eyes of the children, competition with siblings was a positive motivation for attending Koran courses; frustration, boredom or the harsh treatment of the *hoca* (Muslim priest) were equally legitimate but negative reasons for children's refusal to attend.

These general findings are based partly on the statistical analysis of interview texts. In the following section case studies on four families are presented and the qualitative and anthropological aspects of the interviews and research findings are explored. I chose four families for case study according to the following sociological criteria: the families show similarities in terms of parents' occupational background; all the families chosen have rather large households (Family A had 8, family B 7, families C and D 6 persons per household respectively); the families lived in different neighbourhoods, their children attended different schools, in one of the two types of the Bavarian school system; the parents came all from village or small town background, were ethnically Turks and Laz, from the Black Sea and north eastern provinces of Turkey; and the parents have been living in Germany and in Nürnberg for 15 to 21 years.

Apart from these general common social and economic indicators, one important dimension divides the families into two groups: Families A and B do not belong to or support any organisation of political Islam,[9] whereas families C and D (at least the parents) do. On the basis of this classification, the following questions are raised comparatively. Firstly, how different are parents who are organised within political Islam from those who are not, in terms of their attitude towards the non-Muslim environment, and their approaches towards educating their own children? Secondly, are children of parents who are followers of political Islam and those who are not, different from one another in terms of being influenced and controlled by parents in a systematic and authoritarian way? Thirdly, to what degree do biographical and migratory particularities account for the differences in parental attitudes towards religious socialization? Lastly, to what extent do gender roles and gender based power relations within the family account for the type of religious practice and religiosity?

The four case studies

Family A lives in a low rent flat owned by the community, which is run-down and too small for the eight family members, including six children and two parents. The father (aged 40) is a Turk from the central Black Sea region of Turkey. He has primary school education and is an unskilled worker in a metal factory. He has been living in Nürnberg for 18 years and came to Germany after his mother, who had remarried after divorcing his father and was already working in Germany. The father still has a brother and a half-sister living also in Nürnberg and his mother has returned to Turkey. He is good humoured and open, but authoritarian towards his children and his wife. His wife (aged 33) is a Turk, from the same village as her husband but not his relative. She is illiterate, has been living in Nürnberg for 17 years and works as a part-time cleaner. The mother migrated after marrying and has no close relatives of her own in Germany. She is a jovial character, but has an insecure status and little respect within the family because of her illiteracy and temperament, or so she claimed. She believed herself to speak sufficient German and proudly declared that she solved all her problems with bureaucracy on her own. The parents have six children; the eldest son is 16, the two daughters are 15 and 14, and the three younger sons 13, 11 and 5½ years old. The eldest son is in a vocational training school (Berufsschule), the eldest daughter in Sonderschule (special school for pupils with learning problems), the next daughter and the son in secondary school (Hauptschule) and the next two boys in primary school (Grundschule); all of them were in Turkish classes. Apart from the eldest son, who seemed to be an important character in the family,[10] I met all the family members, visited them twice and interviewed the parents, the 14 year-old daughter and the 11 year-old son.

The family biography is marked by a striking but not too exceptional migratory practice: all the children were born in Nürnberg, but except for the youngest son, all of them were sent to the father's village to be taken care of by grandparents. The mother continued working after maternal leave (up to 6 months after the delivery) and the five children stayed in Turkey until 1984. In other words, the whole family came together only six years ago and the children were separated from their parents for 5-10 years.

Family B also lives in a low rent housing estate, but in a better furnished flat than the first family. Seven people (two parents, three daughters and two sons) live in the three room flat. The father (38 years old) is a Turk, was born in a village in north-eastern Turkey but resided in various small towns and in Istanbul before migrating to Germany, following his elder brother. He remained in Germany as a worker after marrying his wife, who is the daughter of another labour migrant from the same province but a different village. The father has primary school education and has been living in Nürnberg for 19 years; his two older brothers have returned to Turkey, but his nephews are settled in Nürnberg. He worked as an unqualified worker in a metal factory until recently and at the time of the interview he was unemployed. He is an open and outspoken person, with very critical views concerning the Turkish community in Nürnberg, German society in general, as well as his own family and person.

The mother (35 years old) came to Germany 20 years ago to join her parents. She finished primary school in Turkey and has done a brief vocational training in Germany. She has been working as a factory worker on and off, making breaks of 3-4 years after each child although she has been continuously employed for the past six years. She has relatives in Nürnberg and in the vicinity. The parents have many friends and acquaintances among the migrants from the same province. The children include three girls aged 15, 14 and 9 years and two boys aged 10 and 5. The eldest daughter has a very conspicuous 'tom-boy' role in the family; not only does she look like a boy, but behaves and is seen like one.[11] She seems to have a very influential position within the family, supervising the youngsters' homework and giving them permission to leave the house. She has mainly male friends, and attends the Turkish class of a Gymnasium, having attained the highest educational qualifications of all the family. The other children are in secondary and primary schools. The 14 year-old daughter attends a Turkish class but the 10 and 9 year-old siblings are in German classes. I visited the family twice and interviewed the parents, the 14 year-old daughter and her 9 year-old sister. All the children were born and brought up in Nürnberg and were never separated from the parents.

Family C lives in a community housing estate, with well-kept houses overlooking a communal park. Their rented flat is very tidy and decorated with a lot of hand-made embroidery, reflecting the taste of wealthy village families. The household is composed of six persons, two parents, three sons and a daughter. The two oldest sons are married and have separate households in Nürnberg. The father (50 years old) is a Laz Turk, comes from a village in the Black Sea region, has been living in Nürnberg for 21 years and migrated after his father, who also worked in Germany but died after returning to Turkey. He did not finished secondary school and worked first as cutler in Turkey and then as turner for 20 years in Germany in four different metal factories. In 1990 he started a partnership with his brother (also in Germany), his son and daughter and is now self-employed as travelling salesman in eastern German provinces, selling bluejean products from Turkey in open markets. He belongs to a mosque association and is in the running committee. The association, known as *Milli Görüs*, is affiliated with the conservative-religious Turkish Welfare Party (*Refah Partisi*) led by Erbakan (for the origins of this party see Toprak (1981), Sar-bay (1985) and Çak-r (1990: 214-25)).

His wife (aged 47) is also a Laz Turk, from the same province but a different village, and has been living in Nürnberg for 16 years. She is illiterate, has worked in agriculture in Turkey and is now a housewife in Germany. She has no kin in Germany but does have a brother in France. She has an open personality, is very homely and self-content. She lived 13 years with her in-laws in Turkey, four years separate from her husband, joining him in 1974. She is not directly involved in the mosque organization but feels herself deeply religious; her head is covered with a scarf at home and outside. The parents have many friends and acquaintances from their home province, as well as relatives among migrants in Europe. They have six children: they are aged 26 (son), 25 (son), 22 (daughter), 12 (son), 10 (son) and 9 (son) years old. The eldest son works in a factory, the second son is now a partner in his father's trade and the daughter is trained as hairdresser, although she also works with her father and brother. The other children are all at school (secondary and primary), attending Turkish classes. This is a conspicuously 'Muslim family' in terms of lifestyle and outlook, especially those of the parents. All the children have gone to Koran courses and the whole household fasts during Ramadan. I interviewed the parents and one of the younger sons.

Finally, *Family D* lives in a spacious and well furnished flat. The furniture and decorations in the living room are designed for large gatherings. The father explained that this was related to his mosque activities and to the fact that they often receive many guests. The household includes two parents, three children and the wife's sister, altogether six persons. The father (48 years old) is a Laz Turk, from a small town in the Black Sea region. He has been married three times, and from his first and second wives he has a son and a daughter. The daughter is married, has children and lives in a separate house in Nürnberg. The father had not completed his secondary education and owned and managed restaurants in various small towns in Turkey. He has been living in Germany for 19 and in Nürnberg for 14 of them. After migrating to Germany he worked in a big factory as car upholsterer. In 1984 he started his own private business as upholsterer and his workshop is under a small mosque opposite his house. He is in the mosque organization and spends much time in the mosque for prayers and for running its affairs. This religious association is affiliated with Cemalettin Kaplan and is considered to be one of the most radical from the Turkish state's point of view (see Biswanger and Sipahio-lu 1988; Gür 1993; Schiffauer 1997).

The father, with whom the interview was rather long, seems to have much experience in the politics of Islam and made a lengthy statement on the public aspects of Islam. He was also keen to know my aims and the possible uses of my research. He made it clear, that he was talking to me to fulfil his duty of delivering the political message on Islam, but that he chooses his personal contacts mainly from Islamist circles. He apologized for his wife, saying that she did not wish to talk to me because the interview was to be recorded. I could talk to her sister instead, from whom the following information was gathered.

The mother is 37 years old, comes from the same village as her husband, has primary school education and has been living in Germany for 15 years. She speaks little German and is a housewife. The children are 14 (girl), 11 (boy) and 6 (girl) years old respectively. The sister-in-law is a dependent of the father but is an illegal immigrant. All the children go to German classes, the youngest one to a nursery school run by the Evangelical Church. The eldest daughter wears a headscarf and has attended Koran courses. The 11 year-old boy still attends them. I interviewed the father and the son only.

Analysis of cases

Family A's general views of the migrant experience and their relation to German society is marked by a strong dichotomy in which the two value systems are mainly incompatible with each other. Both of the parents emphasize the incompatibility of the influences from the social environment (not only the German environment, but also partly including the Turkish community) and the education at home: children learn proper manners at home but forget it outside, according to the father. The parents, however, are not in agreement with each other over their educational styles, priorities and methods. The father seems to be the authority at home and also controls the mother's relations to her children. He feels himself superior to his wife in knowledge, education and his ability to control his temperament: he believes that his wife is illiterate and has an irritable temperament. He tells his children to obey only himself and not to mind the mother if she scolds them. She partly agrees with this control over her and is extremely concerned about the proper education especially of her daughters, expressing her frustration at having failed in education herself. This failure is reflected back on to her by the children's disrespect and disobedience.

Religious education is regarded by both parents as a necessary and fundamental part of their children's moral education. Although they recognize their responsibility for bringing them up as Muslims, they underline the importance of Koran courses and the education in the mosque. What they expect from these courses is less the perfect acquisition of Arabic prayers and religious prescriptions, but more something to counter the effects stemming from the social environment. The father explains the use of religious education, for instance, as preventing the daughters from using excessive make-up and the sons from cursing and using slang. Although he does not insist that his daughters wear headscarves, the mother says she wants her daughters to be protected from bad manners and bad habits. Her perception of Islam and how it is related to their life is shaped by an exoteric concern and definition of religion. She believes that Islam is mainly learned in Koran courses and that what she teaches her children about the religious rituals of everyday life (e.g. keeping oneself ritually clean, showing due respect for food and being able to distinguish ritually 'pure' from 'dirty') is not central to Islamic education. She also believes that learning the prayers, performing the *namaz* (prayer) and reading the Koran are the most important means of reaching salvation (*öbür dünyada abdest, namaz, oruç kurtar-r; ana-baba, karde- de-il*, literally one would be saved in the other world through the ritual cleaning, prayers and fasting one has done, not through parents or siblings). These goals are, however, very difficult to reach. She could not do it herself. Although she still wants to cover herself, perform *namaz* regularly and learn to read the Koran, she claims she cannot for two reasons. Firstly, it does not come from her heart/mind (*içinden gelmiyor*) and secondly, the conditions in Germany are unsuitable. Both parents express their desire to perform all the religious prescriptions and rituals regularly, and idealize the convenience of 'circumstances back home'. Nonetheless, they are also self-critical and realistic and admit that they neglected religious practice back in Turkey. They also acknowledge that there are Muslims in Germany who do perform everything properly and regularly. For the mother, religion signifies an area of failure in terms of self and educational accomplishments. Nevertheless, it is a fundamental part of their values and belief system.

As for the children, religious education for the 11 year-old son and the 14 year-old daughter (who were separated from the parents for 6 and 9 years respectively) began in Turkey and continued in Germany. The girl attended courses in the mosque in Turkey and later on with her sister and brothers in

Nürnberg. She does not currently practise any of the basic rituals except for fasting occasionally in Ramadan. Although she talks favourably about attending Koran courses, she cannot elaborate why this should be good. Due to problems at home and at school, religion seems to be a secondary issue for her. She makes efforts to fulfil her parents' expectations but these are apparently too great for her to cope with. She is notably withdrawn and unassertive compared to her younger brother, who takes initiatives, acts on his own, and has different views on religion and Islam. Like his sister, he conflates the categories of ethnic and religious identities, such that Turks and Muslims are synonymous, like Germans and Christians. Moreover, his classification of sins and religious merits coincides with the classification of good and bad deeds from the non-religious context. In other words, 'good' or 'bad' religious deeds are placed in the context of migration: among the sins he mentioned were stepping on bread (showing ritualistic respect to bread and to similar processed food), but also using heroin and selling hashish (one of the greatest evils of the European society, according to migrants with different political views).

Family B, although similar to Family A in terms of household size and composition, as well as occupational status, differs from them in terms of the power constellation and gender roles within the family. In Family B the parents seem to share with each other the responsibility for educating their children much more than in Family A. Family B's mother is regarded by her children as an authority making decisions and sometimes contradicting those of their father. She is also emotionally and socially closer to them than their father. The eldest daughter also has a significant role in decision-making and taking responsibility for others.

Their attitude and disposition towards the non-Muslim environment is differentiated and contextual. For the father, the ethnic and religious identity of Turks is inseparable, illustrated in his interpretation of any anti-Turkish slogan like 'Kanaken-Türken'[12] as a sign of hostility towards Turks cum Muslims. Moreover, in his opinion, Turks as Muslims are at the bottom of the ethnic hierarchy in Germany. He sees, nevertheless, a possibility of Muslims and Christians, Turks and Germans getting along with and even marrying each other. There is a difference between Germans who like the Turks and know about them, and those who do not. The mother is also in favour of having German friends and approves of the fact that her children have some. However, she is vehemently against a marriage between Germans and Turks, or between Sunni and Alevi Turks. She explicitly criticizes the Turkish community in Nürnberg, especially the way people judge one other's religiosity.

The mother's attitude towards religion and religiosity underlines the relationship between the two components of religion: practice and belief. In terms of practice, like her husband, she does not consider herself to be a good Muslim, because she does not perform the rituals and prayers as prescribed. Even so, she conducts a continuous vocal and philosophical debate with various voices among the Turkish community on the essentials of being a Muslim. For instance, she criticized a female neighbour, who is *kapal-* (covered according to Islamic prescriptions) and who had reprimanded the mother for not being *kapal-* and not coming to the mosque. According to the mother, she does not sit *kapal-* at home, but by working outside she helps her family and relatives in Turkey, and hence fulfils her duties as a Muslim. One does not need to go to the mosque, but can practice religion at home too. She does not want to send her children to Koran courses, as the older daughters already have many extra-curricular activities (like taekwando and music courses) and heavy work load from school. Like her husband, she fasts now and then and performs the *namaz*, if at all, during Ramadan irregularly.

The father, who was fasting on the day of interview, values religious knowledge highly, but does not insist on any Koran course attendance either. Religious knowledge and a positive disposition towards Islam is thought to be good for the children and the family: he wishes that at least one family member learns to read the Koran. On holy days and upon request, at least someone in the family should be able read the Book and do *sevap* (religious merit) for the whole family. The emphasis on the contagious quality of religious merits and the idea that good deeds could have a communal effect contrasts here with the individualized notion of religious merit and sin found in Family A's parents. The latter stress the importance of each family member performing the ablution (*abdest*), the prayer (*namaz*) and fasting (*oruç*) as the key to religious salvation.

The two daughters of Family B who were interviewed (aged 14 and 10 years) are both articulate and self-confident. The elder sister especially is highly sophisticated in her approach and interpretation of moral and religious issues. She not only questions the value of practice, the essentials of religious belief, but is also ironical, joking about her own attitude and understanding. Although she thinks that she has enough knowledge about religion, she jokingly said that she would 'burn in hell', if one were to believe others, because she wears mini skirts and shorts. Nevertheless, she believes that everyone needs to have a religion. Like her mother, she is very critical towards the prejudices and misunderstandings among the Turkish community concerning the virtue of women. The younger daughter has also not been to Koran courses but says that she enjoys religion classes at school and that she wished to attend the class herself (*içinden geldi*). She is in a German class and among the voluntary afternoon classes in Turkish she attends religion only. Compared to the child in Family A, her categories of sin and religious merit are more abstract and universalistic. She does not know how to do the prayers in *namaz*, but her knowledge and interest in other types of rituals, such as the recitation of *mevlut* for life-cycle rituals or *kandil* is elaborate.[13] She says that she prays regularly on her own for success at school, and also for poor and lonely people.

Family C, in comparison to Families A and B, is more publicly visible as Muslim. The father wears his beard in the 'Muslim' style and the mother wears a headscarf at home in addition to a long coat outside. All the children have been to Koran courses and the father is the vice-president of a mosque organization, known to be associated to '*Milli Görüs*' (National View) in Europe and *Refah Partisi* (Welfare Party) in Turkey. He openly supports the Party, displaying its symbols at home. This public image of the family has two particularities, reflecting the pluralism within the family and the significance of migrant biography.

The power constellation and the gender roles within the family are closely related to two things. First, the father's 'conversion' or return to Islam (*kapanma* according to the mother, a term normally used to describe the female seclusion in dress, covering the body and hair) as juxtaposed to the mother's religiosity, expressed as the maintenance of rural Islam. Second, the children's distance from Islamic practice and rules is publicly declared in the daughter's 'uncovered' (*aç-k*) outlook, her participation in public life and links with German society.

According to the father, his conversion to Islam occurred after he sent his children to Koran courses and became concerned with their slow learning. The mother's view is that his conversion has a much more fundamental and dramatic background; he had a serious alcohol problem and got cured after frequenting the mosque organization regularly. The father interprets his life before and after the conversion from the axis of this crucial experience. He is critical of his failures, of his non-Islamic way of life and his short-sightedness in not recognizing the social justice promised by Islam and seeking it at other places (such as socialist ideology). He recognizes his naivety in thinking that the utterance 'we are Muslims, *elhamdüllillah* (Praise Allah)' would be enough to be a real Muslim (similar to many Turks, who still think so), as well as the shortcomings of his own upbringing in which his father taught him to be just and fair but told him nothing particularly on Islam. By contrast, the mother's views reflect the continuity of her biography, that she was brought up to be very religious at home, that she 'learned nothing from them' (i.e. from her in-laws) and that her life style did not change significantly after migration.

The parents send their children to Koran courses because, according to the father, they cannot teach them Islamic beliefs as well as the teacher (*hoca*) in the mosque. The children learn the basic moral values there and are protected from evil deeds and thoughts. They have contrasting educational views and styles. The father, although he wishes to be close with and friendly to his children, is distant and authoritarian. The mother is emotionally very close to them and always there to fulfil their wishes. She also mediates between the children and their father. An outright conflict between the generations (such as the conflict within the Family A) could be avoided probably because of this mediation. Their daughter refuses to dress herself according to the Islamic code, arguing that she works outside and that she needs to interact fully with German society. Her father insists that the mother should put pressure on her, but the mother argues that one cannot force the children to practice Islam. She understands their daughter and does not think she has failed her religious duties. On the contrary, she proudly declares her pleasure in meeting her daughter's German friends, how they all like her and come to their house to eat Turkish delicacies.

The mother's covered dress style is by no means meant as a challenge to German society and values; she emphasizes how covering oneself and adopting modest behaviour (e.g. going one's own way and not provoking aggressive behaviour through one's own insulting gestures, critical looks or words) is the key for peaceful coexistence with the Germans. Like her husband, she believes she draws more criticism and intolerant behaviour from other Turks than from Germans. Even if commensality and ritual cleanliness are areas of potential conflict between Muslims and Christians, the parents see no serious barriers between the two religions (actually among believers) for getting along with each other.

Their 9 year-old son conforms to his parents' wishes and their control over him by going to the Koran courses in the mosque. He is, however, open in expressing his lack of enthusiasm for them. In his opinion they are boring and he would rather go shopping (*'Kauf'lara'*) or watch television on weekends. He maintains a more scriptualist kind of practice and belief; he performs the *namaz* in the mosque but does not fast (unlike the children in Families A and B, who tried to fast at least for a few days). Compared to the children from the previous families, he is more aware of the concepts and rituals which are central to religion (such as *namaz* prayers, the exact prescriptions concerning the ablution and its annulling), but less knowledgeable about those related to life-cycle rituals or Islamic historiography (such as *mevlut* or *kandil*).

To conclude, although the father adheres to political Islam and uses the points of view and arguments of political Islam (e.g. the relation between the state and religion, the meaning and practice of secularism, women's rights in Islam, Islam and social justice, the value of Koran courses) his family displays pluralistic practices and meanings. His young son has accumulated knowledge on Islam, but has a weak emotional attachment to religion, a fact known and accepted (though criticized of course) by the parents. The mother mediates between the father's and the children's views of Islam and thereby represents continuity in change, the link between different instances of time and space.

The analysis of the interaction within *Family D* will have to be restricted because of the missing interview with the mother. Her (or her husband's?) refusal to be interviewed, however, is already a political point and could be seen as setting the tone for this family's world view. The father used a sermon-like style of speech, with very few questions and making interventions presenting his views and experiences as he chose, often giving the impression of being used to such presentations of political Islam. The father's personal background and his subjective perception of, and identification with, Islam is marked by his effort to sustain some continuity with his social, religious and familial origins. He makes a claim for historical significance[14] by stressing how cultured, educated and holy his ancestors were, as signified by his grandfather's tomb in the ancient central mosque in his home town.[15] Hence, he sees himself as another link in this chain. He also had, however, traumatic experiences in his migrant life. Probably the most important one is that his 20 year-old son has left him. The father did not elaborate what exactly happened to him, but briefly mentioned that he 'lost' his son to 'the corrupt German society'. The father's perception of the non-Muslim environment is therefore characterized by a paradox. Although the German state and its system is just and 'truly secular', since there is no discrimination against the believers or against those who think and dress differently, the German people are 'cold' (exemplified by the lack of any human contact with his German neighbours for many years), their religion is 'erroneous' and their education 'corrupt' (exemplified by the widespread anxiety of Turkish parents for 'losing' their children, through heroin addiction, drug trafficking or prostitution). This paradox, however, is resolved at different levels, by keeping public and private spheres separately. In private, the father has contact with the community of believers only; in public, he maintains a formal contact with the German society and emphasizes the need of mastering their language. That is why he sees no contradiction in sending his children to German classes; as a matter of fact, according to the father, the children wanted to go to them themselves, because they thought other Turkish pupils had bad manners, were aggressive and full of gossip. His daughter does not mind being the only pupil with a headscarf in the classroom, as long as she gets the necessary education usable in the wider society.

Compared with the parents in other families, the father is the only one who addresses himself extensively to the more philosophical and essentialist aspects of Islam. He criticizes the secularist position with arguments from Islamic philosophy, elaborating on the nature of Divine Will, the nature of human beings, the reasons for seclusion and the question of why there is evil in this world. He often quotes from the Koran in Arabic and refers to the Hadith to support his arguments.

The 11 year-old son, in comparison to other children from previous families, has the best knowledge and the most sophisticated understanding of Muslim-Christian differences and resemblances. He performs the *namaz* regularly and goes to Koran courses everyday. He knows, however, that he could not be punished for not praying, because he is too young, according to the recommendations from the Hadith. Unlike the children from Families A and B he fasted only a few times, again following the prescribed practice for his age. Among all the children discussed from the four families, he is the only one who said he spoke with his classmates on the content and core of Islamic and Christian belief systems. He challenged a classmate on how Jesus Christ could be the son of God, when God did not have human qualities but Jesus did. Compared to the other children he makes the clearest differentiation between ethnic and national identities, pointing out that some Germans become Muslims and avoiding any preconceived certainty in identifying Turks and Germans from their looks. Despite being in a German class for two years, he claims to have no German friends. This may be considered normal, since he is in the mosque every afternoon.

Concluding remarks

This chapter has presented two main types of sociological findings concerning the forms of religiosity and religious socialization. In the section on the main trends, I have indicated the general support for Koran courses and the further conditions mentioned for actually sending children there. Various levels of interpreting Islam as knowledge and Islam as a belief system have been exemplified. Furthermore, the general patterns of contextualizing essential religious concepts such as sin, religious merit or fate have been shown for different generations.

The subsequent section turned to four case studies and presented a comparative analysis of parental and children's attitudes and behaviour concerning religiosity and religious socialization. The aim was to show the variety in Islamic interpretations and subjective perceptions without, as Loeffler rightly argues, over-interpreting this diversity by overlooking 'the subjectivity of the individual believer' (Loeffler 1988: 247). Loeffler notes that 'what we perceive as diversity, for the believer is a matter of right or wrong' (*ibid.*). The case studies presented above illustrate another dimension of this subjectivity; that it is not a finished process or a closed system, and that rights and wrongs are individually assessed and reorganized, as much within the family and as in the larger social group. They have shown that diversity could exist within the individual's world view and within the same family, where mechanisms such as contextual differentiation and separation of private and public act as means of accommodation and identity management. Finally, both the diversity and individual strategies are framed within the experience of migration. The migration specific discourse and perspectives are plausibly contained in 'migrant Islam', which proposes the exact contextualization of Islamic identity and formations in migration.

Notes

A slightly different version of this article has appeared in Turkish Families in transition, ed. G. Rasuly-Paleczek, peter lang, frankfurth/M., 1996. I am greatful to Ayse Saktanber for critique and comments on an earlier version.

1 Pnina Werbner (1992) takes an alternative approach to Muslims in Europe, in that she stresses the indexicality of social identity and recommends focusing on multiple identities, if they compose a coherent and consistent set and if they do not, on how the inconsistency is managed.
2 For a very similar use of the term 'migrant Islam' see Saint-Blancat (1993) who uses the terms 'migrant Islam' and 'Islam translanté' interchangeably.
3 The research project, which was undertaken between 1990 and 1993, was financed by the German Research Foundation (DFG) and was directed by the Chair of Islamic Studies, University of Bamberg.
4 The families were selected partly randomly - using a technique similar to quota sampling - and partly on the basis of several criteria: school children were chosen according to their sex, age, area of residence, the school and type of class attended. In the Bavarian education system there are two types of classes. *Zweisprachige Klasse* (commonly known as national classes) are composed of children of one nationality (i.e. all Italian, Turkish or Portuguese) and the language of tuition is primarily the language of that nationality. Turkish children attending 'national classes' are taught by native Turkish speakers mostly sent from Turkey. The other type of class is the *Regelklasse* (commonly known as German classes), in which a minority of foreign children learn together with mostly German pupils and in which the language of tuition is German. The foreign pupils usually have the possibility of doing extra hours in their own national language in the afternoon. The implication of these two types of class for the socialization of children is very significant, especially in terms of establishing early and lasting contacts and friendships among children of varying nationalities.
5 For the effects of such disruptions and separation form parents on children's achievement at school and on their futures, see Glumpler (1985).
6 Cognitive capacities of children and teenagers are bound to be different due to psychological and social factors. In this research however, I have not dealt with the exact depiction of cognitive capacities as I did not aim to develop scales of cognitive development for Muslim children. Cognitive capacities are seen here in general as a developmental process, without necessarily specifying the particular stage or capacity of the child or teenager.
7 This may of course arise from the difficulty of conceptualizing 'Islam' as a 'religion'. It was easier for children to discuss Islam and Muslims rather than religion and religiosity.

8 In another article (Yalçin-Heckmann 1994) I argue that cultural change is easier to acknowledge than religious change or religious syncretism. Hence, young people are more inclined to perceive changes in their own belief system as becoming more 'modern' (culturally) rather than becoming 'syncretic' and borrowing directly from other religious practices.
9 By political Islam I refer to Islamic organizations based in Germany, some 'illegal' in Turkey, with a political agenda for influencing and changing the political system in Turkey. For a comparison of different groups of such political Islamic associations in Germany, see Schiffauer (1992) and Gür (1993).
10 His taekwando trophies were proudly displayed in the living room, and his mother and sister praised his strict religious practice and personal integrity.
11 Her father said that he would not hesitate to leave her alone with a hundred men! He wanted to beat up a 'racist' neighbour who had insulted him and his daughter. Like the eldest son in Family A, the daughter's karate trophies were displayed in the living room.
12 The term has a derogatory meaning, but derives from a totally different context i.e. the French colonial experience in the South Pacific.
13 *Melvut* is a religious poem reciting the birth of the prophet Mohammed. *Kandils* are holy days marking important events in Islamic historiography, such as the birth of the Prophet or the revelation of the Koran to the Prophet.
14 For a discussion of the meaning of historical significance, clan *sharaf* (honour) and community in the Black Sea region of Turkey, see Meeker (1976).
15 This town is apparently known for its 'profoundly religious *hoca* families' (*derin hocalar*), according to a migrant friend from the same province (M. Karaalio_lu, personal communication).

References

Baumann, Gerd (1995) 'Convergence and Encompassement: Two Dynamics of Syncretization in a Multi-Ethnic Part of London', in: G. Baumann & T. Sunier (eds.) *Post-Migration Ethnicity: Cohesion, Commitments, Comparison*, Amsterdam: Institute for Migration and Ethnic Studies: 99-116.

Binswanger, K. and Fethi Sipahio-lu (1988) *Türkisch-Islamische Vereine als Faktor Deutsch-türkischer Koexistenz*, Benediktbeuern:Rieß-Druck und Verlag.

Çak-r, R. (1990) *Ayet ve Slogan: Türkiye'de-slami Olu-umlar*, Istanbul:Metis.

Glumpler, E. (1985) *Schullaufbahn und Schulerfolg Türkischer Migrantenkinder*, Hamburg: Verlag Rissen.

Gür, M. (1993) *Türkisch-islamische Vereinigungen in der Bundesrepublik Deutschland*, Frankfurt/M.:Brandes & Apsel.

Joly, D. (1988) 'Making a Place for Islam in British Society: Muslims in Birmingham', in: T.Gerholm and Y.G. Lithman (eds.. *The New Islamic Presence in Western Europe*. London and New York: Mansell: 32-53.
Leveau, R. (1988) 'The Islamic Presence in France', in: T. Gerholm and Y.G. Lithman (eds) *The New Islamic Presence in Western Europe*, London and New York: Mansell: 107-123.
Loeffler, R. (1988) *Islam in Practice: Religious Beliefs in a Persian Village*, Albany:State University of New York Press.
Meeker, M. (1976) 'Meaning and Society in the Near East: Examples from the Black Sea Turks and the Levantine Arabs (I)', *International Journal of Middle East Studies* 7: 243-270.
Saint-Blancat, C. (1993) 'Hypothèses sue l'évolution de l'"Islam transplanté" en Europe', *Social Compass* 40(2): 323-341.
Saribay, Ali Y (1985) *Türkiye'de Modernle-e Din ve Parti Politikas- "Milli Selamet Partisi Örnekolay-*, Istanbul: Alan Yay-c-k.
Schiffauer, W. (1992) 'Islamic Vision and Social Reality: The Political Culture of Sunni Muslims in Germany', in: S. Vertovec and C. Peach (eds.). *Islam in Europe: The Politics of Religion and Community*, Basingstoke: Macmillan: 156-176.
Toprak, B. (1981) *Islam and Political Development in Turkey*, Leiden: E.J. Brill.
Turner, B. S. (1991) *Religion and Social Theory*, London: Sage Publications.
Werbner, P. (forthcoming) 'On Mosques and Cricket Teams: Nationalism and Religion among British Muslims', in: F. Dasetto (ed.) *Muslim Organisations in Europe*, Paris: l'Harmattan.
Yalçin-Heckmann, Lale (1994) 'Are Fireworks Islamic? Towards an Understanding of Turkish Migrants and Islam in Germany', in: C. Stewart and R. Shaw (eds.) *Syncretism/Anti-Syncretism: The Politics of Religious Synthesis*, London: Routledge.

11 Educational Needs of Muslim Children in Britain: Accommodation or Neglect?

Marie Parker-Jenkins and Kaye Frances Haw

The controversy surrounding the publication of *The Satanic Verses* helped to unmask Muslim discontent in British society and although initial outrage directed at the author appears to have subsided, advocacy in relation to the educational needs of this group has not disappeared. Indeed, as sizeable Muslim communities in Britain become more politically active, there is a pressing need to respond to educational issues. This chapter is based on empirical research into the problem: an examination of the theory of pupil need as identified by Islamic writers; and an inquiry into what is actually taking place in British classrooms.[1] By researching the views of headteachers of private Muslim schools, and headteachers of state schools with significant numbers of Muslim children, the study draws on the experience of school practitioners and their perceptions of reality.

The discussion begins by placing the educational system in Britain into an historical context, providing a review of the aims of Islamic education and an examination of the concept of multiculturalism. Following this, a theoretical framework of needs is considered which is juxtaposed with the findings of the study. The results are then examined to discover areas of similarity and divergence in perception, and furthermore, the extent to which educational needs are being accommodated or neglected. Finally, the chapter concludes with a summary of the work achieved in British schools during the 1970s and 1980s, and explores the social and political ramifications of outstanding needs yet to be addressed.

Background

Events such as the 'Salman Rushdie Affair' and the Gulf War have served to highlight the discontent of some Muslims with British society. While feelings engendered by events such as these tend to ebb and flow, anxieties amongst the Muslim community concerning the education of Muslim children remain constant. Discontent over educational issues which revolve around the Education Reform Act (1988), accommodation of the special educational needs of Muslim pupils within the state school system, and voluntary aided status for Muslim schools serve to underpin and spearhead the concerns of some Muslim parents who feel increasingly disaffected with life in Britain.

The Muslim community in this country is not an homogenous one. It is multi-racial, multi-cultural and multi-lingual and comprises the largest religious minority in Britain today. It is this religious dimension which provides a uniting factor. Since Muslim immigrants first began arriving in the UK from the Indian sub-continent and parts of Africa in the 1950s, they have negotiated long and hard with local education authorities (LEAs) and other appropriate bodies for schools to accommodate the religious and cultural needs of their children (Nielsen 1986; *The Independent* 20/1/89). These efforts have met with only patchy success which has meant that some Muslim communities have felt the need of recourse to more radical solutions by establishing private Muslim schools, for which they are seeking to acquire voluntary aided status (Halstead 1986), or to explore the option of 'opting out' legislated for by the 1988 Education Reform Act.

For those Muslims who see themselves as swimming against the tide of increasing secularisation, the education system provides a focus for the incompatibility of values taught at home and those perceived to be advocated by the wider indigenous population and which are seen to be synonymous with those taught in state schools. Areas around the country which are densely populated by Muslims provide a variety of supplementary or Mosque schools for teaching the Qu'ran in the evenings or weekends (McLean 1985). It is estimated that approximately 90 per cent of Muslim children between the ages of 5-12 attend such schools at some time (Hussain 1990). In this way Muslim parents aspire to keep their children faithful in the face of perceived Western materialism and permissiveness. This generates debate over issues such as cultural diversity, social cohesion, and the extent of minority rights in a democracy. These will be explored within the context of the history of education in Britain, the aims of Islamic education and the concept of multiculturalism.

The development of education in Britain

After 1870, a battle began between the Church of England and the state over the control of education, and legislation passed in 1902 and 1906 established the principle of voluntary maintained denominational schools. These existed alongside those run by the local school boards (now LEAs). The 1944 Education Act added further to the development of voluntary schools creating different categories of government control. What is particularly important to this discussion is that the 1944 Act does not stipulate that only Christian churches or groups may apply for voluntary aided status for their schools. In fact Jewish schools have been established using this procedure and it is through this legislation that Muslim (and to a lesser extent Sikh and Hindu) groups are seeking state funding for their schools. The financial benefits are considerable: the Department for Education and Science may make discretionary grants of up to 85 per cent of the cost of the original purchase and extension of the buildings and pay running costs; while staff salaries are paid by the LEA. In January 1991 according to DFE (Department for Education) figures, about a third of state schools had voluntary status and are denominational. The pupils at these schools accounted for 23% of all pupils being educated in state schools (DFE 1991).

There are no clear figures as to the number of Muslim schools in Britain or pupils attending them. There were 15 private Muslim schools in January 1989 with plans to set up another 20 (*The Independent* 20/1/89). A directory of schools provided by the Muslim Education Trust in December 1989 listed 21, although in varying degrees of establishment and permanence (Haw 1990). A further update provided in April 1992, again lists 22 full-time Muslim schools or pre-schools in England (Islamia 1992). Of these 11 were secondary schools for girls and one at Summerfield near Kidderminster was a boarding school leading to further education in Islamic Studies. The remainder were primary pre-schools or boys schools. These institutions catered for approximately 1 per cent out of an approximate total population of 250,000 Muslim pupils in the UK at that time (*Guardian* 22/7/89, *Education Guardian* 23/3/93). A sample was selected from the approximately 21 Muslim schools for use in the study detailed below.

Muslim parents themselves are divided over the need for a religious basis in the education of their children, displaying the same broad range of attitudes towards their faith - from indifference to fervour - as do Christians and Jews (Swann Report 1985; *Times Educational Supplement* 24/8/90). But generally it is claimed that denominational schools make a significant contribution to parental choice in education because of their religious foundation and perhaps more disciplined ethos. Often these schools are the only means of obtaining a single sex education and for this reason it is not unusual to find Muslim girls taking up many of the few places available to children of other religions in both Roman Catholic and Church of England schools, perceiving them to be upholders of moral values (Centre for the Study of Islam and Christian-Muslim Relations 1985; Nielsen 1987).

The voluntary-aided sector of education is being subjected to examination in the 1990s in an unprecedented manner. This is caused by financial constraints, declining Christian intake, the ERA and the issue of private Muslim schools waiting in the wings for voluntary aided status. One simple answer to the issue of voluntary aided status for Muslim schools is to phase out voluntary aided schools altogether but it has been suggested that no government which wishes to stay in office would risk the wrath of both Roman Catholics and Anglicans by putting this proposal in its election manifesto (*The Independent* 15/7/90). The government report on multicultural education, the Swann Report, specifically rejected the idea of voluntary aided Muslim schools as racially and socially divisive but neither Swann nor the Churches considered the implications of this for the existing voluntary sector schools. This debate is probably just beginning. In the meantime, Muslim schools continue to campaign for public funding and accommodation of their pupils' needs.

Aims of Islamic education

Before a basic understanding of the concept and purpose of Islamic education can be gained it is important that an understanding of the nature and purpose in life from an Islamic point of view is attempted (Mohamed 1991). Yasien Mohamed explains this in the following way. According to Islam we are born in a state of *fitrah*, that is with the innate inclination to believe in and submit to God. It is the responsibility of humans to realize the human being's essential spiritual nature; in this realization lies the knowledge of God. Thus we are not only physical and psychological beings but also spiritual beings. Guidance for an Islamic way of life is expressed in its perfect form in the Qur'anic revelation and according to this God has endowed human beings with the faculties of heart (*'qalb*) and intellect (*'aql*) by means of which we may be able to understand divine revelation or recognize the Creator. In contrast to western secular education, which recognises the capacity for sensory and intellectual perception only, Islamic education recognises that there are faculties for a third level of perception, namely, a spiritual one, which is the highest level of perception in the hierarchy of human cognition. In short, we are the locus through which Islam is expressed; through which total and willing submission to the one true God is realized. This also becomes the aim of Islamic education, which is to teach us how to worship God and so fulfil the task of *Khalifah* on earth.

From this explanation it can clearly be seen that a central tenet of Islam is that spiritual and moral beings are provided with spiritual and intellectual aspects of ourselves through which the full potential of *fitrah* can be realised with the guidance of prophets and divine revelation. From the belief that Islam is in consonance with human nature it follows that it becomes the means by which the full potential of our nature, spiritual as well as material may be realised. It is within the context of this perspective that the aims and objectives of Islamic education have to be examined. The basic aim of Islamic education is the actualization of *fitrah* in all its dimensions within a social context and it is therefore concerned with the development of the whole person - body (*jism*), mind (*nafs*), and spirit (*ruh*) - in and for society. Consequently Islamic education is rooted in definite *a priori* principles which also provide criteria for critically evaluating society and the individual.

The primary purpose of Islamic education is to produce a good person and since it is the spiritual self that forms the most direct link with God, it is important that all aspects of man's personality should come under its control. In Islam the divine revelation in the *Shari'a* provides all the requisite knowledge of truth and falsehood, right and wrong. The task of each individual is to come to understand this knowledge and to exercise free will, by either accepting or rejecting it. The Islamic notion of free will is thus a specific view and one which is perceived to contrast sharply with the notion of personal autonomy that is widely considered to be crucial to the concept of liberal democracy.

The consideration of what is knowledge defines the dividing line between Islamic and Western concepts of education. The difference in perception rests on the fact that whereas western philosophy allows religious knowledge as a distinct form of knowledge in isolation, Islam only acknowledges the validity of the true faith and confines all knowledge to within the parameters of the Qur'an and the Hadith. Clearly these issues have considerable repercussions for those Muslim children educated within the state system which has endeavoured to meet their needs through the implementation of multicultural policies.

The concept of multiculturalism

One of the major issues that emerges from this analysis of the differing aims of Islamic and secular education is whether state education can or should reflect cultural/religious differences in society and is it possible for schools to provide an ethos and common core curriculum which are universally acceptable. In a broad and pragmatic attempt to tackle this question LEAs have attempted to produce overarching policies.

Official government reaction in the 1960s was to pursue assimilationist policies giving exclusive priority to the teaching of English to immigrant children and absorbing them into British culture. Assimilationist conceptions of educational aims often resulted in a disturbing lack of sensitivity, for example, over school dress and diet. Large scale underachievement amongst immigrant children resulted and it appeared that this was due to: low teacher expectation; isolation from mainstream school because of attendance at langauge centres; a tendency for them to be declared as educationally subnormal; and a general dissatisfaction with a system which undervalued them and what they had to offer (Rampton Report 1981).

Thus an integrationist model evolved in the 1970s which attempted to shift the emphasis of thought and policy away from cultural imperatives and towards political integration from a position of expected equality. This was to be achieved through provision of equal educational, social and economic opportunities (Mullard 1985). The refined version of this latter model has come to be known during its decade or more of currency as cultural pluralism/multiculturalism and it is accompanied by a multiplicity of interpretations. Responses to multiculturalism have varied widely. At its worst it has been accused of presenting children with caricatures of their own cultures such as the saris, samosas, and steel bands approach (Stone 1980; Troyna 1987; Leicester 1989). Further, during the 1980s a variety of texts reflecting on multiculturalism were published (for example Craft and Bardell 1984; Tomlinson 1984; Banks and Lynch 1986; Verma 1989) in a belief that theoretical correctness would provide the solution to the problem of dealing with the intractable difficulties which arise between individuals and groups in every society.

While the multicultural/anti-racist debate is subjected to continuous reappraisal, particularly since the implementation of the ERA, to some Muslims it has meant the adoption of a liberal approach which has not adequately addressed their religious/cultural requirements. The failure of the state system to provide an Islamic education in any sense is seen by Muslims to arise largely because of the multi-faith approach to religious education specifically, and other curricular areas in general which have been adopted under the auspices of multi-culturalism. The debate has been further complicated by the implementation of the national curriculum which can be interpreted as a rejection of many multi-cultural initiatives in favour of a Eurocentric or Britocentric agenda.

Campaigners for Muslim schools have challenged the efficacy of multiculturalism to enable Muslim children to retain and develop their distinctive identity or to redress racism. This highlights the failure of those educational initiatives which have been implemented to date to effectively address the needs of a plural society. An analysis of the literature produced by Muslim organisations which have concerned themselves with educational issues and which articulate the concerns that Muslim parents experience when faced with the British state education system will be examined next to identify categories of need.

Theoretical framework

A brief résumé of the educational needs of Muslim children provides a useful theoretical framework against which to measure the practice of accommodation or neglect as highlighted in the study. This account draws predominantly on the work of Islamic writers who identify three main categories of needs: religious/cultural, curricular, and general. Further the analysis should be seen within the context of the principles of Islam outlined earlier, and the implications of what it means to be a Muslim with specific duties and obligations which accordingly fall to parents and children.

Religious/cultural needs

The first need is for *religious workshops*. The opportunity to practice the faith in accordance with Islamic principles is an important aspect of everyday life. For Muslims, a major aspect of their faith is the duty to pray five times a day; an obligation which does not cease on schooldays. Muslim pupils face the dilemma of being unable to fulfil obligations of their faith within the confines of the classroom. Flexibility in the timetable to allow midday prayer and attendance at Friday prayers are advocated. Similarly, the provision of a prayer room and ablution facilities are required to assist this activity (McDermott and Ashan 1980).

School assemblies form another need. Collective acts of worship have always been a part of the school day in Britain and section 25 of the 1944 Act reaffirms this aspect subject to withdrawal on conscientious grounds. This principle has latterly been incorporated into the 1988 Education Reform Act. The new legislation adds that the act of worship 'shall be wholly or mainly of a broadly Christian character' (section 7). Where there is a sizeable proportion of pupils from other faiths, schools may request permission to hold alternative acts of worship by applying to the local standing advisory council for religious education. Religious *instruction* is likewise countenanced in terms of Christianity:'any agreed syllabus shall reflect the fact that the religious traditions in Great Britain are in the main Christian' (section 8(3)). Interestingly, this clause goes on to say 'whilst taking into account the principles and practices of the other principal religions represented in Great Britain.' These religious clauses have direct impact on Muslims and other faiths. Some Muslim parents feel that a Christian-orientated worship is unacceptable and are encouraged to invoke their right to absent their children (Muslim Educational Trust (MET) 1992, Iqra Trust 1991a). Indeed, notwithstanding the tide of secularisation, state schools in Britain are perceived as Christian schools. Invitations to Imams and Islamic scholars to visit and give talks for all children is recommended (McDermott and Ashan 1980) as well as the provision of Islam being taught in schools (Anwar 1982).

Following on from religious needs, the *celebration of important festivals* should be permitted, such as Id-al Fitr and Id-al Adha which will necessitate absence from school. Exercising discretion in this instance is in keeping with the tradition in Britain of permitting days of absence for religious celebration, pursuant to section 39 of the Education Act (1944).

A further aspect of the Muslim faith concerns *diet and fasting*. The provision of halal meat within the school catering facilities is required (Iqra Trust 1991a, Karim 1976). Fasting occurs during the month of Ramadam and secondary school pupils in particular, are encouraged to practice this aspect of the faith. The provision of rooming other than the dining area is a concession required for those pupils abstaining during religious occasions (Iqra Trust 1991a). Schools without provision of halal meat should serve vegetarian food, ensuring that no animal by-products are incorporated (MET 1992).

On the point of *school dress*, Muslims are expected to practice a level of decency in all activities. School dress is an everyday practical need which therefore has specific relevance to Muslim children.[2] In keeping with Islamic principles of modesty, there is a need for girls to cover themselves using for example, shalwar kameez and in some instances the hijab or headscarves (Karim 1976, Mabud 1992). School dress extends to clothing for physical education and sports. Recommendations have been that Muslim girls should be permitted to wear tracksuits and leotards for such lessons. There is a general taboo against mixed group activities such as physical education and swimming from the start of puberty (Karim 1976). Standards of modesty have application for *both* females and males, so while physical training may need to be arranged on a single sex basis, individual rather than communal showers are also required.

Curricular needs

The curriculum can be used to address issues in general such as language and customs, or specific problems such as prejudice and racism. There are also aspects of the curriculum which can cause specific concern for Muslim parents and their children, and withdrawal from class because of unacceptable or offensive curricula is a possibility to accommodate Muslim sensitivities. This may not be educationally desirable since such a move flies in the face of efforts to foster multiculturalism but it may not be possible to satisfy the religious convictions of all parents.

It is not uncommon for parents of both religious and non-religious backgrounds to question the content and delivery of *sex education lessons*. For Muslims, there is ample evidence to suggest that sex education conflicts with Islamic principles and both male and female pupils are encouraged to withdraw from such lessons (McDermott and Ashan 1980; Anwar 1982; Mabud 1992).

Choice of *language instruction* has come under review. Under British law, the Education Reform Act (1988) stipulates that a modern language must form part of the compulsory foundation subjects for all 11-16 year olds. While French, German or Spanish has traditionally been taught as second languages, schools are being encouraged to provide language options in Urdu, Gujerati or Arabic which may be more relevant to Muslim pupils. Prior to the implementation of the National Curriculum, Urdu for example was offered for the General Certificate in Secondary Education and it is this initiative which should be promoted (Mabud 1992). This is in keeping with the Bullock Report (1975: 286) into minority educational needs which stated: 'no child should be expected to cast off the language and culture of the home as he crosses the school threshold.' Furthermore, provision for mother tongue education is contained within a directive passed by the European Economic Community in 1977 which places a commitment on Britain to effect suitable measures (Liell and Sanders 1984).

Changing the formal curriculum to reflect an *Islamic dimension* is promoted (Anwar 1982; Hulmes 1989; Muslim Educational Trust 1992) and encouraged as a way to raise esteem and cultural identity (Sarwar 1983). Set within the National Curriculum Guidelines, there is potential scope for inclusion of non-Western perspectives within the options of subjects such as history and geography. Indeed the history syllabus could be used to reflect the Muslim contribution to Science and civilisation in order to remove the negative perceptions of Islam and Muslims (Muslim Educational Trust 1992).

There is a lack of consensus among Muslims over the suitability of *dance and music* in the curriculum. However there is some belief that both activities are un-Islamic and Muslim parents should ensure their children are excused from participation (Karim 1976). Conversely, the Muslim Educational Trust (1992) states that provided guidelines are followed, Muslim pupils can take an active role in music, or dance if it takes place in single sex groups. Art, is encouraged in Islam, according to the Trust, and the curriculum should be broadened to include the study of Islamic art and architecture.

Schools are urged to stock *Islamic books* to provide relevant information on Islam and British Muslims. The authenticity and factual accuracy of such books needs to be checked according to the Muslim Educational Trust and it urges schools to consult with 'reputable' Islamic/Muslim organisations in Britain. Likewise, the need for more Muslim teachers within the education system is advocated (Sarwar 1991; Union of Muslim Organisations 1989).

General needs

There are a variety of needs which fall within the organisational management of schools and which concern issues related to schooling in general. One of these is *Home-School Links*. Enlisting parental support is an important aspect of any attempt to accommodate Muslim needs within the school system. This can be made easier if the school recruits Muslim teachers who satisfy national and or local regulations as well as seeking advice from multicultural advisers. Muslim teachers may perform pastoral as well as academic roles, provide guidance on questions of dress, religion and the nature of the curriculum both formal and 'hidden'. They provide an important source of reference for pupils and may serve as positive role models (McDermott and Ashan 1980). The Iqra Trust (1991a and 1991b) formed to promote knowledge of Islam in Britain, suggests that home-school links can be fostered by the formation of liaison teams in schools with special responsibility for Islamic understanding. A lack of knowledge of the British education system, as well as the language itself, can lead to Muslim parents feeling isolated from mainstream school life (Joly 1989). Effective home-school links with the community in which the school is situated is therefore a specific need (Bastani 1988, 1989).

Private Muslim schools have tried unsuccessfully to obtain *voluntary aided status*. This would place them in the same category as the more than 7,000 Anglican and Catholic schools, and 21 Jewish institutions which currently receive government funding (Commission for Racial Equality 1990). Private Muslim schools which boast long waiting lists, increasingly clamour for public funding along the lines presently afforded other denominational schools in Britain (Halstead 1986, Smith 1990). The lobby for voluntary aided status for Muslim schools continues as a struggle for equity in funding and to provide what some Muslim parents feel is the ideal environment to cater for their children's needs.

The phasing out of *single sex schooling* in the 1970s prompted the formation, in Bradford, of the Muslim Parents Association. The organisation was formed to represent the Muslim interest and from this time a number of Muslim private schools have been founded along single sex lines and in accordance with Islamic principles (Barrell and Partington 1985). Muslim parents express a preference for single sex schooling; predominantly for girls but also expressed for boys (Anwar 1982, Mabud 1992, Iqra Trust 1991a). The option of single sex tutoring *within* a coeducational environment has been introduced by some of the state schools participating in this study.

Involvement in *school governance* in order that a school has a representative view of Muslim interests has been advocated (Mabud 1992, Iqra Trust 1991a). Muslim organisations are also encouraged to become more pro-active in attempts to bring about change within the educational system. Accordingly, and notably in London, Birmingham, Leicester and Bradford, there has been increasing involvement over issues at school and local government levels (Joly 1989, Nielsen 1986). The Iqra Trust and Muslim Educational Trust advocates Muslim participation at all levels of the educational consultative process in a more balanced partnership.

The study

Following on from this brief overview of the educational needs of Muslim children from a theoretical perspective, this paper seeks to examine the ways in which theory translates into practice. It is based on a 12 month empirical study augmenting work previously undertaken by one of the authors in this field (Parker-Jenkins 1991, 1992). The overall purpose of the study was to review the theoretical needs of Muslim children and examine the work being done in schools to accommodate those needs.

A qualitative research approach was employed in the inquiry and a sample of schools was selected. This consisted of 25 per cent of the private Muslim schools in Britain and an equivalent number of state schools in the inner-city areas of London, Leicester, Bradford, Bolton and Derby. These geographical locations are consistent with the documented settlement patterns of British Muslims (Nielsen 1986). The headteachers were the main focus of attention for the study since they were perceived as practitioners in an influential position. This follows previous research by Joly (1989) which showed that initiatives introduced into schools for the benefit of Muslim children came from headteachers. In part the interviews were to be used to assess the gap or discrepancies between the theory as espoused by Muslim writers and conceptualised earlier in this paper, and to gauge the views of practitioners as to accommodation or neglect of needs. Other methodological techniques used to elicit information were; participant observations of the schools, analysis of school prospectuses and school records. A pilot study was conducted earlier in which teachers, pupils and governors were also interviewed but the focus of this paper is limited to the responses of headteachers. Finally, a semi-structured interview schedule was used and no guidance was given based on what the research team had discovered from the initial literature review.

Criteria for selection of the schools was as follows. Of the Muslim schools, institutions were identified from previous research conducted by the authors, which were not transitory in nature and which had been established for a minimum of five years. The lack of state funding for Muslim schools in Britain since their formation in the 1980s has meant that many have struggled to survive and some have subsequently closed. Each of the Muslim schools were to be easily contactable, with a headteacher perceived to be open and co-operative in research. Some of the Muslim schools contacted were wary of public attention and were difficult to penetrate denying access to non-Muslims and outsiders. The schools in the study consisted of four secondary and two primary, with at least 40 pupils on roll, and demonstrated evidence of good practice, with an established and well planned curriculum. All of the selected Muslim schools were headed by practising Muslims but only one had an all-Muslim staff, the rest relying on non-Muslim teachers to be sensitive to the Islamic ethos.

Similarly, a selection criteria for non-Muslim schools was formulated. A comparative number of state schools were identified with between 30-90 per cent of Muslim pupils enrolled. Again four secondary and two primary schools were used in the study, but no single sex boys school. This is because the majority of Muslim schools established in Britain have invariably been for girls and it was intended to replicate similar situations. At the time of the research, there were 62 state schools in Britain with a Muslim intake of 90-100 per cent, and 230 such schools with a 75 per cent intake (Islamia Party of Great Britain 1992). Again the headteacher was identified as being open and co-operative in research, and particular emphasis was placed on identifying schools with evidence of good practice and well conceived policies and knowledge of accommodating Muslim children. Many of the schools were recommended by local education authorities in areas with high numbers of Muslim residents. Overall, the children in this study were representative of 37 different countries of origin, the majority of Asian descent; predominantly first generation British Muslim by birth; with a small proportion consisting of second generation and newly arrived immigrants.

A final note should be added within this section on methodology regarding access, confidentiality and anonymity. Access was negotiated and re-negotiated when appropriate throughout the study. The vast majority of interviews were taped, and a strict code of confidentiality and anonymity was applied. Interviewing of headteachers, whether Muslim or not, was conducted in an atmosphere of non-challenging trust between interviewer and interviewee, and the researchers aimed to provide scope and opportunity for the Muslim voice to be heard.

Results of the study

There were both similarities and differences between the perception of headteachers in state schools and private Muslim schools over Muslim children's needs. Similarity lay in the issue of religion and religious observance where all interviewees acknowledged religious needs. For example, school dress, provision of prayer room facilities, and flexibility in homework setting for children attending madrassah or supplementary school in the evenings, were all highlighted as aspects of religion affecting school life. Where the respondents differed in opinion was over the conceptualisation of religion in the lives of Muslim children. Headteachers of Muslim schools all expressed the need for children to have a spiritual dimension permeating their lives in and out of school. This is understandable given that the *raison d'être* of Muslim schools is to promote an Islamic ethos throughout the school and consistent with the theoretical perspective provided earlier. They spoke of the importance of faith, prayer, and pride in being a Muslim which they felt children should be taught. Furthermore, for them Islam included moral education and responsibility for the community whereby 'the world and faith go hand in hand'. Accordingly, children should be taught to be productive British citizens and maintain their Muslim identify. One Muslim headteacher said: 'we find a kind of imbalance in the present system and we are trying to correct the balance so that the individual will be a useful member of society and at the same time be a good follower of Islam.' Conversely, headteachers of state schools saw the religious dimension observances in terms of providing for specific, practical needs of Muslim children rather than as an entire spiritual dimension to their schooling.

There was an interesting response regarding prayer room provision which appeared in the pilot study and in subsequent interviews with headteachers of state schools within the study. The latter group felt the need was not significant and some reported the lack of use of the prayer room within the school. Perhaps the issue is not simply one of the availability of a prayer room but also the way in which the system is set up to allow Muslim children to feel comfortable about using it, perhaps they feel under peer pressure not to. Or is the prayer room provision a political statement rather than a personal need? Similarly, gender may be a factor here, since boys rather than girls may be in the habit of visiting the Mosque to pray, and in some communities Muslim girls only pray at home. Within Muslim schools the role of the headteacher was found to be significant in that he/she often assumed responsibility for leading prayer times and pupils witnessed this commitment to the faith. Furthermore, it is understood that within the Muslim schools all children took part in prayer times as it forms an important and normal aspect of the school timetable and accordingly prayer rooms were continually used.

The largest single need expressed by headteachers of state schools was not religion, or religious related needs as expressed overwhelmingly by their peers in Muslim schools. Rather, the need for English language acquisition was recorded from 83 per cent of state school heads compared with 33 per cent of Muslim school respondents. The cultural context of the majority of the Muslim children in this inquiry is that they are second language users and this has profound implications for academic attainment, assessment and testing. Furthermore, the geographical location of the state schools in the study were areas of high ethnic minorities, and headteachers noted the lack of opportunity for their Muslim pupils to interact with indigenous children thus further inhibiting their English language competency. (This need was not highlighted by any of the selected theorists, a point which will be addressed in the conclusion.)

Beyond this, the main needs identified were as follows:

i) Effective home school links: this was identified as a need by 50 per cent of the headteachers in state schools in comparison with 33 per cent of the Muslim headteachers.

ii) Balanced curriculum: again 50 per cent of the headteachers in the state schools identified this as a need in comparison with only 16 per cent of the Muslim headteachers.

iii) Better resources: this emergent category of needs was not mentioned by state school heads but 83 per cent of Muslim headteachers identified this as a need.

iv) Education as a preparation for life: this category did not feature in the responses of the headteachers of state schools. In comparison 33 per cent of Muslim headteachers identified this as a need.

v) Racism awareness and monitoring: 50% of the headteachers in state schools identified this as a concern but this did not feature in the responses of their counterparts in Muslim schools.
vi) School transportation needs: this is largely a concern of the headteachers in state schools, featuring in 50 per cent of their responses but not in the responses of the headteachers of Muslim schools.
viii) Teacher awareness: the Muslim headteachers did not identify this as a need but 33 per cent of the headteachers in state schools identified this as an area of concern. One state school headteacher said: 'of course there is no typical Muslim family ... but the onus is on us to know about Muslim pupils' backgrounds as completely as possible.' Similarly, 'there is a greater need for the teachers to be informed ... I don't think the education needs to be different, I think we need to be sensitive to the different issues which affect the lives of Muslim children.'[3] Another state school headteacher expressed home-school links thus: 'we recognise that the parent is the first educator of the child bringing to school complementary skills and what we are trying to do is work through a sense of partnership and really trying to involve parents in the educational process of their children'.

Headteachers of Muslim schools did not perceive the home-school link issue as being of such paramount importance, although it was identified as an area of concern. This is possibly because the Muslim schools studied were predominantly set within a local and identifiable community in which language and culture were common between the home and school. Trust and co-operation were regarded as having ensured the survival of the private Muslim school based on a level of not simply home-school relations but also community-school relations.

The responses of both categories of headteachers suggested support for a balanced curriculum. Using positive role models and images from Islam, curriculum should be developed away from an ethnocentric bias and the Islamic contribution to knowledge made evident. Where the curriculum was felt to be unacceptable, some of the state schools in the study provided the opportunity for exemption although one added 'as a headteacher I have a constant battle to keep the Muslim students within the mainstream while at the same time accommodating their serious needs.'

Education as a preparation for life was identified as a need within Muslim schools only, but the headteacher of one state school raised a problem associated with this broad area that Muslim children in contemporary society had to face: 'it is difficult for Muslim girls who are valued in school but are called racist names out of school.'

Public funding for Muslim schools was not expressed specifically, but the need for better resources featured highly and this would come about if voluntary aided status was obtained, as discussed earlier in this paper. Resources were not identified by state schools, but improved transportation facilities were noted in order that Muslim children could avail themselves of extra curricular activities outside the normal school day. Better provision of transport was not stipulated by Muslim school headteachers possibly because the Muslim school is normally a community school serving a population within a narrow geographic area and transportation is less likely to be a significant issue. At secondary level particularly, state schools serve a wider catchment area and the question of transportation is likely to be more problematic, particularly for girls.

Single sex schooling was not highlighted as a major concern, and as noted earlier some schools in the study are experimenting in single sex tutoring within the co-educational environment. Hindu, Sikh, Afro-Caribbean and white indigenous parents may also prefer this type of arrangement, particularly in light of suggestions that single sex education can lead to higher academic attainment.[4] Muslim needs in school diet were seen as being accommodated with a variety of arrangements and this was not perceived to be a major problem. Nor was the question of school dress a problem, as all schools in the study designed or adapted uniform in such a way as to be acceptable to Muslim parents. From the responses of Muslim headteachers specifically, the hijab was seen as demonstrating Muslim identity through attire. It represents Muslims negotiating their position and presence in a European setting; the symbol chosen to preserve identity and clearly the visibility of Islam in schools both Muslim and non-Muslim.

To summarise this analysis of the results, English language needs was the major concern of state school headteachers while within Muslim schools, the major perceived need was a total spiritual dimension to Muslim children's lives which the headteachers were attempting to accommodate through school ethos and the curriculum. Overall both categories of headteachers identified effective home-school links and a balanced curriculum; and a variety of other needs centred on resources, transportation, teacher awareness, racism monitoring and education as a preparation for life although a different emphasis was placed on their needs depending on the category of school. Finally, one state school headteacher said she did *not* feel Muslim children had special needs:

I would perceive the educational needs to be the same as for all children. I make no sort of separation for the fact that our children come from parents of the ethnic minorities. At the end of the day we have got to prepare children for life and that means living within the social settings that people within Britain live.

Conclusion

From this study into the educational needs of Muslim children in Britain, some concerns have been addressed thus far. Structural change in the school system has ensured that school dress, physical education, school diet, and prayer rooms were to a great extent been accommodated in the 1970s and 1980s. This is consistent with Jeffcoate's (1981) view that good multicultural education should be sensitive to 'special needs' and make special provision in terms of language, religion, diet and dress. These accommodations have been based on local and individual school effort and the findings are consistent with the documented initiatives of local education authorities particularly in areas with sizeable numbers of ethnic groups (Nielsen 1986). This study suggests that needs highlighted in category one of the theoretical framework outlined earlier are by and large accommodated by headteachers as ones which can most easily be addressed by the school within the confines of their own establishments. Further, they are seen as 'goodwill' gestures in a balancing act which aims to offset and deflect the accommodation of those needs described in categories two and three which are the potential minefields that multicultural and anti-racist initiatives have thus far failed to address. These initiatives have not proceeded in a uniform manner: Troyna and Williams (1986) and Troyna and Ball (1987) point to the fact that there have been significant differences in the way terms such as 'education for equality', multicultural and antiracist education have been conceived and implemented by professional officers and teachers. Moreover, whereas there was some degree of autonomy for LEAs which provided the opportunity for the initiation and development of such policy, the aftermath of the Education Reform Act (1988) has witnessed a gradual disappearance of that 'space'. This has led Troyna and Selman (1989: 35) to conclude that: 'in the likely absence of further initiatives along antiracist lines at ERA level the responsibility for change lies more than ever with those at the chalkface.'

Key areas of need which remain do not concern the practical everyday aspects of school life but rather are concerned with academic attainment. English language acquisition, a balanced curriculum and effective home-school links, which featured significantly in the responses of the headteachers of state schools, all revolve around academic concerns, performance and success. The characteristics of this next layer of needs are that they are heavily resource-led, require a very high level of commitment from headteacher and staff; and strike at the very nature of the national curriculum which is centrally determined. Jeffcoate (1991) stated that a key principle of education and for a multicultural society is: 'that it should afford the different ethnic groups equality of educational opportunity.'

Muslim children will not be seen to be recognizing their true potential within the educational system if they lack competence in the English language. Further, second language acquisition should not act as a barrier to attainment but this accommodation will require increased financial support and resources. This raises two questions pertinent to this discussion. Are Muslim children receiving equality of opportunity through existing arrangements for English language acquisition in Britain? What is this likely to imply in terms of equality of outcome? Clearly, the next phase of needs require more than tinkering with the educational system but concerted effort to ensure that Muslim children are not disadvantaged.

A movement away from an ethnocentric curriculum towards one based on global knowledge and international perspectives would require a movement away from a Eurocentric or Britocentric bias. Notwithstanding the perceived strait jacket character of the National Curriculum, there are possibilities to use the document to raise the image of ethnic minorities, or as Leicester (1989: 42) suggests to move away from an education 'perceived through ethnocentric spectacles'. Finding the right balance between the indigenous and minority cultures as expressed in the curriculum continues to be an area of concern. It is no longer possible to make the school curriculum responsive and sensitive to Islam without simultaneously negotiating with the National Curriculum. There are, nevertheless, benefits to be gained for both the Muslim and non-Muslim child: 'the achievement of respect for others lies in knowledge - the concept of respect for self is achieved in a similar way' (McGee 1992: 18).

The next phase of needs moves beyond practical, structural changes in the school system and strikes at the heart of educational policy in this country and the implementation of a National Curriculum. This has been described by Eggleston (1990) as being assimilationist in general, clearly expressed in the National Curriculum documents in which compulsory sections are British or Eurocentric and alternatives to the Western perspective lie in options which can be followed or ignored. Only very committed schools can ensure that there is a move away from the ethnocentric curriculum.

From this study, it is apparent that what is required is greater refinement in the assessment of needs as applied to Muslim children. This is in terms of: what needs are expressed, and by whom; what needs are accommodated or neglected; and at what level and to what extent? This study has suggested that there is a discrepancy in perception between what the selected Islamic writers feel are legitimate needs and what headteachers identify as needs, particularly within the state school sector where the vast majority of Muslim children are taught in the UK. Explanation for this may lie in the level of concern over spiritual matters rather than a lack of concern over academic performance on behalf of the theorists. Either way we need to be more specific about: general needs of all Muslim children e.g. school dress, diet and prayer room provision; specific academic needs resulting from socio-economic background and particular linguistic concerns; and individual needs as people in their own right. Clearly while educationalists must respond sensibly and sensitively to groups need, there is also the importance of recognizing the needs of the individual Muslim child as in any school setting. Again, this study was limited to schools in which the majority of children were first-generation British Muslims of Asian descent, and a major need was found to be English language acquisition. This will not necessarily hold true for third- and fourth- generation Muslim children whose linguistic and educational needs may well be very different. First-generation Muslims will have specific needs, concerns and anxieties, but as time, knowledge and experience passes between generations the situation changes and therefore needs change. In short the momentum of responding to Muslim needs should be maintained but it is now more essential that educationalists and policymakers employ greater sophistication in diagnosing levels of needs, and in assessing success or failure in efforts made thus far.

Notes

1 The empirical research was conducted as part of a funded project by the University of Nottingham to explore the educational needs of Muslim children in Britain.
2 There is not complete consensus as to whether Muslim girls need to cover their heads and the tradition may be cultural rather than religious in origin. For further discussion on this theme see Hussain (1984) and Werbner (1981). In terms of implications for physical education, see Carroll and Hollinshead (1993).
3 Teacher awareness was identified as a factor of importance in a recent study of Asian parents in Tower Hamlets, see Tomlinson and Hutchinson (1990).

4 For further information on this see: Bone (1983), Steedman (1984), Deem (1980 and 1984) and Willis and Kenway (1986).

References

Anwar, M. (1982) *Young Muslims in a Multicultural Society: Their Needs and Policy Implications*, Leicester, The Islamia Foundation.
Ashraf, S. A. (1986) 'Foreword' to Halstead, J. M., *The Case for Muslim Voluntary-Aided Schools: Some Philosophical Reflections*, Cambridge: The Islamic Academy.
Banks, J. A. and Lynch, J. (eds) (1986) *Multicultural Education in Western Societies*, London: Holt, Rinehart and Winston.
Barrell, G. and Partington, J. (1985) *Teachers and the Law*, London: Methuen. 6th edn.
Bastiani, J. (1988) *Parents and Teachers*, Windsor: NFER-Nelson.
Bastiani, J. (1989) *Working With Parents*, Windsor: NFER-Nelson.
Bone, A. (1983) *Girls and Girls-Only Schools; A Review of the Evidence*, Equal Opportunities Commission.
Bullock Report (1975) *A Language for Life*, London: HMSO.
Carroll, B. and G. Hollinshead (1993) 'Ethnicity and Conflict in Physical Education', *British Educational Research Journal* 19(1): 59-76.
Centre for the Study of Islam and Christian-Muslim Relations (16/10/85.) Report of seminar held at Westhill College, Selly Oak, Birmingham on 'Citizenship and religious education: Multifaith and denominational schools'.
Commission for Racial Equality (1990) *Schools of Faith*.
Craft, A. and Bardell, G. (eds) (1984) *Curriculum Opportunities in a Multicultural Society*, London: Harper Educational.
Deem, R. (1980) *Schooling for Women's Work*, London: Routledge and Kegan Paul.
Deem, R. (1984) *Co-education Reconsidered*, Milton Keynes: Open University Press.
Department for Education (1991) *The Parent's Charter. You and your Child's Education*, London: HMSO.
Eggleston, J. (1990) 'Can Anti-racist Teaching Survive the 1988 Education Act?', *Multicultural Teaching* 8(3): 9-11.
Halstead, M. (1986) *The Case For Muslim Voluntary-Aided Schools Some Philosophical Reflections*, Cambridge: The Islamic Academy.
Haw, K. (1990) 'Muslim Girls' Schools: A Question of Race,Gender or Religion?' Unpublished MA dissertation, Sussex University.
Hulmes, E. (1989) *Education and Cultural Diversity*, London: Longman.
Hussain, F. (1984) *Muslim Women*, New York: St. Martin's Press.

Hussain, M. (1990) Personal correspondence, 27 November 1990, Headteacher, Madrassa Karima, Supplementary School, 14 Berridge Road, Nottingham NG7 6HR.
Iqra Trust (1991a) *Meeting the Needs of Muslim Pupils*, London: Iqra Trust.
Iqra Trust (1991b) *Participating in School Governing Bodies*, London: Iqra Trust.
Islamia Party of Great Britain (1992), *Common Sense*, August, Milton Keynes: IPGB.
Islamia: National Muslim Education Newsletter (1992), Issue No.18, April.
Jeffcoate, R. (1981) 'Why Multicultural Education', *Education 3-13* 9(1): 4-7
Joly, D. (1989) 'Muslims in Europe: Ethnic Minorities and Education in Britain: Interaction Between the Muslim Community and Birmingham Schools', Research Papers No.41. Centre for the Study of Islam and Christian-Muslim Relations. Selly Oak Colleges, Birmingham.
Karim, I. (1976) *Muslim Children in British Schools: Their Rights and Duties*, Birmingham: The Straight Path Monthly.
Leicester, M. (1989) *Multicultural Education from Theory to Practice*, Windsor: NFER Nelson.
Liell, P. and Saunders, J. B. (1984) *The Law and Education*, London: Butterworth. 9th edn..
Mabud, S. A. (1992) 'A Muslim Response to the Education Reform Act of 1988', *British Journal of Religious Education* 14: 88-98.
McDermott, M. Y. and Ashan, M. M. (1980) *The Muslim Guide*, London: The Islamic Foundation.
McGee, P. (1992) *Teaching Transcultural Care*, London: Chapman and Hall.
McLean, M. (1985) 'Private Supplementary Schools and the Ethnic Challenge to State Education in Britain', in: C. Brock and W. Tulasiewicz (eds) *Cultural Identity and Educational Policy*, London: Croom Helm.
Mohamed, Y. (1991) 'Knowledge in Islam and the Crisis in Muslim Education', *Muslim Education Quarterly* 8(4): 13-32.
Mullard, C. (1985) 'Multiracial Education in Britain: From Assimilation to Cultural Pluralism', in: M. Arnot (Ed) *Race and Gender. EqualOpportunities Policies in Education*, Pergamon Press: 39-53.
Muslim Educational Trust (1992) Comments on the Government White Paper: Choice and Diversity, London: MET.
Nielsen, J. (1986) 'A Survey of British Local Authority Response to Muslim needs', Research Papers: Muslims in Europe. No.30/31. Centre for the Study of Islam and Christian-Muslim Relations. Selly Oak College, Birmingham.
Nielsen, J. (1987) 'Introduction to Islam and religious education in England, Europe- Research Papers No.3. Centre for the Study of Islam and Christian-Muslim Relations. Selly Oak Colleges, Birmingham B29 6LE.
Parker-Jenkins, M. (1991) 'Muslim Matters: an Exploration of the Needs of Muslim Children', *New Community* 17(4): 569-582.

Parker-Jenkins, M. (1992) *Educating Muslim Children*, Nottingham: School of Education, University of Nottingham.

Rampton Committee (1981) *West Indian Children in our Schools*, Cmnd 8273. London: HMSO.

Sarwar, G. (1983) *Muslims and Education in the UK*, London: Muslim Educational Trust.

Sarwar, G. (1991) *British Muslims and Schools*, London: Muslim Educational Trust.

Smith, G. (1990) 'The Next Ten Years', *Muslim Educational Quarterly*, 1(5): 26-27.

Steedman, J. (1984) 'Examination Results in Mixed and Single-Sexed Schools', in: D. Reynolds (ed.) *Studying School Effectiveness*, London: Falmer Press: 87-101.

Stone, M. (1980) *The Education of the Black Child in Britain*, London: Fontana.

Swann, M. (1985) *Education for All: A Summary of the Swann Report on the Education of Ethnic Minority Children*, Windsor: NFER-Nelson.

Tomlinson, S. (1984) *Home and School in Multicultural Britain*. London: Batsford.

Tomlinson, S. and S. Hutchinson (1990) *Bangladeshi Parents and Education in Tower Hamlets*, London: Ace-University of Lancaster Research Project.

Troyna, B. (1987) 'Swann's Song: the Origins, Ideology and Implications of Education for All', in: T.S. Chivers (ed.) *Race and Culture in Education*, Windsor: NFER-Nelson: 26-43.

Troyna, B. and Ball, W. (1987) *Views From the Chalkface*, University of Warwick. 2nd edn.

Troyna, B. and Selman, L. (1989) 'Surviving in the Survivalist Culture: Anti-racist Strategies and Practice in the new ERA', *The Journal of Further and Higher Education* 13(2): 22-36.

Troyna, B. and Williams, J. (1986) *Racism, Education and the State: The Racialisation of Education Policy*, Beckenham: Croom Helm.

Union of Muslim Organisations, Youth Council of UK and Eire (1989) Seminar on ERA 1988.

Verma, G. K. (ed.) (1989) *Education for All: A Landmark in Pluralism*, London: Falmer Press.

Werbner, P. (1981) 'Manchester Pakistanis: Lifestyles, Rituals and the Making of Social Distinctions', *New Community* 9(2): 216-229.

Willis, S. and J. Kenway (1986) 'On Overcoming Sexism in Schooling: To Marginalize or Mainstream', *Australian Journal of Education* 30: 132-149.